WHO LEARNS WHAT FROM CASES AND HOW?

✿ ✿ ✿

The Research Base for Teaching and Learning With Cases

WHO LEARNS WHAT FROM CASES AND HOW?

The Research Base for Teaching and Learning With Cases

Edited by

Mary A. Lundeberg
University of Wisconsin–River Falls
Barbara B. Levin
University of North Carolina
Helen L. Harrington
The University of Michigan

 LAWRENCE ERLBAUM ASSOCIATES, PUBLISHERS
1999   Mahwah, New Jersey   London

Lawrence Erlbaum Associates, Inc., Publishers
10 Industrial Avenue
Mahwah, New Jersey 07430-2262

Cover design by Kathryn Houghtaling Lacey

Library of Congress Cataloging-in-Publication Data

Who learns what from cases and how? : the research base for
   teaching and learning with cases / edited by Mary A.
   Lundeberg, Barbara B. Levin, and Helen L. Harrington.
       p. cm.
   Includes bibliographical references and index.
     ISBN 0-8058-2777-3 (cloth : alk. paper). — ISBN
   0-8058-2778-1 (pbk. : alk. paper)
     1. Case method—Study and teaching—United States.
   2. Teachers—Training of—United States. I. Lundeberg,
   Mary A. II. Levin, Barbara B. III. Harrington, Helen L.
   LB1029.C37W56 1999
   370'. 71'1—dc21   99-17946
                                                      CIP

Books published by Lawrence Erlbaum Associates are printed
on acid-free paper, and their bindings are chosen for strength
and durability

Printed in the United States of America
10 9 8 7 6 5 4 3 2

Contents

Not a Case?"
Sigrun Gudmundsdottir   177

Chapter 9   Culturally Relevant Teaching With Cases:
               A Personal Reflection and Implications
               for Pedagogy
               Sonia Nieto   179

               Commentary on "Culturally Relevant
               Teaching With Cases: A Personal Reflection
               and Implications for Pedagogy"
               So-young Zeon   197

Chapter 10   Revisiting Fieldwork in Preservice Teachers'
               Learning: Creating Your Own Case Studies
               Susan Florio-Ruane   201

               Commentary on "Revisiting Fieldwork
               in Preservice Teachers' Learning:
               Creating Your Own Case Studies"
               Helen Featherstone   225

PART IV: FUTURE DIRECTIONS

Chapter 11   Reflections on Methodologies and Future
               Research
               Mary Anna Lundeberg, Barbara B. Levin,   231
               and Helen L. Harrington

               References   241

               Author Index   259

               Subject Index   265

               Contributors   273

Foreword: A Rationale for Case-Based Pedagogy in Teacher Education

Katherine K. Merseth
Harvard University

As teacher-educators contemplate the 21st century, they face a clear and compelling challenge to offer strong teacher education programs that will help teachers become as effective as possible in influencing student learning. The complex conditions of student learning, the increasing diversity of school populations, and the rapidly changing knowledge base about teaching combine to make this challenge particularly daunting. It is clear that teacher-educators must find ways to provide aspiring teachers with approaches, experiences, and ways of thinking that will enable them to perform effectively in their classrooms.

Every aspect of teacher education—its program content, structure, and pedagogy—must be re-examined to determine necessary changes for more effective teaching in the nation's classrooms. Indeed, the required reforms will likely touch several key factors known to be essential to successful teaching practice, including increased opportunities to deepen and extend teachers' understanding of subject matter, greater exposure to curricula and methods that will help develop broad and creative repertoires of desirable instructional practices, extended participation and experience in supportive learning communities, and sufficient time both to reflect on how these knowledge bases interact with each other and how to apply them. This seems a tall order for teacher-educators. And yet, there is a small but courageously determined group of teacher-educators who believe that the use of cases and case methods offers a particularly promising strategy to help meet these demands of 21st century teacher education programs. And, it seems, the group is growing in size and activity.

The *case idea*, as Sykes and Bird refer to this pedagogical approach (1992), is not a new concept in teacher education. As early as 1920, case materials were being used in teacher education programs in New Jersey and Massachusetts. In the middle of this century, professional educators noted the apparent success of case-based instruction in the professional fields of law and business and sought to introduce it into programs to train school administrators (cf. Sargent & Belisle, 1955). Interuniversity programs to share case materials were established (UCEA, 1987) and essays about the pedagogy (Hunt, 1951) began to appear in educational journals. Although activities related to this pedagogical approach in the field of education were never large or particularly well organized, they nevertheless existed in a steady state throughout the 1960s and 1970s.

With the accelerating school reform movement of the early 1980s (A National Commission on Excellence in Education, 1983) and an increasing awareness of the importance of teachers (Carnegie Forum, 1986), interest in case pedagogy began to grow (Merseth, 1981). Influenced in part by the public recognition of the method by Lee Shulman in his Presidential address to the American Educational Research Association (AERA) in 1985 and the advocacy of the approach by a number of professional organizations such as the American Association of Higher Education (AAHE) and the Carnegie Forum on Education and the Economy (1986), some members of the education professorate began to take note of this approach. By the late 1980s, more essays and commentaries advocating the effectiveness of cases and case methods began to appear in the teacher education literature (Carter, 1989; Carter & Unklesbay, 1989; Greenwood & Parkay, 1989; Kleinfeld, 1988; Shulman & Colbert, 1987, 1988; Sykes, 1989). Soon other professional organizations such as the American Association of Colleges of Teacher Education (AACTE) and the AERA were holding preconference workshops on the approach at their annual meetings and journals such as the *Journal of Teacher Education* and the *Teacher Education Quarterly* were sponsoring special issues on the topic of cases in teacher education (Ashton, 1991). The number of voices talking about cases and case methods in teacher education was increasing.

In the early 1990s, a number of case books were on the market (Kowalski, Weaver, & Henson, 1990; Silverman, Welty, & Lyon, 1992) and books and articles about cases and case methods were plentiful (Doyle, 1990; Kagan, 1993; McAninch, 1993; Merseth, 1991a, 1991b; Shulman, J., 1992; Shulman, L., 1992; Wasserman, 1993). Notably, most of these materials advocated the use of cases as a pedagogical approach in teacher education. Any empirical basis for the claims was rarely evident. Indeed, a review of case-based pedagogy for the *Handbook of Research on Teacher Education* (1996) wryly commented on this mix in the early 1990 literature between advocacy and empirical knowledge: "The collective voice of its proponents far outweighs the power of existing empirical work" (p. 722).

Since the mid-1990s, the tone and nature of the literature about the use of cases and case methods in teacher education has changed. Today's work in the field seems to reflect a much greater awareness about the need to understand, through empirical research, the appeal as well as the effect of this approach. Although the pedagogy still has great chasms to cross with regard to developing a well-founded and codified knowledge base, scholars are turning their attention to several exciting research issues inherent in this approach. However, before examining this work and the particular methodological and design challenges that face researchers in this field, it is important to ask why cases and case methods have sustained the interest of teacher-educators for the last two decades. What is the appeal of these materials and pedagogical approach? Understanding what the hopes and aspirations are that teacher-educators ascribe to this pedagogy will help frame the subsequent discussion about design and method of the empirical research. Just what is it that teacher-educators hope cases will do?

THE APPEAL OF CASE-BASED INSTRUCTION
IN TEACHER EDUCATION

It is no secret that many preservice teachers experience dull, formulaic teacher education programs characterized by uninspired teaching methods, a fragmented and superficial curriculum, and inadequate time to connect theory and practice (Goodlad, 1990; Holmes Group, 1986, 1995). For many, the situation is no better once teachers are on the job. All too often teachers are left disappointed by inservice programs that are too theoretical, too narrow, too irrelevant, or just too boring. All teachers need abundant opportunities to reflect on their own experiences, to deepen their understanding of subject matter, and to gain a wider repertoire of pedagogical practices. Without a focus on the teacher and the teacher's role, no advances will be made in student learning. The recent report of the National Commission on Teaching and America's Future summarizes the view of many: "On the whole, the school reform movement has ignored the obvious: What teachers know and can do makes the crucial difference in what children learn" (Darling Hammond, 1998, p. 5). Many teacher-educators see case-based instruction as a particularly promising approach to help students of teaching to help formulate "what teachers know and can do." In particular, they believe that case-based instruction can help students of teaching develop skills of analysis and problem-solving, gain broad repertoires of pedagogical technique, capitalize on the power of reflection, and experience a positive learning community. A brief review of each of these beliefs follows here.

Cases and Case-Based Instruction Help Students to Develop Skills of Critical Analysis and Problem-Solving. One of the most widely cited advantages of case-based pedagogy is its ability to help students develop skills of critical analysis, problem-solving, and strategic thinking (Doyle, 1990; Hunt, 1951; Kleinfeld, 1991a; Lundeberg & Fawver, 1993; Merseth, 1991a; J. Shulman, 1992a; Wasserman, 1994). For example, Hunt suggested that the method provided

> the power to analyze and to master a tangled circumstance by selecting important factors; the ability to utilize ideas, to test them against facts, and to throw them into fresh combinations...for solution of the problem; the ability to recognize the need for new factual material or the need to apply technical skills; the ability to use the latter experiences as a test of validity of the ideas already obtained. (p. 178)

Some 40 years later, Wasserman (1994) states that "cases promote students' ability to discern the essential elements in a situation, to analyze and interpret data, and to use data to inform action" (p. 606). Well-designed cases in teacher education are claimed to help students to observe closely, spot dilemmas, identify relationships, and formulate organizing principles.

Cases and Case-Based Instruction Encourage the Development of Higher Order Cognitive Thinking and the Generation of Multiple Pedagogical Techniques. Through their construction, cases are often seen as stimulants for preservice and inservice teachers to examine and discuss alternative instructional strategies and to construct new ones. By combining discussions of content and pedagogy, cases offer an instructional approach that encourages the development of pedagogical content knowledge—that skillful blend of content and pedagogy first noted by Professor Lee Shulman (1986) of Stanford University—that is especially key for the implementation of new reform-based curriculum materials and standards. Perhaps the field evidencing the greatest amount of inquiry in this regard is mathematics. Barnett (1991) and her colleagues at WestEd have done important work on this topic. Others suggest that cases can promote increased technical rational thinking (Moje & Wade, 1997). Discussions can range from a close consideration of the techniques present in a particular case to the consideration of an alternative approach offered by the instructor or one of the case discussants.

The rich context and realistic presentation of many cases also can allow participants to try their own hands and voices at articulating plausible action plans in a realistic, yet safe environment without harm to real subjects (Merseth, 1991b). Because the environment created in case discussions is both safe and bounded, participants are free to advance several possible theories and courses of action and to develop multiple perspectives (Harrington, 1996). In this situation, case participants can build new understandings by listening to the interpretations and suggestions of others in the discussion. With this pedagogy, no actual individuals are harmed by an ill-designed strategy or a poorly crafted intervention.

Cases and Case-Based Instruction Often Foster Reflection.   A number of scholars advocate case-based instruction as an effective means to develop habits of reflection about teaching. For example, Richert (1991b) claims that "cases require teachers to reflect on practice" (p. 122), whereas Kleinfeld (1992b) suggests that cases can stimulate "the habit of reflective inquiry" (p. 47). Richert (1991b) stated that "cases provide the potential for connecting the act of teaching with the cognition and feelings that motivate and explain that act. They offer a vehicle for making the tacit explicit" (p. 117). Harrington explores the development of habits of reflective inquiry through the use of cases (Harrington & Garrison, 1992). Others proclaim the power of cases to enhance reflection, but limit their case sources to those written as self-reports of individual experience (e.g., Shulman & Colbert, 1989; Shulman, Colbert, Kemper, & Dmytriw, 1990). This use stresses the internal process of writing cases rather than the external process of discussing them (Shulman, J., 1991). Those who write about the ability of cases to foster reflection argue that cases stimulate learning from experience—whether it is from their own experience or the experience of others.

Cases Help Present a Realistic Picture of the Complexities of Teaching.   Finally, many case advocates feel that cases can help illustrate the complicated aspects of teaching. Through the description of actual schools and classrooms, these cases also open a window that illuminates the contextual influences on teaching and learning. Challenging instructional situations in schools often present "not one well-defined issue but many ill-defined issues, intertwined like the fibers of a thick rope" (Kleinfeld, 1988, p. 9). Harrington (1996) explored the ability of students to discern multiple complexities and dilemmas within a case description. Thus, cases can describe realistic issues and hold them still for analysis and examination, sometimes making them less overwhelming than the actual event. Cases discussions also challenge teacher's notions of authority in classrooms. Barnett and her colleagues at WestEd have explored the influence of case discussions on teachers' perceptions of the locus of control and authority in content based discussions (Barnett & Tyson, 1994).

CLAIMS ABOUT CASE-BASED INSTRUCTION AND EMPIRICAL RESEARCH

With many claims about the use of cases in teacher education programs being espoused, it is important to determine the degree to which these claims are substantiated by solid empirical research. Is the excitement about case-based instruction in teacher education well founded? Will the ongoing work in this area help teacher-educators understand the nature of the pedagogy and its most effective use? Further, we are interested in the nature of the inquiry in this field. What are the type of questions being asked and what are the most common methodologies in use? Are there any particular design and methodological issues that are especially problematic or challenging in this field of research? It is exciting that this volume seeks to answer these questions.

Up until the mid-1990s, the match between the claims of case users in teacher education and a solid empirical research base was remarkably weak. With a few notable exceptions, the literature regarding cases and case-based instruction in teacher education was advocacy-based. However, this lack of research base was not limited only to teacher education. In the field of business administration, often seen as the godfather of case-based instruction, researchers also noted a paucity of empirical work (Masoner, 1988; Merseth, 1991a). Essentially, the conversations about case-based instruction over the last two decades has been full of heat, but with very little light. Only recently have teacher-educators seriously attempted to define an empirical basis of this movement.

There are many reasons for the slow development of an empirical base. First and perhaps most important are questions of design. Good research depends on good designs and good designs in turn depend on the nature of the research question, the amount of control or comparability across contexts, and the desired end product. Good designs flow from clear goals; unfortunately, it seems that teacher education researchers have not always been entirely clear about their goals for using cases in their classrooms.

Sometimes we want to use cases to teach "problem-spotting skills" or to encourage "habits of reflection." Other times we seek to impart very specific subject matter (as in the case of mathematics teacher education cases) or specific skills (such as disciplinary approaches or special education techniques). Because of the wide array of purposes, a mismatch sometimes can exist between what the case researchers say they want to achieve and what actually happens.

Second, a strong empirical base depends on an ability either to control for the many confounded variables that are at work when the case method is in use, or else to offer a clear explanation for their interaction. And this issue of control in the design leads to a third limiting factor in the development of a strong empirical base: the difficulty researchers have in generalizing their findings. There are also multiple questions about method. Given the interactive nature of case-based instruction and the heavy influence of context, it is often not clear which methods will sustain the most robust inquiries and solids conclusions.

The important contribution of this book becomes clear in the context of these challenges. These chapters offer important insights and explorations of these issues for those of us interested in research on case-based pedagogy. Taken together this work will enhance our knowledge of case-based instruction in teacher education in a most significant way.

Preface

Despite a long history of using case-based teaching in the professions, research on using cases has received emphasis only since the 1980s (Merseth, 1996). The inclusion of a chapter on cases and case methods in teacher education by Katherine Merseth in the 1996 edition of *Handbook of Research on Teacher Education* (Sikula, 1996) attests to the innovative position of cases and case pedagogy in teacher education (the first edition of the *Handbook* did not include a chapter on case methods). Our intent in putting together this edited book is to organize and present major empirical work done to date on cases and case-based pedagogy, and hopefully, to stimulate continued research and dialogue about case-based pedagogy.

Because of the relative newness of case-based pedagogy in teacher education, there are multiple definitions regarding the meaning of the case method embedded within the research on cases. Furthermore, although there are many claims made about the efficacy of case-based teaching methods (e.g., Merseth, 1991a; Shulman, J. 1992a; Sykes & Bird, 1992), the research base is less well defined (Merseth, 1996). We think this edited volume is timely not only because it contains a comprehensive review of much of the scholarship to date, but also because it encompasses a wide range of perspectives on cases and studies are frequently qualitative and time-consuming. They range from interviews to discourse analysis and content analysis to the use of questionnaires. A third goal is to clarify what we do not yet know about cases and case pedagogy. Finally, the commentaries on each chapter are intended to provoke further dialogue regarding cases and case pedagogy. As these chapters suggest, investigations into the power that case pedagogy holds for fostering the development of teaching has only just begun.

The book is organized into three sections that, we think, address some of the most important questions all teachers ask of themselves: What kind of learning am I attempting to foster? How might I best structure the learning environment to foster learning? How do my own understandings and the understandings of my students interact with the learning and teaching in which we engage? The focus of this book, as just discussed, is how cases may or may not help us answer those questions.

PART I: THE LEARNING FOSTERED
THROUGH CASE-BASED PEDAGOGY

Lundeberg (chap. 1) presents a model of research related to the kinds of understandings about teaching and learning preservice teachers may discover though the use of cases. Cases contribute to preservice teachers' discoveries of knowledge about the complexity of teaching and the diversity of learners by enabling them to apply theoretical and practical knowledge to specific school contexts, and to reason critically about classroom dilemmas and propose courses of action. Through vicarious engagement in case stories, preservice teachers make discoveries about themselves as future teachers and as learners. As preservice teachers write about and discuss case situations they develop metacognition with regard to one's own teaching, and examine their beliefs about teaching. Using cases also enables preservice teachers to discover how colleagues' perspectives, values, and ideas may influence changes in their understanding of teaching and learning. This influence of learning through social interaction helps preservice teachers to value social, ethical and epistemological growth.

In her chapter, Harrington (chap. 2) focuses on written case analyses. She discusses how asking prospective teachers to complete written analyses of cases can be used to both foster and assess development in students' performance of thought. Students' written analyses of cases provide insight into changes in how prospective teachers think about and resolve educational dilemmas embedded in cases over time; that is, growth in their professional development. She conceptualizes professional development as an increase in the ability to make reasoned decisions, warrant claims, and reflect on assumptions when making professional decisions. This framework is illustrated through the work of three students.

Barnet and Tyson (chap. 3) examine the role that case discussions play in fostering inservice teachers' professional autonomy. Using case discussions of mathematics teaching as a site for inquiry, they focus on how case discussions enable teachers to develop a deeper understanding of the content they teach; an appreciation of the multiple ways both students and teacher may understand content and how those understandings influence both the teaching and learning of the content; and how teachers begin to develop a more critical stance on teaching and learning. Noddings, in her comments on the chapter, while reminding us to be careful about the language we use, highlights the multiple benefits that members of the learning communities established through case discussions derive from those discussions.

Moje, Remillard, Southerland, and Wade (chap. 4) illuminate what teacher-educators can learn from the use of cases. They describe their deliberations as they systematically studied their uses of cases in their university classrooms. They critically examine their own purposes for using cases, their data from transcriptions of case discussions, and the intended and unintended outcomes for preservice teachers engaging in case-based pedagogy. Zeichner's commentary on chapter 4 seconds the notion of self-study by teacher-educators that goes beyond merely deciding whether case discussions are a valuable pedagogical tool for preservice teachers' learning.

PART II: STRUCTURING THE LEARNING ENVIRONMENT WITH CASES

As Levin suggests in chapter 5 on case discussion, "the more we know about the factors that influence teachers' understanding of thinking about cases, what can be learned from cases, and how to conduct case discussions effectively, the better we will be able to determine when, with whom, and how best to use this potentially powerful pedagogical tool for teacher education." The chapters in this section focus attention on factors that structure the learning contexts cases are embedded in and how those factors influence the educative power of cases.

Cases are not presented to students or teachers as is—that is, as something to be read independent of the other activities in which students are engaged. Rather, they are embedded within the context of specific classrooms or staff development efforts. They provide a focus for the complex and interactive dynamics of teaching and learning. Levin discusses the empirical research that focuses on the role of the facilitator in planning and carrying out discussions of cases. She also compares the research conducted with the claims made for the efficacy of the case method and concludes with suggestions for future research, especially action research conducted by instructors using cases with their own students. Silverman, in her commentary on Levin's chapter, reinforces the importance that style plays in case facilitation.

Although much of the scholarship on cases is grounded in the examination of cases as written texts, increasingly various forms of technology are being used to expand what can be accomplished with case-based pedagogy. Richardson and Kile's chapter (chap. 6) on learning from videocases begins with the rationale that videocases have high face validity because they "project a moving picture of a classroom context, teaching, and students' responses." In their definition of a videocase, they include written materials in addition to hypermedia technology. After describing three examples of research studies using videocases, they acknowledge that videocases (or any representation of reality) are to some degree unauthentic and less complex than reality. The major methodological question raised concerns how to measure change in preservice or inservice teachers, particularly changes in beliefs and deep understandings as well as actions. In his commentary, Griffin asks how cases bring preservice teachers into a relational engagement with the practice of teaching, and the necessity of moving teacher–student relationships beyond content toward issues of caring, justice, and democracy.

If there are any shared understanding among scholars and researchers using cases, it a recognition of the importance of case discussions. In her chapter on case discussions, Levin (chap. 7) captures the richness and variety in the investigations that have been conducted on this important aspect of case pedagogy. In sharing what has been learned about the value of case discussions she also raises equally important questions about what we do not yet know including how the structure of discussions interacts with what is learned from cases. She reminds us that the most important focus for our research on cases must be on what students learn and why. Shulman's commentary adds to the questions raised, as she cautions us to consider the style of the facilitator and the substance of cases selected.

PART III: RETHINKING CASES

The next three chapters move beyond the traditional boundaries of research on cases and case-based pedagogy. The authors articulate, in their own voices, either the questions they have about cases or how they use them in their own practice. They move our consideration beyond the broader questions raised in previous chapters—about who learns what from cases and how the structure of the learning context influences what is learned—to prompt us to consider some of the particulars embedded in our work with cases.

Carter (chap. 8) raises fundamental questions about not only what we consider a case, but about the questions those of us working with cases raise as well. She juxtaposes a discussion of storied knowledge and narrative with how teachers come to know about teaching. She suggests a careful consideration of the questions that prompted the work presented and reviewed in this volume, as well as additional questions that may contribute to a better understanding of what it means to prepare teachers for the complexity and ambiguity of their work. Gudmundsdottir, in her comments on the arguments raised in Carter's chapter, reiterates the privileged nature of story as a way to understand practice.

Nieto (chap. 9) provides insight into how she views and uses cases. For her, the power in cases is the way they illuminate the lived experience of children, particularly those who represent the increasingly diverse students that prospective teachers will teach. Whereas Carter (chap. 8) makes an argument for the importance of teachers' stories, Nieto builds a powerful argument for students' stories and how they might begin to help teachers and prospective teachers come to understand the unique and complex lives each of their students live. She points out how cases can be used to help prospective teachers see their students through sociocultural and sociopolitical lenses that, for the majority of teachers, their own experience would never provide. Even if cases are not or should not be viewed as representative, they are instructive.

Florio-Ruane (chap. 10) bridges Carter and Nieto's chapters. She suggests that asking students to write their own cases provides them with opportunities to gain access to their own stories and the ways in which they might limit understanding of students' stories. She provides a way to help students make sense of what they are seeing in classrooms, so that they gain deeper insight into the complexity of classrooms, the multiple factors that influence teaching and learning, and the role their own experience and stories play in how they make meaning. Featherstone, commenting on the chapter, cautions that helping students see and understand their own or other's stories requires careful and thoughtful guidance.

Together, these three chapters suggest that well-crafted cases are one way to capture the richness and multilayered complexity of teaching. In addition, they can be used to provide those whose experience is limited with a way to begin to understand that "one" answer or one interpretation is almost never sufficient. Each prospective teacher and teacher's story enhances their own and others' understanding. Each student's story provides insight into how to best foster their learning and development. These stories of teaching that teachers or students of teaching write and use provide one way to begin to peel away the layers in what it means to teach.

In the final chapter, we look across all of the chapters and the work reviewed in them to examine patterns in the research discussed. We reflect on some of the major questions about the methods and procedures used to study what is learned from cases; we highlight the strengths and weaknesses of the ways in which case-based pedagogy is enacted; and we suggest direction for future research based on those reflections.

ACKNOWLEDGMENTS

We sincerely appreciate the ideas contributors have provided to this volume. The timely nature of their work and broad perspectives shared will stimulate advances in future research. Thanks also to Naomi Silverman, our editor at Lawrence Erlbaum. Our deepest thanks to family members, Laura Lundeberg, Bill Fox, Robert Barry and David Brown, for their continued support throughout this project. Finally, we acknowledge the support we have given each other.

—*Helen L. Harrington*
—*Barbara B. Levin*
—*Mary Anna Lundeberg*

PART I

THE LEARNING FOSTERED THROUGH CASE-BASED PEDAGOGY

1

Discovering Teaching and Learning Through Cases

Mary Anna Lundeberg
University of Wisconsin—River Falls

There has long been an assumption, albeit not been much research, that using cases in the education of teachers fosters understanding about teaching and learning. This assumption has been founded on several ideas concerning the situated, narrative nature of cases; the likelihood of knowledge transfer to future teaching situations; the role of conflict in changing beliefs and broadening perspectives; and the motivational value of framing and constructively resolving "real-life" teaching dilemmas (Berliner, 1992; Carter, 1992, 1994; Harrington, 1995; McAninch, 1993; Silverman & Welty, 1996). Preservice teachers are more likely to transfer knowledge if it is situated in "real-world" classroom contexts (Bransford & Vye, 1989). However, situated learning is complex, and some of the claims thus far have been overstated (Anderson, Reder, & Simon, 1996).

In this chapter, I present research related to the kinds of understanding about teaching and learning preservice teachers may discover though the use of cases. To illustrate some of these, I constructed a model based on case research. Cases contribute to preservice teachers' discoveries of knowledge about the complexity of teaching and the diversity of learners by enabling them to

1. Apply theoretical and practical knowledge to specific school contexts,

2. Reason critically about classroom dilemmas and propose courses of action. Through vicarious engagement in case stories, preservice teachers make discoveries about themselves as future teachers and as learners. As preservice teachers write about and discuss case situations, they
3. Develop metacognition with regard to one's own teaching, and
4. Examine their beliefs about teaching. Using cases also enables preservice teachers to discover how colleagues' perspectives, values and ideas may influence changes in their understanding of teaching and learning. This influence of learning through social interaction helps preservice teachers to
5. Value social, ethical, and epistemological growth.

After explaining this model by examining research on using cases with preservice teachers, I present some research showing how the ways we use cases affects the knowledge acquired by preservice teachers, and finally, discuss some the methodological limitations of research in this area.

OVERVIEW OF THE MODEL ON DISCOVERIES ABOUT TEACHING AND LEARNING

A model outlining what cases contribute to preservice teachers' discoveries about teaching and learning is shown in Table 1.1. This model is the focus of this chapter. Although each of these "discoveries" are presented separately in this chapter, they are not mutually exclusive and overlap to some degree. As Table 1.1 shows, the first category includes theoretical and practical knowledge. Although these two kinds of knowledge are often separated in the literature on developing teachers' knowledge (e.g., Fenstermacher, 1994), they are combined here. Professors use cases for many different purposes and may chose to focus on one kind of knowledge, such as practical or theoretical, to the exclusion of the other. However, many professors use cases to generate theory from practice, or to encourage teachers to apply theory in a practical classroom situation, and to discover when and how theories may be useful or not useful. In contexts such as this, the distinction between theory and practice becomes muddied.

A second but related area, as shown in Table 1.1, is the development of reasoning. This category includes both problem-finding as well as problem-solving. The ability to think reflectively and to alter one's plans or decisions based on the context are important discoveries about teaching and learning.

TABLE 1.1

Discoveries About Teaching and Learning Through Cases

Theoretical and Practical Understandings	Reasoning
Transfer, strengthen, clarify formal knowledge	Critically analyze complex situations
Use performance (procedural) knowledge	Identify issues and problems
Develop conditional knowledge	Use cognitive flexibility
Develop practical knowledge	Recognize assumptions
	Consider consequences
	Practice reflective, ethical decision making
Metacognition	*Beliefs*
Develop self-knowledge	Explore tacit knowledge
Recognize own assumptions	Clarify and question personal beliefs/values through agreement and disagreement
Awareness of problem-finding	Alter previously held beliefs
Consider personal/professional goals	Formulate and strengthen beliefs
Plan for future situations and relationships	
Realize how personal perspectives affect decisions	
Social, Ethical, and Epistemological Growth	
Value learning communities, shared inquiry	
Open-mindedness and responsibility	
Compare and evaluate perspectives	
Acknowledge limitations of experience	
Understand that knowledge is transformable	
Consider the contextual, uncertain nature of teaching	
Become critically reflective and concerned for social justice	

Developing metacognition—that is, gaining an understanding of how one handles classroom challenges and becoming aware of how one forms plans and goals—is an area of self-knowledge that case pedagogy fosters. Case discussions also encourage teachers to explore their beliefs related to teaching and to become open to new ideas through agreement and disagreement with peers. Finally, the use of case pedagogy enables teachers to compare and evaluate their own and others' perspectives, to become more open-minded and to develop learning communities engaged in critical reflective inquiry. This form of discovery includes epistemological development as well, in which teachers understand that teaching and research are contextual, social, and ethical enterprises. Research on whether using cases foster discovery about teaching and learning in each of these areas is discussed next.

Construction of Theoretical and Practical Knowledge

Teachers' knowledge can be categorized as either formal or practical (Fenstermacher, 1994). Formal knowledge is theoretical in nature and consists of facts and propositions that arise from research, whereas practical knowledge is oriented toward performance and arises from the situations and experiences of teachers. Some researchers (e.g., Kennedy, 1988) have argued that theoretical or principled (i.e. formal) knowledge is an essential component of teacher education, but only a part of what is necessary for the professional education of teachers. The idea that teachers construct understanding from case discussions (Carter, 1992, 1994; Sykes & Bird, 1992) is in contrast to more traditional notions that cases be used to apply theories in teacher education classes or "translate theory to practice" (Greenwood, 1996; McAninch, 1993). McAninch argued that cases be used to develop teachers' capacity to "observe the particular through a theoretical perspective," which she believes is "key to professional practice" (p. 87). She thus advocates using cases after students have gained a basic understanding of general concepts and theoretical ideas to further their theoretical understanding.

Although teacher educators may have neglected the practical component in favor of theory (e.g., Fenstermacher, 1994), there is no reason to continue to perpetuate this dichotomy. Depending on the context of case use and the goals of the instructor, it seems plausible that cases may be used to do both to some degree (Moje & Wade, 1996; Sykes & Bird, 1992). For example, Barnett (1991) found that case discussions enabled teachers to use their practical teaching knowledge in developing theoretical pedagogical knowledge, and in considering how to use such knowledge (procedural knowledge) and under what conditions this knowledge applies (conditional knowledge).

Lundeberg and Fawver (1993) found significant changes in preservice teachers' ability to connect theoretical principles to situated problems. They collected two kinds of data: (a) students' pre- and post-written analysis of a dilemma-based case at the beginning and end of the semester; and (b) students' self-reported written explanations of changes in beliefs at the end of course units on development, learning, instructional psychology, and measurement. During the first unit in this course, preservice teachers wrote a preassessment analysis of a case, entitled "Life in a high school classroom."

This case presented a principal observing a ninth-grade general mathematics class of a veteran high school teacher, and provided several pages of "typical" classroom instruction, interaction, and decisions (Greenwood & Parkay, 1989, Case 6). The teacher was a conventional, textbook-oriented mathematics teacher: He presented a problem, asked recitation questions, and did not probe students' thinking or encourage alternative forms of problem-solving. Moreover, he was somewhat sexist in his interaction with students, particularly with one female pupil who was having difficulty.

In this course, preservice teachers discussed twelve short cases at the end of each chapter in their textbook (Good & Brophy, 1994) designed to emphasize theoretical principles and eight complex cases (one case at the end of each unit) from a book of cases portraying teaching dilemmas (Greenwood & Parkay, 1989). Thirteen weeks later, during the last week of the education course, preservice teachers reread this same case ("Life in a High School Classroom") and wrote a second, postassessment analysis of it. After preservice teachers completed the second case analysis, they compared their first and second analyses using a metacognitive guide that asked students to count and to qualitatively compare the number of issues, perspectives, theories and decisions in their pre- and post-case analysis. Changes in the number of issues, perspectives, theories, and decisions by gender and by age were analyzed using MANOVA. Also, interrater reliability between preservice teachers' self-scores and scores given by an independent rater (blind to gender, age, and pre/posttest status) was calculated to test the validity of preservice teachers' self-scores.

Table 1.2 presents the earlier and later scores of traditional (under 22 years of age) and nontraditional age (22 years old or older) men and women on the number of theories evident in their written case analyses. As Table 1.2 shows, preservice teachers connected twice the number of theoretical principles on the later assessment compared to the earlier, a significant change. With regard to theory application,

> more than one-third of the preservice teachers (38%) said they were now able to cite specific relevant theories that applied to the case. Twenty-three percent (23%) reported providing more in-depth discussion of theories; 10% thought they were better able to connect problems in the case with theories, and 8% said they knew more theories. (Lundeberg & Fawver, 1994, p. 293)

In a later study exploring the relation between case discussions and pedagogical knowledge, Lundeberg, Matthews, and Scheurman (1996) found that almost half of the students (45%) reported that cases helped them connect educational psychology concepts to real classroom situations, as this comment illustrates:

TABLE 1.2

Mean Pre- and Postscores of Theories by Gender and Age

Age Group	Traditional	Nontraditional
Women		
Pretest	1.3 (1.3)	1.1 (1.4)
Posttest	3.1 (2.0)	3.6 (2.2)
Men		
Pretest	0.6 (0.8)	1.4 (1.5)
Posttest	2.3 (2.0)	3.0 (2.4)

Note. $N = 70$; (Women = 41: nontraditional age [over 22] = 14, trad. = 27; Men = 29: nontraditional age = 15, trad. = 14); Differences between pre- and post-scores were significant: $F (1, 66) = 75.55, p < .001$.

I think the case analysis has given me the opportunity to apply concepts/theories in a more practical sense. I have learned that recognizing issues will come in the form of listening to and researching a student's life. As a teacher I will be much more likely to remember Ed Psych concepts from story situations than from textbook reading. (p. 11)

With the exception of the research based on teachers discussing cases about mathematics pedagogy (e.g., Barnett, 1991; Barnett & Tyson, 1993a; Barnett & Ramirez, 1996), and multicultural education (J. Shulman, 1996a), little research has explored the development of either formal or practical knowledge through cases. We know, however, from work on expert reasoning in domains such as law, that knowledge interacts with reasoning (jurisprudence), and that reasoning about cases develops further knowledge (Lundeberg, 1985, 1987).

Reasoning and Reflective Decision-Making

Reasoning and reflective decision-making involve several components, such as the ability to identify, frame, or find a problem; consider problems from multiple perspectives; provide solutions for problems identified; and consider the consequences and ethical ramifications of these solutions (Harrington, 1995; Lundeberg & Fawver, 1994). Some researchers include developing students' awareness of their assumptions and limitations in their thinking as a component of reflective decision-making (e.g., Harrington, 1995), but I include that aspect of thinking under the section on metacognition, because it seems to me we are encouraging students to think about their thinking and how it may have influenced their case analyses. Many of us who use cases based on dilemmas do so to develop preservice teachers' critical analysis, problem-solving in complex ethical situations, and reflective practice (Harrington & Garrison, 1992; Lundeberg & Fawver, 1994; Merseth, 1991a).

> Dilemmas present situations for which there are competing, often equally valid solutions. Using dilemma-based cases in preservice programs helps students begin to understand and accept the tentativeness in knowing, with certainty, what action to take; provides opportunities to marshal and evaluate evidence for judging alternative interpretations and actions; and can illuminate the moral dimensions of teaching. (Harrington, 1995, p. 2)

Through the process of reasoning about cases, preservice teachers engage in problem-finding and problem-solving (Harrington, 1995; Kleinfeld, 1991; Lundeberg, Matthews, & Scheurman, 1996). Some educators have noted the difficulty preservice teachers have in analyzing a problem situation:

> In teaching such cases, I am often taken aback by the great difficulty many education students have in analyzing a problem situation. Many students see problems as no more than common-sense, obvious difficulties. They have not developed the idea that problems are constructed and can be constructed in more and less fruitful ways. Many education students also have little notion of how to think about a dilemma; they come up with nothing more than a quick reaction and a single solution. (Kleinfeld, 1991, p. 7)

Harrington (1995), Silverman and Welty (1996), and Lundeberg (1995) have corroborated Kleinfeld's (1991) observation that preservice teachers need some structure and guidance in framing problems to counter their tendency to construct a problem from only one perspective. We do not know, however, whether simply modeling various perspectives in analyzing problems or explicitly teaching students to frame problems from more than one perspective is preferable in improving students' ability to analyze a problem situation.

Harrington (1995) refined an analytic frame to code-written case analyses by examining the reasoning preservice teachers used to "identify the case, b) identify and ground alternative perspectives on the case, c) propose a solution, d) identify positive and negative consequences of the actions in the case and in their recommendations, and e) critique their solution and analysis" (p. 7). She found that over the course of the semester preservice teachers had begun to improve their reasoning. Although the majority were able to identify the problem in the case, only half explicitly used facts and issues from the case to ground their identification of problems. Although preservice teachers also improved in considering more perspectives of others not directly involved in the case (e.g., the community, parents), more than half (58%) focused on the perspectives of key participants in the case. The majority of preservice teachers (92%) based their solutions on moderate or multiple sources of evidence and most also considered some consequences of their solutions. However, only 15% of the preservice teachers critiqued their analysis and "reflected on their own assumptions and how they may have influenced their interpretation and resolution of the case" (Harrington, 1995, p. 15). Other researchers using this analytic framework reported improvement in preservice teachers' reasoning (e.g., Levin, 1997).

Using a less complex coding scheme, Lundeberg and Fawver (1993) compared the number of issues, solutions, and multiple perspectives (e.g., teacher, pupil, researcher) in preservice teachers' earlier and later case analyses (this methodology was described in the previous section). Table 1.3 presents earlier and later scores of traditional and nontraditional age men and women on the number of issues, solutions, and perspectives they generated in their case analyses at the beginning and end of the semester. Students' differences on identifying issues and proposing solutions earlier and later in the class were significant. There were also notable age differences: Nontraditional students proposed considerably more (twice the number of) issues and solutions than traditional age students. Additionally, there were identifiable gender differences: women generated significantly more issues and solutions than men. Moreover, examination of earlier and later assessments means showed that female nontraditional students gained the most in identifying issues.

With regard to growth in perspective, as Table 1.3 illustrates, both women and men analyzed the case from a greater number of perspectives at the end of the semester. Students reported using one or more of the following perspectives in analyzing cases: principal, teacher, researcher, pupil, school board member, school, and personal experience/opinion of the preservice teacher. Students' explanations showed that preservice teachers became more student-centered. The largest single category of change in perspective was in the addition of a student perspective. Almost one third (28%) of the preservice teachers reported thinking about the case from the pupils' point of view, with some of those preservice teachers identifying individual pupils in the case by name.

Most of the research on enhancing reasoning and reflective decision-making through case pedagogy has been done in the context of actual courses. Thus, it is impossible to determine whether the case discussions and written analyses or some other aspects of those teacher education courses contributed to the development of reasoning reported in these studies.

TABLE 1.3

Mean Pre- and Postscores of Issues, Decisions, and Perspectives by Gender and Age

Age Group	Traditional	Nontraditional
*Issues**		
Women		
Pretest	5.1 (3.1)	3.1 (1.8)
Posttest	6.3 (2.2)	7.2 (3.7)
Men		
Pretest	2.6 (1.3)	3.9 (2.3)
Posttest	5.0 (2.6)	6.0 (3.02)
*Decisions**		
Women		
Pretest	2.9 (1.5)	2.1 (2.6)
Posttest	4.3 (2.1)	5.7 (4.2)
Men		
Pretest	1.8 (1.5)	3.3 (1.7)
Posttest	2.6 (2.9)	4.9 (2.3)
*Perspectives**		
Women		
Pretest	1.9 (1.1)	1.5 (0.9)
Posttest	2.6 (1.5)	2.4 (0.9)
Men		
Pretest	1.6 (0.9)	2.1 (1.5)
Posttest	2.4 (1.3)	2.2 (0.9)

Note. Numbers in parenthesis are standard deviations. $N = 70$ (Women = 41: nontraditional age [over 22] = 14, trad. = 27; Men = 29: nontrad. age = 15, trad. = 14);

* Pre- and post-differences were significant at the .001 level.

Nontraditional students proposed significantly issues and solutions than traditional age students: $t (69) = 5.1, p < .001$; and $t (69) = 4.55, p < .001$ respectively.

Women generated significantly more issues and solutions than men, $t (69) = 7.58, p < .001$; and $t (69) = 3.38, p < .001$ respectively.

Female nontraditional students gained the most in identifying issues; this two-way interaction between age and sex was significant, $F (1, 66) = 7.93, p < .01$.

However, Lundeberg, Matthews, and Scheurman (1996) asked preservice teachers whether they thought they learned anything through case analyses, after these teachers had re-examined two cases they had written about over the course of the semester. Of these teachers, 65% thought that case analysis contributed to their abilities to recognize, find or see new aspects of a problem situation. Case-based pedagogy enabled students to recognize problems and see new aspects of problems, as this quote illustrates: "I recognize problem areas more readily and also am able to see solutions quicker. My ability to communicate has improved, and this is very important as a teacher" (p. 11).

Similarly, case discussions promote reflective reasoning on current teaching practices (Moje & Wade, 1996). In interviews debriefing teachers on their views regarding what they learned from case discussions, one teacher explained:

> I think it [reading a teaching case] can cause you to reflect more, especially those of us who have been teaching, on what you do. Do I do the same thing? Do I have the same reasons? Or, why do I do what I do? You tend really to internalize what you're reading. (Moje & Wade, 1996, p. 1)

Although these self-reported statements may not necessarily carry over into classroom actions, there is some indication that the vicarious teaching experiences provided by cases develop students' reasoning and reflective decision-making. Likewise, discussion of cases may provide a safe environment for teachers to take pedagogical risks, imagine themselves trying out new teaching strategies or picture themselves "correcting" pedagogical mistakes they may have made. This sort of vicarious risk-taking involves thinking about one's thinking (or metacognition), a form of self-understanding fostered by the case method.

Metacognition

Metacognition involves thinking about and being aware of how one thinks (Pressley & McCormick, 1995). Teachers use a number of strategies to reach students in a variety of situations. Using metacognitive knowledge about when and where to use certain strategies and with whom, under which teaching contexts, is an important aspect of pedagogical knowledge. Another essential component of metacognitive knowledge for teachers is the ability to reflect on how one's past and future thoughts, assumptions, and beliefs guided classroom actions. Adults as well as children often fail to monitor their cognitions (Garner & Alexander, 1989; Pressley &

McCormick, 1995). Because of the complexity of classrooms, teachers may react to situations based on past experiences rather than carefully thinking about how their assumptions, thoughts, and beliefs influence their decisions.

Complex cases of teaching dilemmas have provided a rich context for teachers and preservice teachers to examine and reflect on their knowledge, assumptions, and beliefs (Barnett & Sather, 1992; Lundeberg & Fawver, 1994). If students analyze a case more than once and compare their recent written analysis with previous ones, they become aware of growth in their ability to transfer theoretical knowledge and consider additional perspectives (Lundeberg & Fawver, 1994; Lundeberg, Matthews, & Scheurman, 1996). Preservice teachers also engage in metacognition when they are asked to write a reflection comparing what they first thought about a case (prior to case discussion) with what they think after the discussion, as this students' reflection illustrates: "I have learned as a result of this case that there are many perspectives to any problem. It's not like I didn't know that before, but to actually experience seeing the different perspectives in action brought it to life. I realize now how my perspectives affect my decisions as a teacher" (Dana & Floyd, 1994, p. 13). Both inservice and preservice teachers used "cases as tools to think about, question, and critique their own teaching" (Moje & Wade, 1996, p. 48). Likewise, Lundeberg and Fawver (1994) found that preservice teachers used cases as a tool for thinking about and planning to use certain classroom strategies in their future teaching. This preservice teacher reported becoming aware of her own metacognition, as well as her plans as a future teacher to encourage metacognition in students:

> One way that my previous conceptions have changed is that I've always stated that you should try to sneak in the material, not let them realize that they're learning it. It is very important, I've come to realize, that the student be aware of how and why they are learning the material. I know that it is in my best interest to teach the students strategies and model them myself. Students can apply these strategies to the classroom and later on in life. Thinking things aloud will help others also. It's like a brainstorming session; it may stimulate further ideas. I want my students to be able to make sound decisions based on the facts, their own beliefs, and their own judgment. (Lundeberg & Fawver, 1994, p. 294)

In future studies, researchers might use protocol analysis of preservice teachers analyzing cases to study whether metacognition develops over time as students gain more experience with case analyses. Verbal protocols of reading have provided much insight into how learners construct knowledge during the reading process (Pressley & Afflerbach, 1995). Protocol analysis before and after a case is discussed in class would add to our understanding about how (or whether) individuals' beliefs change through case discussions.

Beliefs

Beliefs influence how teachers interpret theories as well as practical situations, and affect both pedagogical actions and ethical decisions (Richardson, 1996). The relation between beliefs and practice seems to be reciprocal; that is, beliefs influence practice and practice influences beliefs. Cases are a kind of pseudo-practice that provide vicarious opportunities for teachers to test new ideas in a low-risk situation (Moje & Wade, 1996). Cases may also alter beliefs about learning; for example, preservice teachers reported changing from believing that students receive knowledge from teachers to believing that students create meaning: they construct knowledge (Lundeberg & Fawver, 1994). In that study, students reflected on and acknowledged changes in their beliefs. Because beliefs may often be implicit, changes in beliefs are complicated to assess though an outsider's (e.g., researcher's) lens. Is it enough for researchers to identify what they interpret as changes in beliefs, or do such changes in beliefs need to be acknowledged by the learner as a new conception?

Preservice teachers' beliefs may interfere with current concepts and theories in our field (Anderson, et al., 1995). For example, if teachers believe students are to blame for bias in classroom interaction and take no responsibility for it, gender or racial bias will continue. Unless teachers alter their beliefs, they are unlikely to change their practices, because beliefs influence classroom practice (Peterson, Carpenter, & Fennema, 1989). Preservice teachers' beliefs are tenacious (Holt-Reynolds, 1992)—research suggests that beliefs draw their power from previous vivid episodes or events in students' lives, and are influenced minimally by theories and knowledge that are semantically stored (Pajares, 1992). Thus, traditional teaching methods such as lecture or simply reading a case may do little to alter beliefs. Indeed, even readers of persuasive text rarely change their beliefs; typically these readers reject disconfirming evidence (Chambliss & Garner, 1996).

The early literature on cognitive change suggests that teacher-educators can encourage students to alter beliefs by helping them become aware of their own beliefs, and recognize conflict between existing beliefs and alternative beliefs (see, e.g., Posner, Strike, Hewson, & Gertzog, 1982). More recent theorists of conceptual change emphasize that these original models are excessively rationalistic, and that social interaction plays an important role in changing students' conceptions (Solomon, 1987).

J. Shulman (1996) expressed the importance of discussion and facilitation when she said "cases, even with commentaries, do not teach themselves" (p. 155). Challenges from their peers and the facilitator have
enabled people to confront misconceptions and change attitudes (J.
Shulman, 1996), and to understand and respond to cultural diversity (Dana
& Floyd, 1994). Social interaction during discussion, particularly of conflicting views and values, promoted social construction of knowledge and
changes in thinking (Dana & Floyd, 1994; Levin, 1995; Lundeberg,
Matthews, & Scheurman, 1996). Lundeberg, Matthews, and Scheurman
(1996) found that although the case itself served as the anchor for
preservice teachers to develop situated knowledge, it was the discussions in
large groups that encouraged preservice teachers to develop new perspectives.

Studies that report changes in beliefs regarding gender or ethnicity (e.g.,
Lundeberg & Fawver, 1994; J. Shulman, 1996) used large group-facilitated
case discussions. In contrast, Moje and Wade (1996) used small-group case
discussions, followed by large-group reporting; they found that teachers
viewed teaching as a technical act and did not discuss issues of ethnicity,
class, or gender. Future research might examine the degree to which the
kind of case used (e.g., dilemma-based vs. narrative) and the method of facilitation affects changes in perspectives, beliefs, and attitudes. Do
preservice teachers value the changes in beliefs they have made after listening to their peers? This question and others form the basis of the last component of the model.

Social, Ethical and Epistemological Growth

When preservice teachers adopt new perspectives and change their beliefs,
do they value becoming more open-minded? Do preservice teachers become more likely to consider ethical questions and the moral consequences
of decisions when analyzing a case? Do they understand that teaching is
contextual, that their knowledge is limited and that pedagogical knowledge
about teaching changes over time? How teachers view knowledge and
"truth" is a window into their epistemological development and may determine how they interact with others, and whether they consider the multiple
perspectives of these involved in the educational process (children, parents, school board members, principals, and the cultural or community context). This discovery of the limits of our understanding about teaching and
learning and the potential for continual growth in understanding is of ut-
most necessity in preparing teachers for the diverse, complex, and ambiguous challenges inherent in today's schools.

Although there is healthy disagreement in the field regarding how to incorporate cases into preservice and inservice education, most case propo-

nents stress the importance of case discussions in creating shared learning communities among students, broadening their perspectives to include moral dimensions of teaching, and enabling students to construct situated, case-specific understandings (Barnett & Tyson, 1993a; Harrington & Garrison, 1992; Levin, 1995; Lundeberg, Matthews, & Scheurman, 1996; Merseth, 1996; Silverman & Welty, 1996). In discussing the relation between teaching and knowing, Harrington (1994) wrote: "The knowledge of most worth is brought into being dialogically. It is said and heard in multiple ways—transformed in the sharing—enriched through the multiplicity. Dialogue allows students to become aware of what they share in common, as well as the uniqueness of each of them as individuals (p. 192).

The powerful influence of case discussions on students' perspectives has been corroborated by Levin (1995), as well as by Harrington and Garrison (1992). Levin (1995) found people's ability to analyze cases far superior when they had opportunities to discuss cases rather than simply writing about the cases. Cases are "value-laden, if not explicitly, then certainly implicitly ... dialogue allows us and our students to transcend the limitations of our own experience and values" (Harrington & Garrison, 1992, p. 717).

Drawing from Dewey's (1933) work on open-mindedness, responsibility, and wholeheartedness, and work on critical reflection (e.g., Zeichner & Tabachnik, 1991), Harrington, Quinn-Leering, and Hodson (1996) assessed preservice teachers' development in these areas. The operationalized open-mindedness as "recognizing and acknowledging the validity in other perspectives," responsibility as "considering the moral and ethical consequences of choices," and wholeheartedness as "identifying and clarifying limitations in one's assumptions when making decisions" (p. 26). Using qualitative methodology, Harrington et al. categorized preservice teachers' critical reflections on cases into three levels. Level 1 had a unitary focus (teacher-centered), Level 2 had multiple foci (typically considering both teachers and students), and Level 3 had an inclusive focus, considering broader socio-moral contexts, issues, and consequences, such as "assumptions about schools, families, society, and the influence of educational policies and practices" (p. 34). Most students' written case analyses were in Level 2, with a few reaching Level 3. This coding scheme was used later by Levin (1997), who analyzed students' reflections on a case before and after a case discussion. Levin (1997) found that most students moved from a unitary focus to a multiple foci for open-mindedness, responsibility, and whole-heartedness, but less than 20% had an inclusive focus.

Cases provide a situational context for students to connect ethical questions with theoretical concepts. For example, in her case analysis written at the end of the semester, this secondary education mathematics student analyzed the interaction in a case to raise questions concerning equity:

> How can John be made aware of his differential treatment of males and fe-
> males? What can John do to be more equitable in regard to gender? John
> called on 14 males during his lesson and praised 11 of them for their re-
> sponses. He only called on 8 females, none of whom did he praise. John needs
> to call on and praise females more often. He should also encourage his female
> students. This is essential especially in math and science areas. In order to
> achieve in mathematics, females need encouragement from their teachers.
> Also, to promote equal opportunity in the classroom, male and female stu-
> dents should be called on and praised equally. (Lundeberg, 1993a, p. 163)

In this example, a preservice teacher used her knowledge of gender equity in
classroom interaction to frame a problem in the case and to propose some
solutions. Lundeberg (1993a) found that while less than half of the students
(46%) identified sexism as a problem in their initial case analysis at the beginning of the semester, the majority (92%) included this as an ethical problem in their analysis of the case 14 weeks later. Some preservice teachers
have also indicated an awareness of their epistemological development, as
this quote illustrates: "I find in our case study discussions, I am always interested in how everyone handles the situation. I tend to see things in black or
white. I realize now there are many answers to one problem" (Lundeberg &
Fawver, 1994, p.295). Similarly, in their work with inservice teachers,
Barnett and Tyson found that case discussions affected teachers' views regarding the sources of knowledge: teachers shifted from authority to autonomy—that is, from thinking that knowledge stems from external sources to
thinking that knowledge can be gained from internal sources and peers (see
Barnett & Tyson, chap. 3, this volume). Case discussions empower teachers, providing them with a stronger sense of autonomy as well as pedagogical
content knowledge (Barnett & Tyson, 1993a). However, case discussions
do not necessarily lead to critical reflection or epistemological development. Undergraduates who view the world in a dichotomous fashion may
struggle with the notion that although teaching is contextual, it is not individualistic, and that although multiple perspectives are valuable, this does
not mean that "anything goes" (see chap. 4, this volume).

Assessing social, ethical, and epistemological growth presents a major
methodological challenge, because of the value-ladenness inherent in assessing this form of knowledge. So far we think that using cases with
preservice teachers fosters the development of their theoretical and practical knowledge, reasoning, beliefs, metacognition, and social, ethical, and
epistemological growth. However, we know little about how this happens,
apart from some self-report and anecdotal data. One way to learn more
about how the use of cases develops understanding of teaching and learning

is to examine how preservice teachers' knowledge changes as we alter our case methods, which is the topic of the next section.

How the Ways We Use Cases Affect Discoveries
in Understanding

Lundeberg, Matthews, and Scheurman (1996) found that how we use cases affects understandings preservice teachers discover. Should cases be used at the end of an instructional unit to demonstrate students' understanding of ideas, or at the beginning of a unit to serve as an anchor for instruction? Because Lundeberg and Scheurman disagreed about when to use cases and whether cases should be used more than once, they decided to use action research to resolve their dispute. The first question they asked was whether students learn more when theory (e.g., a unit of instruction) comes before story (the case) or whether the story (case) should come first? Lundeberg, Matthews, and Scheurman (1996) answered this question by examining pre- and posttest differences in preservice teachers' problem-framing and decision-making under two conditions: analyzing a case after a unit of instruction, and analyzing a case prior to a unit of instruction. In addition to the question "Which should come first, theory or story?," Lundeberg, Matthews, and Scheurman (1996) asked a second question: "Should cases be used more than once?"

Lundeberg, Matthews, and Scheurman (1996) collected preservice teachers' earlier and later written analyses of the case ("The Glory that was Greece," Greenwood & Parkay, 1989) and students' reflections on changes in their analyses. All students discussed the case in pairs on computers, in order to identify problems, justify their reasoning, and propose possible solutions. Each pair turned in their analysis and were given points for participation. After student pairs completed their repeated case analysis, they compared first and second analyses and reported what (if anything) they learned from analyzing the case again.

In the first semester, 47 students first learned about motivation, analyzed the case, studied a unit on learning, and analyzed the case a second time. Students worked with a different partner on the first and second analyses. The first analyses were collected after students studied the unit on motivation, but prior to the unit on learning. Thus, the case served as an anchor for the unit on learning. Later analyses were collected after students studied the unit on learning.

In the second semester, 18 students studied learning, analyzed the case, studied a unit on motivation and analyzed the case again. Thus, in Semester 2, the case then served as an anchor for the unit on motivation. Analyses were first collected after students studied the unit on learning but prior to motivation. Subsequent analyses were collected after students studied the unit on motivation. Students worked with the same partner. Because they had the same partner, prior to writing their second analysis, Semester 2 students were given a computer disc that had their first analysis on it. We purposely altered this procedure in Semester 2, so that additional concepts added in the second analysis could not be attributed to a new partner's perspective.

For data from both semesters, Lundeberg, Matthews and Scheurman (1996) used content analysis (Merriam, 1988) to categorize students' responses to their metacognitive reflections and to categorize concepts and theories that students included in their case analysis. Concepts and theories were classified as either relating to learning or motivation according to how these ideas were presented in these units in the students' textbooks (Good & Brophy, 1994 or Woolfolk, 1993). If a statement was too vague—for example, "the students aren't motivated"—it was not counted as a concept. If a student mentioned the same concept twice, it was only counted as one concept, unless they provided additional reasons for using the concept again in their case analysis, or a very clear and different example of the concept. This counting procedure was the same for both semesters. All three authors worked together to initially categorize concepts and then resolved any later discrepancies through discussion. (See Lundeberg & Scheurman, 1997, for additional methodological and statistical details.)

Using Cases as an Anchor for Instruction Fosters Theoretical/Practical Knowledge

Students who were given instruction after they initially grappled with identifying problems and solutions in a case integrated more concepts in their case analysis than those who were given prior instructions. Figure 1.1 shows the ratio of concepts identified from the students' first to their second case analysis. This ratio was obtained by dividing the number of learning and motivation concepts students gained in their second analysis by the number of learning and motivation concepts they identified in their first analysis. As Fig. 1.1 indicates, for both learning and motivation concepts, the gain ratio is higher when instruction was given second rather than first. With instruction prior to case analysis, students gained between 1.2 and 1.4 additional concepts from their second analysis of the case. With instruction following their initial case analysis, students more than doubled the number of concepts they initially identified. In conversations with students, they anecdotally reported actively connecting concepts to the case during the unit of instruction when given the case first. Analyzing the case first seemed

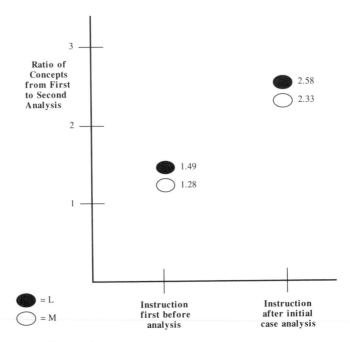

FIG. 1.1. Effects of repeated case analysis on concept integration.

to serve as an anchor for concepts in both semesters and in both units of instruction (learning and motivation).

Repeated Exposures to a Case Strengthened Theoretical/Practical Knowledge

Does revisiting a case after students gain additional knowledge build further knowledge? Lundeberg, Matthews, and Sheurman (1996) expected that students would integrate new ideas from the recent (second) unit, but that the concepts initially identified would remain essentially the same or even diminish.

Figure 1.2 shows the effects of repeated case analysis on concept integration. As Fig. 1.2 illustrates, students integrated concepts both by repeated analysis of a case and by learning principles in educational psychology. Data from both semesters shows a similar cross-over effect. In Semester 1, by using a case as an anchor for the instructional unit on learning, students integrated far more concepts in their second analysis. However, students with previous instruction from the unit on motivation continued to integrate more motivational concepts as well: this was surprising. Repeated case analysis strengthened students' integration of knowledge. We found this pattern

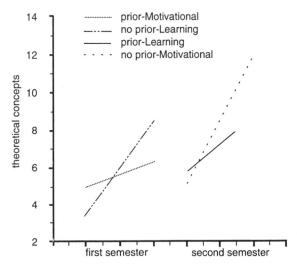

FIG. 1.2. Gains in conceptual knowledge from using cases either before or after instruction in motivation and learning.

again in Semester 2, where the case was used as an anchor for the unit on learning.

Repeated Exposures to a Case Strengthened Reasoning and Metacognition

Lundeberg, Matthews, and Scheurman (1996) asked preservice teachers' whether they thought they learned anything from analyzing a case more than once. Of the students, 11% reported that repeated analysis allowed them to identify more problems and another 11% identified more solutions. As one student said, "When I first started reading cases, I would think, so what's the problem here? And then we would discuss the case and I would hear other students finding these problems. Now I'm able to read and find problems in these cases too" (p. 11). Twenty-nine percent of students commented that the repeated analysis permitted them to go more in-depth, which allowed them to generate more ideas and examine the case further. Almost one quarter (23%) reflected on metacognitive development. These students described how repeated case analysis provided them with a measurement of learning and progression of views: "Yes, it [repeated case analysis] demonstrated what we learned since the last case analysis. [It] Also shows how our views have changed over the course of the semester on this case" (p. 9).

Social, Ethical, and Epistemological Growth

In response to a question asking preservice teachers whether they thought they learned anything from case analysis, over a third of our students wrote that analyzing cases opened their minds to different viewpoints, as these quotes illustrate: "My mind has opened a little more with the exposure to different view points. I've developed more self-confidence." "It's [case analysis] has taught me to take in all views. To see not only from a teacher's view but from a student's, principal's, and other faculty" (Lundeberg & Scheurman, 1997, p. 793).

Preservice teachers believed that case discussions enabled them to change their ideas, and valued this exposure to alternate perspectives, as this student said: "If we deal with them [problem situations] now, even unrealistically, we are still exposed to new ideas. By discussion, we can test our theories and ideas, and learn others! It is through discourse that we can alter previously held convictions, and learn new things" (p. 793). While these self-reported beliefs may not necessarily carry over into classroom actions, there is some indication that the vicarious teaching experiences provided by cases coupled with discussions of theories and experiences contribute to the epistemological development of some preservice teachers. According to Belenky, Clinchy, Goldberger, and Tarule (1986), "connected knowing" is a personal, cooperative approach to learning that values tying theory to experiences, in contrast to "separate knowing," an adversarial, impersonal approach to objective reasoning, which focuses primarily on abstract theories. In an analysis of discussion interaction, I found evidence of preservice teachers (primarily women) connecting previous experiences to cases and raising ethical concerns. Ethical considerations were case-specific—that is, the content of the case contributed to the kinds and percentage of ethical questions that emerged from case discussions. If we are to encourage preservice teachers to discover moral and ethical dimensions involved in teaching and learning, we need to provide appropriate case contexts for them to wrestle with these questions.

REFLECTIONS ON METHODOLOGY

What kinds of discoveries about teaching and learning do preservice teachers make through the case method? The evidence cited here suggests that case discussions develop teachers' theoretical as well as practical knowledge. Moreover, case discussions enhance preservice teachers' reasoning and may foster metacognition. Perhaps most importantly, case discussions increase participants' awareness of their beliefs and values and seem to promote social, epistemological growth.

The methodology used to study pedagogical knowledge has primarily been teacher research: professors studying the knowledge gained by students in their own classes. While there is important insider knowledge utilized in studying ones' classroom, there are also potential biases that may stem from the instructor's intuitions and expectations (see Lundeberg, Levin, & Harrington, chap. 11, this volume, on methodology).

Researchers have used numerous tools, such as writing, interviews, and self-reports, to measure growth and changes in pedagogical knowledge. Studies that combine multiple data sources and perspectives (e.g., product measures with self-reports or interviews) seem more veridical, as are studies that use more than one researcher perspective in examining the data. Some researchers provide data consisting of only one or two strong examples; in such cases, it is impossible to discern how widespread these examples range. Other researchers categorize, count, and provide percentages, but neglect to use statistics, which could shed light on significant changes. A question as yet unanswered has to do with a quantitative assumption some researchers make: that more is better. If students identify twice as many issues in a postcase analysis as in a precase analysis, is that necessarily better? Should one judge the quality of the issues identified? If so, how? Perhaps one of the major methodology questions as yet not clarified is "what counts"? What is the nature of the changes in preservice teachers' thinking, reasoning, critical reflection, beliefs, or values that we need to examine? What is the fate of the "old" understandings, beliefs, and so on? Has preservice teachers' understanding about teaching and learning become more integrated and less fragmented?

Other methodological issues, such as reliability and validity of self-report measure and problems with using written products to evaluate students' understanding are discussed in chapter 11, on methodology. Regardless of the methodological challenges we face in studying whether (and how) cases help our students discover understanding about teaching and learning, intuitive knowledge is not enough. Gathering empirical evidence to systematically test our assumptions will enable us to reassess our goals and to improve our practice. Future research might refine our understanding of how the pedagogical contexts we use influence what students discover through cases.

Commentary: The Case for More and Bigger Cases

Michael Pressley
University of Notre Dame

There has been plenty of evidence generated since the 1970s that students benefit from opportunities to confront problems together—that general thinking skills improve from opportunities to wrestle with specific dilemmas. For example, when students reason together about moral dilemmas, their ability to reason about moral dilemmas in general improves (Enright, Lapsley, & Levy, 1983). When students work on mathematical problems together, the more they try to explain their reasoning to others, the more they learn about mathematical problem-solving (Webb, 1989). Thus, the case made by Lundeberg and other contributors in this volume—that students of teaching can learn a great deal about teaching by interacting over teaching dilemmas presented in cases—makes good sense.

Including case analysis in teacher education makes excellent sense from another perspective as well. Despite the stereotype that teachers mostly go it alone, running their own show once the classroom door is closed, teaching is a profession that demands the ability to think with others. The most obvious set of others that teachers must think with is their students. For example, not a morning goes by in many elementary classrooms when the teacher does not think through a number of problems with students, from reasoning with Johnny about which book he might read next, to discussing with Susie how most efficiently to contact her mother to let her know that Susie is ill. After school, that same teacher may have a conference with a parent that requires substantial joint problem-solving, for example, over a plan to improve a child's reading through a coordinated school and home effort. Sometimes such meetings include not only the teacher and parent but also other professionals, such as special education teachers and school psychologists. Teachers must also reason with others as part of the decision-making required in every school. Faculty members reason together about problems in a school not only during formal faculty meetings, but also informally in the faculty room. Moreover, as respected professionals in the larger community, teachers often sit down with others to confront important civic concerns.

Reasoning well with others is a skill that needs to be developed—for many, it is anything but a natural ability (e.g., Schrage, 1990), with many teachers clearly lacking the ability to oversee classes so that teachers and students think well together (e.g., Haroutunian-Gordon, 1991). Although educational psychologists are convinced that such social shared cognition should be developed in students (Resnick, Levine, & Teasley, 1991), unfortunately, little work has been reported that was explicitly aimed at developing shared cognition abilities in teachers. My guess, however, is that there is a great deal of improvement of shared cognition abilities as teachers reason about cases. If I had a frustration in reading Lundeberg's chapter, it was that I wanted to know more about how reasoning together improved as students of teaching became more experienced in confronting cases together.

Summarizing to this point, I am convinced that much cognitive growth occurs because of the case experiences Lundeberg describes. Nonetheless, even the most complete of written case studies is simplistic relative to the complexities of actual classrooms. I am certain of this point because I have spent much of the 1990s in elementary classrooms confronting the questions: "What is going on in these classrooms, and why?" The result of this immersion in classrooms has been a much more complete theory of comprehension strategies instruction than existed previously (Pressley et al., 1992), a conception of literacy instruction in Grade 4 and 5 classrooms that was full of surprises (Pressley, Wharton-McDonald, Mistretta, & Echevarria, 1998), and a summary of effective Grade 1 instruction resembling rocket science in its complexity (Pressley et al., 1998). All of this work came from the in-depth analysis of individual classrooms, with each classroom seen as a case study and generalizations gleaned by making comparisons across the individual classroom cases. My work as an educational theorist improved enormously by immersing myself in individual cases.

This recent work convinces me that much can be learned from complete immersion in particular classrooms, treating each such classroom as a case study requiring that the observers answer the questions, "What is going on here, and why?" As my colleagues and I did such work, we discussed, argued, and reasoned together a great deal. It was a real growth experience for all who were involved in the work, and I hope that others interested in teaching also will partake of such an experience, expecting that what is known about teaching will increase greatly if teacher educators immerse themselves in living and breathing cases of teaching, especially excellent teaching.

As I reflect on how much my colleagues and I learned, I am convinced that beginning students of teaching would also benefit from such immersion. Thus, I think the case approach needs to upgrade a bit, getting beyond reading and reflecting on written cases to observing it (and reflecting on) real classrooms. If this suggestion is taken seriously and is implemented, students of teaching will begin experiencing the professional world they will be entering, much as students of other professions are introduced to their professional worlds. This past half-year I was immersed in medical treatment at a major teaching hospital. That hospital was filled with young residents who spent much of their time watching older and more accomplished professionals do their work. They also spent a good deal of time in conference with peers and senior physicians, discussing at length the cases they were seeing in the hospital. When I visited with my attorney a few months ago, the firm was filled with summer interns, law students who were immersed in the world of a law firm as part of their training. These young lawyers spent much time with one another talking about the experiences they were having, including much reflection on dilemmas they faced in their work.

In the first pages of *Genesis*, the Judeo-Christian world is instructed that it is not good for people to be alone. Moreover, only when that loneliness was broken did Adam begin to come to knowledge, with everything changing when Eve entered Adam's life. Thus, the constructivist tenet that knowledge is better constructed together than alone is only a recent version of wisdom that is at least as old as the most ancient of the Hebrew scriptures. However, that in no way diminishes the contribution of Lundeberg and others in this volume, who are advancing curriculum that has promise for changing everything in teacher education, transforming it from a curriculum that students mostly study alone to one that is confronted by students of teaching in intense interaction with one another. I look forward to much more work on case-based teacher education that requires students of teaching to think together, including the immersion of students of teaching in real classrooms, confronting the dilemmas of figuring out what is going on and why.

2

Case Analyses As a Performance of Thought[1]

Helen L. Harrington
University of Michigan

Preparing effective and responsible educators has never been easy. As teacher-educators become increasingly aware of factors that influence that process, it becomes more important to have a clear sense of the "kind" of teacher we hope to prepare, the best methods to accomplish that, and how to find ways to determine if we have been successful and, if so, in what ways. Whatever focus a program has, whether it is on preparing reflective practitioners, effective pedagogues, transformative intellectuals—or any other "kind" of teacher—common concerns include how to help new teachers learn to deal with teaching's complexity and ambiguity, make informed decisions, and recognize and move beyond assumptions and beliefs that may limit their ability to foster the learning of all students.

In this chapter, I discuss how asking prospective teachers to complete written analyses of cases can be used to both foster and assess their development. Although the power of case discussions has most often been high-

---

[1] The term *performance of thought* comes from Wolf, Bixby, Glenn, and Gardner (1991). A performance of thought is an approach to assessment that promotes as well as monitors learning. They are multidimensional, respond to learners, and support learning opportunities through design intended to index depth of understanding.

lighted in the research on cases (see Levin, chap. 7, this volume), students' written analyses can provide insight into changes in how prospective teachers think about and resolve the educational dilemmas embedded in cases, and thus indicate growth in their professional development. Professional development has been conceptualized in a variety of ways. For the purposes of the work discussed here, professional development is conceptualized as an increase in the ability to make reasoned decisions, warrant claims, and reflect on assumptions when making professional decisions. First I discuss the framework used to direct the work discussed here, including brief discussions of professional development, case based pedagogy, and performance assessment. Next, drawing from the work of three students, I discuss how their thinking changed over the course of one semester of professional education. I conclude with the implications of utilizing students' written analyses of cases as a way to assess their development as professionals.

GUIDING FRAMEWORK

Professional Development

Teachers must be prepared to deal with ever-changing environments, the ambiguity inherent in those changing environments, the political and ethical nature of the decisions they make, and the consequences of their choices. They must be prepared to work not only in the schools of today and in schools that will be significantly different in the future, but to initiate change in today's schools as well. In addition, an expanding knowledge base requires an understanding that knowledge is constructed, built on previous knowledge, coupled with experience, transformable, evolving, and consequential. Although learning how to foster the learning of all students—the intellectual heart of teachers' work—under conditions of ambiguity is one of the key responsibilities educators must assume, teacher preparation programs must also find ways to prepare professionals who are as concerned with issues of social justice as they are with effective pedagogy (see Griffin's commentary following chap. 6, this volume). In order to achieve any of these aims, expectations must be clearly conceptualized and the means employed given as much thought as the ends desired.

However, regardless of the ends desired, reasoned decision-making as a means to those ends is essential. The work of educational scholars provides ways to understand various aspects of professional reasoning. Toulmin, Rieke, and Janik (1984) provide a framework for reasoned argumentation. Their work suggests that reasoned decision making includes a claim, grounds to support the claim, a warrant to connect grounds and claim, evidence for the warrant (what Toulmin and his colleagues identify as the theoretical or experimental foundations), qualifiers to temper the claim, and consideration of rebuttals. Encouraging the development of reasoned argumentation in teachers should better prepare them to deal with the dilemmas encountered within teaching's ambiguity and complexity in effective and responsible ways.

Professional decisions should also be based on the best evidence available. In teaching, that evidence will be wide-ranging, including both formal theory and practical experience. However, adults in general often fail to provide evidence of any kind to substantiate their interpretations (Kuhn, 1992). Some are not able to generate anything other than pseudo-evidence, or as Kuhn explains it, "a scenario, or script, depicting how [a] phenomenon might occur" (p. 162). Although Kuhn's work suggests that educational attainment plays a part in adults' willingness and ability to present reasoned arguments, King, Wood, and Mines (1990) found that even college seniors often fail to use evidence in support of the arguments they make. They also found that these same students often do not see the relationship among interpretations, judgments, and evidence. Many undergraduate college students see interpretations as being little more than opinion; they neither seek evidence to evaluate conflicting interpretations or provide evidence for their own interpretations. Providing prospective teachers with a way to think about what they value, how they ground arguments, and the evidence they use to support both may lead to more thoughtful action. This in turn should help them better understand how theory and practice can be used to inform each other.

Being disposed to make reasoned, warranted decisions can be subtly undermined, however, by unrecognized assumptions that place limitations on the ability to assess what constitutes best evidence. Epistemic, sociocultural, and psychological assumptions ground beliefs and forms of knowledge and act as filters on reasoning (Mezirow, 1991). Although it is impossible to recognize all assumptions, particularly those that are "regarded as too true to warrant discussion" (Douglas, cited in Bowers, 1988, p. 98), students of teaching should be provided with opportunities to become aware of the assumptions that may limit their effectiveness as professionals. Brookfield (1991) presents a model of critical thinking that includes awareness of assumptions, contexts, alternatives, and being reflective and critical of each. Critical thinkers are aware that their worldview is embedded with assumptions. They further recognize that these assumptions reflect, in part, the contexts they as individuals participate in. They are also aware that other contexts generate other assumptions leading to alternative perspectives. In addition, critical thinkers are able to imagine alternative perspectives. They are also skeptical of both other perspectives and their own perspective. Brookfield's model suggests that although reasoning may be the tool that helps individuals choose among alternatives, being aware of and questioning assumptions precedes choosing among alternatives. What means will help teacher-educators encourage their students to reason and think in these ways? How might our achievement of these aims be assessed?

Case-Based Pedagogy

As the work discussed in this volume indicates, one approach currently being advocated as a pedagogical technique with the potential to foster prospective teachers' professional development in the ways just discussed is case-based pedagogy. Cases based on dilemmas or teaching's illstructuredness, as opposed to other types of cases, are designed to highlight teaching's ambiguity and complexity (Harrington & Garrison, 1992; J. Shulman, 1992a; Sykes & Bird, 1992). The use of dilemma-based cases, in particular, helps students become aware of their reasoning, the evidence they use to ground their reasoning, and the assumptions they bring with them to their understanding of educational dilemmas (Harrington, 1995). Case-based pedagogy also encourages accountability and knowledgeable professional commitment by providing students of teaching with opportunities to hold each other accountable for the interpretations and solutions generated—for warranting claims in effective and responsible ways. The case method does this by providing intending teachers with opportunities to reflect on various courses of action, both through dialogue with others and in the reflection accompanying their own writing (Levin, 1995; Lundeberg & Scheurman, 1997).

The case method may also allow us to do something else and in the process help us determine if our means are aligned with our ends. When we use students' written case analyses to illuminate how they think and reason about the dilemmas encountered in teaching, they can be used to determine if students' professional development is strengthened as they progress through our programs. The way prospective teachers think about and address teaching's dilemmas when they enter programs should become more reasoned, warranted, and reflective as they progress through their professional preparation. Students' written analyses of cases can provide insight into this development when they are viewed as a performance of thought—as a new form of assessment.

Performance Assessment

Whatever method of assessment is used in teacher preparation, it should reflect the overall goals and aims of programs. The model of teacher development being suggested here requires an alternative conception of assessment—one that is embedded in activities that reflect what individuals are expected to do as professionals. Acknowledging teaching as complex and ambiguous necessitates a form of assessment that focuses on conditional knowledge and teachers' thought processes as much as it does on declarative and procedural knowledge. Because development, whether professional or personal, is a process and not an end point, longitudinal forms of assessment are necessary. We also need to go beyond assessing prospective teachers' behaviors, knowledge, and skills to assess how they think—how they frame problems, generate solutions to those problems, and how all those choices inform their future thinking and action. Scholarship on performance assessment provides direction.

Current forms of assessment have been criticized on the basis of their content, format, impact, and absence of criterion related validity (Haertel, 1991) and for their focus on learning as individually achieved, fixed, and linear (Wolf, Bixby, Glenn, & Gardner, 1991). One of the limitations in most current forms of assessment in relation to the assessment of teaching is the failure to acknowledge the ill-structured nature of the teaching and learning process. As Haertel (1991) noted, "there are many areas of professional practice where it is impossible in principle to specify a single correct answer or a single acceptable instructional procedure" (p. 7) or as Wolf et al. (1991) note, there are "culturally variegated forms of excellence [and] contrasting approaches to displaying understanding" (p. 32). Recommendations include developing types of assessment that use "multi-method approaches embedded in existing settings" (Ewell, 1991), allow the extended responses necessary to capture critical understanding (Haertel, 1991), and "offer vigorous and wise diagnostic information rather than rankings on normal curves" (Wolf et al., 1991, p. 31).

A move away from a group, common-denominator approach to assessment to a more individualized approach is particularly important in teacher education. We cannot teach our students all they need to know, but we can help them develop as learners who are able to deal effectively and responsibly with the growing complexities of teaching. The common-denominator approach supports a knowledge transmission model; the individual development approach supports the development of teachers as critical inquirers into their own practice. The individual development approach to teacher assessment is similar to the types of assessment called for by Haertel (1991) under a professional model of teaching:

> Teacher assessment under a professional model would be very different from [assessment under a bureaucratic model]. Professional teacher assessments would be designed to ensure a high standard of professional practice, not to elicit an approved canon of answers to multiple-choice questions that trivialize teaching's complexities ... or to monitor conformity to a checklist of

approved classroom behaviors. Because professionals are expected to exercise judgment and discernment in their work, there are many areas of professional practice where it is impossible in principle to specify a single correct answer or a single acceptable instructional procedure. Thus professional teacher assessments would necessarily be more complex and open-ended than current examinations and observation systems. (p. 7)

Students' written case analyses may provide precisely this kind of assessment. They do not ask for one "correct" answer, but rather require students of teaching to exercise judgment and discernment in their analyses of the problems embedded in practice. The analyses of dilemma-based cases can be considered a "performance of thought" (Wolf et al., 1991) and used to assess prospective teachers' development over time. Wolf, et al. propose that assessment that is a performance of thought is multidimensional and captures an individual's "craft … as it is exercised in the context of his [sic] longer undertaking" (p. 35). They also suggest it is "longitudinal enough to inquire into the processes through which he developed his understanding. It should offer information about his ability to amplify his own thought by connecting it to tools, resources, and other thinkers" (p. 35). Additionally, Wolf et al. propose that this kind of assessment "ought to be keen enough to index the student's depth of understanding: whether he acts only as a correct summarizer or whether he develops a point of view—with all the risk of having to meld values and experience with information and data" (p. 35). Case-based pedagogy can provide this kind of assessment (Harrington, 1995; Harrington & Quinn-Leering, 1996; Harrington, Quinn-Leering, & Hodson, 1996). Students' written analyses can provide rich information about the processes through which prospective teachers develop their understandings, if and how they amplify thought by connecting it to multiple resources, and whether they are summarizing or developing their own, warranted point of view. Written case analyses can also be used to illuminate students' development over time.

LOOKING AT STUDENTS' THINKING

To provide insight into how we might use students' written analyses of cases to examine their development, I discuss the work of three preservice teachers in some detail. Although the focus of much of the research on cases is fostering student development, often limited detail about the substance of students' thinking is provided. Because the main argument presented here is on how cases can be used as a performance of thought, it seems crucial to provide readers with enough information to decide for themselves if that argument is valid.

The work discussed here was completed by three students enrolled in an introductory teacher education course. A critical interpretive analysis (Lincoln & Guba, 1985) of their written analyses of the first and last of three cases[2] included in the course was completed focusing on change in the aspects of professional development just outlined. The first student, Ann,[3] was selected for an outstanding first analysis wherein she thoughtfully reasoned about the dilemmas embedded in the case and solidly warranted her interpretations, recommendations, and reflections. She was the only student of the 22 students enrolled in the course to do so. The second student, Barbara, was selected because she expressed difficulty with written analyses throughout the semester both in the introductory course and in her other courses. She indicated that she was never sure what was expected of her even when given explicit feedback throughout the semester. Although Catherine, the third student selected, had difficulty with the first analysis, she completed the course very successfully. She indicated that she was not sure how to complete the case analyses initially, but the feedback she received with her first analysis enabled her to complete the assignments to her satisfaction. These students represent a range in students' ease or difficulty in completing written analyses of cases.

Students were required to complete their analyses in preparation for a case discussion that served as the culminating activity for sections of the course addressing school and society, teaching, and professional ethics. Cases were selected in light of the readings and the focus of the section of the course that each was aligned with. Students were provided with explicit directions for their written analyses at the beginning of the semester. They were asked to identify and discuss the following: the facts and issues in the case and how they would prioritize them; based on that, how they would identify the case; how different perspectives might inform the interpretation of the case; what their recommended solution was and why; the possible consequences of their solution; and how they would critique their solution and analysis.

Three levels of coding were used to analyze Ann, Barbara, and Catherine's first and last written case analyses.[4] The first level examined the students' reasoning. Their written analyses were examined for the structure of the arguments grounding their analyses of the dilemmas embedded in the

---

[2]Cases were selected from *Case Studies for Teacher Problem Solving* by Silverman, Welty, and Lyon (1992).

[3]All names are pseudonyms.

[4] There were 22 students enrolled in the course. The complete set of analyses was used to develop the coding categories.

case (see, e.g., Harrington, 1995). Aspects of the analyses examined included the students' ability to frame the case, if the key facts and issues identified supported how they framed the case and the solutions they generated, and if and how interpretations and solutions were qualified and substantiated. The second level of coding examined the degree to which students made theory to practice connections—how they warranted their interpretations and solutions. Through multiple passes of the set of analyses, three categories of "theory in use" were identified including formal theory or what they were learning in their college based courses, practical theory or how what they were observing in the practicum[5] informed their interpretations, and personal theory or how their own beliefs and experiences informed their interpretation. The final level of coding illuminated the students' ability to reflect on the process of dilemma analysis. Three categories of reflection were identified during the coding process including awareness of assumptions made by characters in the case, awareness of the students' own assumptions, and awareness of limitations in knowledge, both formal and informal.

The Case of Therese Carmen

The first case analysis was due the fifth week of class. Students had been in their practicum placement for approximately 4 weeks. They had completed readings dealing with approaches to teaching, inclusion, diversity, curriculum, and performance assessment. Class discussions centered on the relationship among learning, teaching, approaches to teaching, and the curriculum choices teachers make. The case they analyzed is that of Therese Carmen, a first-grade teacher struggling with implementing a new science curriculum. The authors of the case suggest that the primary topic being addressed is learning but that additional issues include effective teaching, curriculum, and organizational politics. The thinking captured through the students' analyses is discussed next.

Ann. Ann is one of those students who often seems to fade into the background. She is the kind of student who makes infrequent contributions to class discussions and, unless close attention is paid to those contributions, it is easy to miss how thoughtfully she approaches what is being discussed and studied in her classes. Ann's first analysis illuminates that thoughtfulness. Her analysis is well reasoned and substantively warranted. That in it-

---

[5] While enrolled in the introductory course, students were also enrolled in an educational psychology course, reading methods course, and a 6-hour-per week practicum in an elementary classroom.

self is significant; previous research on case-based pedagogy indicates that few students are able to do this in their first analysis (Harrington, 1995). More significant, however, is her ability to reflect on assumptions, both her own and the assumptions of the characters in the case. Ann's ability to deal with the ambiguity and complexity in teaching, connect theory to practice, and critically reflect so early in her teacher preparation program is exceptional. She immediately identifies the facts of the case, drawing quotes directly from the case to support her summary of the facts. Based on the facts, she lists what she sees as the key issues in the case and from that indicates what kind of case it is. As Schön (1979) suggests, problem-framing is as important as problem resolution—if not more important. Ann frames the case in a way that addresses both instructional issues and broader social and moral issues—a teacher's self-fulfilling prophecy and the implications for student learning and development. As she explicitly writes:

> In my opinion, this is a case of a negative self-fulfilling prophecy, which, in turn, leads Therese to have an ineffective teaching method. This is evidenced in her assumptions of the grade level she is teaching. Therese feels that first graders are "defenseless" and "needy." This causes her to format her class in such a way that she is the center of attention and in complete control.

She then proposes a solution that addresses the case as she identifies it, grounding and warranting her analysis with the formal theory she is reading about and learning in her education classes. She uses quotes from texts such as her educational psychology text and readings from the introductory course to support her interpretations. She also draws from her personal experience and from the practical experience she is engaging in during the practicum. In all instances, she clearly provides insight into her reasoning and thinking.

> My lack of experience working with 6-year-olds hinders my ability to propose a flaw- proof solution to the problems that Therese is having in her classroom. However, is there really such a thing as a flaw-proof solution? There are winners and losers in every situation. … I think that my proposal makes the students the obvious winners. If I am correct in basing my solution on the indicators in the Omnibus Guidelines,[6] the students would begin to flourish in their abilities to accomplish the tasks found in the objectives of the curriculum.

---

[6]A text used in class by Jablon, Ashley, Marsden, Meisels, and Dichtelmiller (1994).

As previously indicated, however, what may be most exceptional about Ann's analysis is her reflection on the assumptions embedded in the case and in her own thinking. She identifies assumptions she thinks the characters in the case are making, assumptions that ground her own interpretations, and limitations in both what is presented in the case and in what she knows at this point in her preparation program. She makes excellent use of qualifying language throughout her analysis to illuminate the tentativeness in what she does and can know. Ann's analysis provides clear insight into how she is beginning to reason about the dilemmas encountered in teaching, make theory to practice connections, and how she is reflecting on her own thinking.

Barbara.   In contrast to Ann, Barbara struggles throughout the semester with the ill-structured nature of the dilemmas embedded in cases. She perceives the directions provided for the written analyses as confusing and written feedback on the completed analyses as unhelpful. She struggles, as well, with the structure of the other education courses she is taking during the semester and with the assignments in those courses. She expresses this in class discussions and in written reflection papers.

Barbara's first case analysis is very descriptive and concrete. Although she seems to have a good sense of the "facts" of the case, she limits her identification of the key issues to one issue—an inappropriate curriculum. She presents the information from the case as absolute. For example, she claims "the teacher is frustrated with the program and the children's response to the program, and is uninterested in teaching the material in the requested fashion." She uses no qualifying language in her analysis; she does not question what is presented in the text of the case or her reading of it.

Although she does not specifically frame the case, her solution addresses the issue she identifies. However, she neither warrants nor provides substantiation for her analysis and recommendations beyond her own beliefs. She makes statements such as "I believe that the principal's loyalties should lie first with the teachers, and then with the students in the school," to support her recommendations. She does not question that if the principal supports Therese (the reasoning she uses in the statement just presented), the principal will not be supporting the teachers who developed the new curriculum. In addition, the reasoning she uses later in the analysis is in conflict with her prior reasoning; toward the end of her analysis she makes statements that are in direct conflict with those made earlier by suggesting the principal should place students first—not teachers, as suggested earlier.

Barbara does not draw from what she is reading in her classes, from her experiences in the practicum, or from her personal experience. Her approach is very procedural. She identifies what she thinks the problem is and what Therese should do to address it. She never questions the possibility that her recommendations might not work nor that her interpretations may be limited. She does not question her own assumptions nor the assumptions of the characters in the case. She seems to take what is presented in the case as a given and does nothing to illuminate her own thinking, let alone reflections on her own thinking. In turning the case of Therese Carmen into a well-structured, single-issue case, Barbara's analysis reflects an oversimplification of the complex and irregular nature of the dilemmas embedded in the case as she treats the multidimensionality of the case as unidimensional. The work on cognitive flexibility suggests that although this is not atypical in advanced knowledge acquisition, it can be detrimental to the development of the ability to deal with ill-structured problems (Spiro, Coulson, Feltovich, & Anderson, 1988)

Catherine. There are ways Catherine's first case analysis is similar to both Ann's and Barbara's. Like Ann, Catherine is aware of the multi-dimensionality of the dilemma presented in the case. But, like Barbara, she immediately bounds the case in a somewhat narrow fashion, although not as narrowly as Barbara does. Whereas Barbara dealt with only one issue, Catherine identifies two issues to be addressed—the appropriateness of the curriculum and school politics. However, she never frames the case or integrates the two issues in her analysis, dealing with each issue independent of the other. In contrast to Barbara, however, Catherine provides clear insight into her reasoning. She is also aware of the tentativeness in being able to "know" what the characters in the case may know and uses qualifiers such as "*perhaps* the other teachers" or "Therese *seemed* to know" to convey that tentativeness.

A major weakness in Catherine's analysis is her total reliance on her own beliefs and opinions. She draws nothing from what she is reading or learning in her courses, from what she is experiencing in the practicum, nor from her own experience. Her analysis reflects Kuhn's (1992) findings that adults often fail to provide evidence to substantiate their interpretations with some generating pseudo-evidence, or as Kuhn explains it, "a scenario, or script, depicting how [a] phenomenon might occur" (p. 162).

Catherine does, however, have good insight into the limitations in her own understanding. She clearly indicates that there are many unknowns, conveying this in a variety of ways. She says such things as "there is no information given about ... " and "it is not clear if ... " or "without knowing the ... " to indicate limitations. She is also able to identify how her own assumptions have influenced her thinking and her reading of the case. In addition, although she does not explicitly address the assumptions of the characters in the case, she does indicate tentativeness through her explicit references to the characters' beliefs. In general, the weaknesses in Catherine's first analysis are ones she effectively addresses in later analyses—to frame the case and to provide substantiation beyond her own opinion and beliefs.

The Case of Carol Brown

The prospective teachers' last analyses were due the 13th week of class. Their practicum was in its last week. In addition to what they had read and discussed prior to the discussion of Therese Carmen, they had completed readings addressing broad issues of schooling and society including issues of equity, equality, and excellence. Professional ethics was the focus for the section of the course, for which the case of Carol Brown served as the culminating activity. In addition to readings dealing with professional ethics, students read articles dealing with teaching's moral dimensions and the multiple responsibilities of teachers including the moral and social development of learners. Discussions in class focused on the multiple ways teaching is a moral enterprise and what that implies for teachers' responsibilities and obligations. The case of Carol Brown deals with a first-grade teacher confronting the possibility of the theft of a pencil case. From Carol's perspective, her class is highly diverse and through her hard work has been successfully socially integrated. The authors of the case suggest that the primary topic being addressed is diversity but an additional issue to consider as students discuss the case is moral development.

Ann.   Ann's last case analysis is as rich as her first. She moves from what she sees as the facts of the case to address fundamental issues grounding the case. What quickly becomes apparent in a reading of her analysis is her ability to deal with the complexity and ambiguity in the events embedded in the case in a coherent and integrated fashion. She does an excellent job synthesizing what she sees as the key issues and facts to frame the case holistically rather than dealing with each issue independent of the others, as many students continue to do. She thoroughly substantiates her interpretations, providing clear insight into her thinking. She also uses qualifiers throughout—indicating, for example, when she has limited information or when she feels she is on firmer ground and what those grounds are.

A particular strength in her analysis of the dilemmas in the cases continues to be how she draws from what she is reading and learning in her courses to substantiate interpretations and recommendations. Her applications of theory to practice are very thoughtful and comprehensive. Whereas many students, at this point in the program, seem to be trying theory on—seeing if it fits a particular situation—Ann makes the kind of connections that indicate she has thoughtfully considered the appropriateness of a particular theory or piece of scholarship to the problems at hand. The specifics of the case are used to determine the appropriateness of the scholarship she draws from. She draws from the readings she is doing in her educational psychology course, quoting from them but also explaining her thinking. She also draws from the readings in the introductory course using "formal" learning to both support her interpretations and to ground suggested recommendations. For example, she explicitly states that she has limited experience to draw from, in terms of the age of the students reflected in the case, and finds this a disadvantage. As she says, "I like to use a combination of reading and experience when I make decisions but, of course, that is not always possible, and the best way to make informed, reflective decisions is to substantiate with what we are reading."

Ann no longer draws from her practicum experience, however. She was placed with a teacher whose style was in conflict with what Ann was learning in her courses and with her own thoughts on teaching. In addition, the teacher discriminated against specific students in class—the African-American students. Over time, this became apparent to Ann and to the university supervisor working with her. Although Ann did not reference the practicum experience in her analysis she did so in other written work, reflecting thoughtfully on what she was observing and how she would counter or avoid that in her own practice.

As in her first analysis, an awareness of assumptions is apparent throughout Ann's final analysis. She also continues to use language to indicate the tentativeness in what is known and explicitly specifies what she has or has not addressed. For example, she indicates "I conveniently avoided what to do about the missing pencil case." She then provides her reasoning for doing so: "That involves things like searching desks or continuing to bring up the issues. For one thing, I lack information about the legality of such measures and/or the possible effects of doing such things to first graders. Thus, that is one area that I do not have enough information to make an accurate, substantiated decision."

Ann continues to draw thoughtfully from what she is reading, learning, and experiencing. She attends to limitations in her knowledge, in the knowledge of others, and in the assumptions that embed each. She is developing her own point of view, one that is grounded and warranted.

Barbara.   Although Barbara does frame the case of Carol Brown, something she did not do in her first analysis, she never indicates what she thinks the key facts or issues in the case are. Indeed, her initial summary or framing of the case provides no support for why she identifies the case as she does. Someone unfamiliar with the case would not be able to determine her possible reasoning. She also continues to present information as absolute, using few qualifiers as she interprets the events in the case. Barbara still provides little insight into her own thinking. The arguments embedded in her analyses do not appear to be reasoned arguments in that she provides few connections among the various aspects of the analysis. Using Toulmin et al.'s (1984) framework, Barbara makes a claim about what Carol Brown is a case of, although she does not provide grounds to support that claim and therefore does not provide warrants to connect grounds and claim nor evidence for those warrants. What she does attempt to provide grounds and evidence for, however, is her evaluation of Carol Brown's approach to teaching. She also presents some substantiation for her recommended solutions.

Although Barbara draws from what she is reading in her various courses and her own experience to support her interpretation of Carol Brown's approach to teaching, 65% of her analysis is devoted to events in the case independent of their relevance to the case as she defines it. She appears to attempt to match what she is reading in her various courses with what is occurring in the case. For example, she cites readings from her reading methods course to support Carol Brown's use of an "author's seat." She describes the technique, providing support through scholarship she has been reading and discussing in her methods course, but does not indicate how she sees that as relevant to the case as she identifies it. So, even though she does appear to make theory to practice connections, there is little coherency in her analysis. She provides no insight into how she understands what she is learning. For example, she cites what she has been reading about prosocial behavior, moral development, and conflict resolution as evidence warranting her solution but draws no distinctions among them nor how they might relate to the specific issues or facts of the case.

A noted change in Barbara's last analysis is her attention to the assumptions being made by the characters in the case. She specifically addresses assumptions she believes can be damaging to the students such as the teacher's assumption that it may be a "poor" student who stole the pencil case and assumptions the teacher is making about other students in the class. Although Barbara provides a rationale for why she thinks this may be damaging, she relies solely on her own beliefs to support her interpretation.

> Carol is making an assumption about the more affluent children in her class. Even though their parents are wealthy, the children may not get every single thing they desire. If a wealthy child is accustomed to getting everything s/he

wants, and his/her parents say no to a new pencil case, s/he may feel justified in taking John's case. After all, "Suzy" wanted it, but her parents said no. Since Suzy usually gets everything she wants, can she see any reason not to take it, particularly if no one is looking?

As she critiques her recommended solutions (but not her analysis) she also acknowledges limitations in her own experience and what she has learned or is learning. She also reflects on how she would approach the situation herself, suggesting she would turn to an authority such as her principal or colleagues with more experience. Barbara's analysis is just that, analysis without synthesis; events are treated independent of one another. She continues to have a great deal of difficulty with the ill-structured nature of the case. In addition, she is unable or unwilling to reflect on her own thinking, providing little or no insight into her reasoning.

Catherine. Catherine draws from all of the strengths of her first analysis and builds on them to provide a reasoned, reflective analysis of the case. In her last analysis, in contrast to her first, she clearly frames the case and explicitly identifies the issues she believes are the key to the resolution of the dilemmas faced by Carol. She provides insight into her thinking and draws from multiple sources of evidence to substantiate her interpretation of the facts, issues, and recommended solutions. She continues to use qualifiers effectively to convey the tentativeness in what she can know about the events in the case.

The greatest improvement is noted in how effectively Catherine draws from what she is reading and learning in her classes. It is clear how carefully she considers how what she is reading and learning can inform specific aspects of practice. In contrast to many other students, Catherine does not rely on a limited number of sources but draws from multiple readings and classes to provide a solid foundation for her interpretations and recommendations. She also provides clear insight into the specific ways the readings inform her thinking. She continues, however, to draw in a very limited way from her own experience and does not mention at any time what she is experiencing in the practicum.

As in her first analysis, it is clear that she is well aware of assumptions that have influenced her analysis of the events in the case. She explicitly addresses those she believes are most relevant and how they have influenced how she thinks about the dilemmas in the case. She is equally aware of limitations in what can be known and how her limited experience may color her analysis. She continues to address the assumptions of the characters in the case by identifying what she interprets as their beliefs. It is left to the reader, however, to determine the specific ways these beliefs may be limitations. In learning what the "rules" of written analyses are, Catherine is able to complete an analysis of the dilemmas embedded in cases in a reasoned, reflective way.

DISCUSSION AND IMPLICATIONS

The intent of this discussion has been to illuminate the insight written case analyses provide into students' thinking. In examining Anne, Barbara, and Catherine's analyses we find that they were encouraged to address the dilemmas of teaching in reasoned ways, draw connections between theory and practice, and critically reflect on their own way of making meaning—they are learning to make reasoned, responsible, and reflective decisions. In addition, their analyses can be viewed as a performance of thought in that they provide rich information about how those understandings develop and how students develop the ability to amplify thought by connecting it to multiple resources (Wolf et al., 1991) They illuminate, as well, whether students are summarizing other positions or developing their own warranted point of view. As would be expected, there is wide variety in students' ability to do so.

Some students, like Ann, approach the dilemmas embedded in cases in mature ways very early in their preparation program. Other students, like Barbara, continue to struggle with the ambiguity and complexity encountered. Still other students like Catherine progress once they learn the "rules." But all students, as exemplified here, develop over the course of a semester. Written case analyses provide insight into at least three aspects of that development: the students' ability to make reasoned decisions, warrant their interpretations, and reflect on assumptions.

As students analyze the dilemmas in cases their thinking becomes more reasoned over time. Providing them with a way to frame their analyses encourages them to understand and make the connections among claims, grounds supporting claims, and the evidence that warrants claims. Writing case analyses also provides students of teaching with opportunities to reflect on their own thinking and on the thinking of others. Although cases can be used to encourage all students to make more reasoned decisions, some will have more difficulty developing reasoned practice than others. The work of Spiro et al. (1988) is instructive in helping us to understand students who may have difficulty dealing with the ambiguity in cases. Some students, like Barbara, seek to limit the complexity and ambiguity in cases by dealing with the issues one at a time, and drawing no connections among them. They simplify the ambiguous structure in order to deal with it. They also match the theory they "know" to the events in each case, ignoring the specific contextual complexity in each case. They do not reflect on their own thinking—do not reason about their own reasoning—or on the tentativeness in what can be known with certainty. They treat what is given as absolute, questioning neither their interpretations or the interpretations of the characters in the case. Written case analyses provide insight into how students will deal with the complexity and ambiguity encountered in teaching and, in doing so, may be used to help students deal with that complexity in more effective ways. Future research may provide insight into that possibility.

Although case-based pedagogy also helps students of teaching learn to warrant their interpretations and decisions, we have no assurance they will do so in practice. It is instructive, nonetheless, to consider the different ways they warrant claims and actions within their written analyses. When they rely on only their own beliefs, as both Barbara and Catherine do initially, it is important to provide them with opportunities to consider how what they are learning can also inform their thinking. The use of cases can be a particularly powerful way to help students make explicit practice to theory connections. They have time to consider how what they are learning and reading can inform the decisions made in classrooms; they can discuss applications of formal knowledge with their peers in case discussions; and they can compare and contrast the effectiveness of decisions based solely on experience or theory, or a combination of both. When cases are drawn from real events in classrooms, theory becomes more than an abstract body of knowledge learned in college classrooms; it becomes a tool used by reflective practitioners. Students begin to "practice" responsible and thoughtful ways of approaching the dilemmas in teaching. They begin to consider as well, as Ann does, how multiple sources of evidence—both experience and formal knowledge—can inform professional decision-making. All three students, over the course of the semester, begin to draw from what they are reading and learning to help them better understand the events in the cases. The events in the case, in turn, may help them better understand what they are reading and learning. Future research may provide insight into this reciprocity.

In order for teachers to make reasoned decisions that have a strong evidentiary base, they must also be aware of assumptions that act as filters or, in some instances, blinders to their understanding of the teaching and learning process. Case-based pedagogy offers numerous opportunities for prospective teachers to become aware of how assumptions ground what they and others know. Each student discussed above became more aware of assumptions over the course of the semester. They were, as well, sensitive to multiple "kinds" of assumptions. They reflected on how their own assumptions influenced how they interpreted the events in the case as well as the solutions they recommended. Some students were also sensitive to how the assumptions of the characters in each case might have influenced the actions they took and their interpretations of the events. Finally, they became more sensitive to how much assurance they could have (what they could assume) in what they knew based on their own experience, what they have learned at this point in their program, and the information presented in the case. By sensitizing themselves to their own assumptions in the course of completing written case analyses, students of teaching may become more sensitive to assumptions held by others. Case discussions can further serve to help students become more aware of and attentive to the influences of assumptions.

Students' written case analyses can also be used to assess how students are "thinking" about teaching—they can be used as a "performance of thought." They capture multiple aspects of student thinking. They reflect how students reason in that they include a claim (how students frame the case); grounds to support the claim (the connections they draw among facts, issues, and the claim); warrants used to connect grounds and claims (how they substantiate their thinking); evidence for the warrants (the formal, informal, and personal theory they draw from); and qualifiers and consideration of rebuttals. Cases provide students with opportunities to reason about real problems that educators encounter in practice. Although the students themselves are not practicing educators, dilemma-based cases do "capture [an individual's] craft ... as it is exercised in the context of his [sic] longer undertaking" (Wolf et al., 1991, p. 35) and provide opportunities to assess how students of teaching might approach those dilemmas in practice. The analysis of cases can also be used to provide insight into prospective teachers' development over time. They illuminate the processes that contribute to students' understanding of teaching's complexity and ambiguity as well as the connections students of teaching make between their own thinking and the resources, skills, and theory they are presented with in their formal preparation program.

Although case-based pedagogy seems to offer significant potential for strengthening the preparation of teachers, cautions must be raised. In the work discussed here cases are only a part of the work students engage in. They are provided with other opportunities intended to foster their reasoning, responsibility, and reflectiveness. It is impossible to determine exactly how much cases play a role in fostering students' development. The use of cases, however, does provide a structure for helping prospective teachers learn how to deal with dilemmas in teaching and illuminates that development.

Acknowledging the ambiguity and complexity in teaching requires that we are less intent on giving students the answers they need and more intent on helping them develop the ability to find their own answers. The work reported here and in the other chapters in this book suggests that case-based pedagogy offers multiple opportunities for fostering students' professional development. Teachers must make reasoned decisions. They must choose among alternatives to find the best answers for the specific students in their care. They must do so in light of the specific contexts in which they find themselves working. They must, as well, be aware of how their own experience serves to both inform and confound the decisions they make. These are not skills to be transmitted to students of teaching within the course of their professional preparation program. They are ways of thinking or habits of mind developed over time. New models of professional development require new forms of preparation and assessment. Case base pedagogy may provide both.

Commentary on "Case Analyses As a Performance of Thought"

Anthony G. Rud, Jr.
Purdue University

The previous chapter focuses on how to prepare effective and responsible educators. These two attributes are especially important in today's schools. Teachers should reach out and teach students not only subject matter, but also about the wider society and the role of a citizen in a democracy.

To accomplish these aims, teachers must be able to choose among a variety of strategies. Informed choice requires reflection and deliberation. Reasoning should be a social process, and thus a teacher must state reasons for doing what she does, and let others examine and discuss these reasons. Privately held beliefs silence the articulation of a community based upon shared ideas and norms. Many minds together are better than one, at least in teaching and learning.

In her chapter, Harrington asks more of professional development than many teacher educators do. Dwelling with ambiguity and complexity are not easy tasks, especially for college students. In order to prepare future teachers, an atmosphere hospitable to conflicting ideas must be supported. If we are to prepare effective and responsible educators, they must have considered the many facets of schooling. These complexities include the social context of schooling (Liston & Zeichner, 1991), a contested arena where the roles schools play in society and in social transformation are significant.

Harrington assumes that her case-based pedagogy would give students practice in reasoning skills, and she demonstrates that this can happen. However, I wonder if these same students had any practice in reasoning before they came to higher education and their professional education se-

quence. I note that Harrington's first student, Ann, was the only one of 22
who presented an "outstanding first analysis" of a case.

Matthew Lipman (1991, 1996) and his colleagues at the Institute for the
Advancement of Philosophy for Children have argued over the years that
higher education is too late to begin practice with reasoning. Lipman's "philosophy for children" curriculum assumes that children can begin to reason
as early as the primary grades. Practice in analytic reasoning, using the standard of warranted assertion Harrington promotes, occurs extensively in the
preadolescent part of Lipman's program.

What if students had such practice even before coming to the university,
where they might reflect upon teaching and what it means to be a teacher? I
was particularly struck by the fact that the concurrent practicum had little
influence on written analyses of Harrington's students. It seems ironic that
students will spend years before getting to college in classrooms with various
teachers, and yet few teachers ever share rationales of their own practice
with their students.

My daughter's second-grade teacher bucked the trend in her rural South-
ern school. She devised teaching strategies heavily reliant on Deweyan and
Foxfire concepts and practices. She shared these ideas explicitly with her
youngsters, and in greater detail with parents. We all knew why her room
was so arranged, or why she taught reading in a particular way.

Teaching via transmission does not accommodate such reflection on
method. Deweyan models such as Lipman's philosophy for children pedagogy explicitly encourage reflection upon method by all involved. The
teacher is a facilitator, among equals in a circle of dialogue.

In addition to investigating the preparation in reasoning that may occur
before college, another promising area of future research might be an
inservice model where cases are used. I have joined many others in successfully using cases in a doctoral program in educational leadership. Likewise, I
would like to see how veteran teachers reacted to cases through written
analyses. Many teachers still work in isolation, and do not have the opportunity to relate and compare their teaching to others, or to use professional or
other literature to illuminate the nuances of their work (Rud, 1993).
Written case analysis, perhaps even posted on a listserv or website so that
topic strands of discussion and commentary could be followed, would go far
to help break these walls of professional and personal isolation.

Harrington is careful to acknowledge that cases are only part of the work
these students do. Using other means to develop a reflective habit of mind,
or what some have called the "critical spirit" (Siegel, 1988), are vital.
Written analyses of cases, and pedagogies like it, are perhaps what university
educators are equipped at doing and assessing best. Close contact with field
experience supervisors, and student interaction over case analyses, would

provide additional insights into how student knowledge and performance are developed. Cases are a valuable tool for professional development. Let us make the use of cases even stronger by investigating ways they may be used to strengthen reasoning both before, and after, college.

3

Case Methods and Teacher Change: Shifting Authority to Build Autonomy

Carne S. Barnett
Pamela A. Tyson
WestEd, San Francisco

Lisa joined mathematics case discussions at the insistence of her fellow teachers, three of whom had participated the year before. She rarely contributed to the early discussions. When she finally ventured into the conversations, she asked questions that others might have been reluctant to ask, such as, "I'm like the kid [in the case], I don't understand why 100% isn't 100."

Lisa's confidence and trust grew with each monthly discussion. She began to tap her fellow teachers in the group as resources for new ideas and teaching materials. Instead of skipping percent this year, as she had done in previous years, she did a six-week unit using "real-world" problems and manipulatives. As she said in an interview, "I'm beginning to trust myself and try new things."

Lisa, like others in her case discussion group, exhibited a growing sense of autonomy with regard to her mathematics teaching. Most of the teachers in this group did not enter the case discussions with strong confidence in their mathematics teaching, yet at their own initiation they began to open their classrooms, seek advice from each other, question their own assumptions about teaching, and engage in collaborative inquiry. The autonomy the teachers demonstrated, both individually and collectively, could be characterized as the empowerment to make decisions, a propensity to self-monitor, a sense of efficacy, openness to criticism, and ownership of ideas.

These outcomes were surprising, in part because the professional development program in which the teachers were participating made no explicit assignment to incorporate these changes into their teaching practice, initiate inquiry projects, or work collaboratively outside of case discussions. These were decisions the teachers made of their own accord. In examining Lisa's story and the stories of others who have engaged in mathematics case discussions, we became interested in understanding more fully what features of the case discussion program contribute to teachers' propensity to autonomously make decisions about their mathematics teaching practice.

Many educational leaders consider autonomy a worthy attribute for teachers to acquire (Driscoll & Lord, 1990; Elliott, 1990; Richardson, 1990). Little's (1990, 1993) analyses of the research literature on professional development support this goal as it relates to teachers' initiative and responsibility. She concluded that the form and content of the collegial relationships among teachers, and the extent to which they stimulate collective autonomy, can be significant factors determining whether teachers feel empowered to make changes in their classrooms. Little (1990) defines *collective autonomy* as "teachers' decisions to pursue a single course of action in concert or, alternatively, to decide on a set of basic priorities that in turn guide the independent choices of individual teachers" (p. 519).

Several respected proponents of the case discussion approach point out how it can contribute to different aspects of autonomous behavior. Wasserman (1993), for example, proposes that "learning with cases promotes personal and professional autonomy. Cases require you to develop your own ideas, to evaluate situations as you see them, to make a decision based on how you see the issues being resolved" (p. 28). Harrington and Garrison (1992) argue that using cases as opportunities for shared inquiry and reflection leads teachers to "question not only what is and why, but what could be" (p. 719). Ingvarson and Merrin (1997) note that through involvement in case discussions, "we have seen teachers set their own demanding agenda for reform and focus their energy on what really matters to them in meeting their own standards and aspirations to do a better job" (p. 13). Although there are numerous claims about how involvement in case methods supports the growth of autonomous teacher behaviors, little research has been carried out to document this (Merseth, 1996).

This chapter documents and provides rich descriptions of autonomy that we observed in the teachers with whom we work. In the first part of the chapter, we describe features of the Mathematics Case Methods Project that were designed to support autonomous behaviors with regard to mathematics teaching. In the second part of the chapter, we present examples that illustrate teachers' autonomous thinking and behavior. At this point we are not making arguments about how participation in math case methods leads to specific changes in teachers and their practice; instead we are juxtaposing the aspects of math case methods that were developed to support teacher autonomy with instances from teachers' self-report data and classroom activities. Comparing such instances of teacher autonomy with the components of the case methods could help us to more clearly define what we mean by autonomy. Thus, this study sets the stage for future studies that could document the breadth and depth of development of autonomy within a group of case discussion teachers.

METHODOLOGY

The goal of this chapter is to more fully illuminate the character of autonomy that we believe is promoted through the case discussion process, and to present compelling examples from our own observations and teachers' self-reports to suggest how it might develop. We are not trying to make causal connections between participation in math case discussions and teachers' development of autonomy in their practice. Instead, this is an interpretative study designed to provide more information about the "structure of occurrences, rather than their general character and overall distribution, and the meaning-perspectives of the particular actors in the particular events" (Erickson, 1986, p. 121). This exploration sets the stage for future work that will document in more broadly and deeply how autonomy develops within a group of teachers.

Because we are not making claims, at this point, about the typicality of our findings, we have surveyed a vast array of data to find exemplars of autonomy demonstrated by teacher responses or practices. These data were part of an ongoing longitudinal study of the Mathematics Case Methods Project that began in 1989. Our data profile for individual teachers varies greatly: for some we have data since 1989, for others we have only recent data. Also, there is considerable variation in the roles that teachers have taken in the project. For example, depending on their skill and experience, they have the option to discuss cases, write cases, facilitate case discussions with peers, or conduct seminars for others to learn how to write or facilitate discussions.

At this point, data have been collected on approximately 100 teachers, kindergarten through eighth grades. Subsets of teachers were chosen to participate in different aspects of the study. An especially rich source of data is the videotapes and audiotapes of the monthly case discussions, held over a 9-month period, with three different groups of teachers. All of the teachers in this study were from a local school district in the San Francisco Bay Area, serving a community that is economically, racially, and linguistically diverse.

Our data include the following:

1. Videotapes and audiotapes of case discussions, as well as transcriptions of these tapes.
2. Videotapes of mathematics lessons and teachers' reflections about their own teaching as shown on videotape.
3. Pre- and postassessments of teachers' understanding of rational numbers.
4. Structured oral interviews, each lasting 45 to 90 minutes.
5. Researchers' notes from case discussions and personal conversations with teachers.

EXAMINATION OF THE STRUCTURE OF THE CASE DISCUSSION PROCESS

Several features of the Mathematics Case Discussion Project were developed with the goal of fostering autonomous behavior in mathematics teaching. We describe these features by first explaining the nature of the cases. Then we examine the role of the facilitator and the norms of the discussion process. Finally, we discuss how the overall framework of the program provides opportunities for autonomy to evolve.

The Nature of Cases.   Either a case can be framed as "an instance of exemplary practice," or it can carry "no presumption that the case itself illustrates either exemplary or ineffective practice" (Merseth, 1991a, p. 2). Our cases (Barnett, Goldenstein, & Jackson, 1994) follow the latter model. They are narratives designed to promote discussion of significant issues; portray a variety of teaching strategies and philosophies; and highlight the complexity, rationality, and flaws in student thinking. These cases were written by fourth- through eighth-grade teachers about the surprises, perplexing situations, and dilemmas they encountered while teaching fractions, decimals, ratios, and percentages.

In addition, the cases portray real-life situations with all the ambiguities that teachers typically encounter in the classroom. Such events frequently do not have clear-cut, generalizable solutions. Thus, the discussion goal is not to lead teachers to the correct answers, but rather to expand their knowledge base so that they can better assess their materials and decisions.

We attempt to frame the cases so that they do not represent or endorse particular teaching strategies. Our aim is to open critical deliberation on all viewpoints, those illustrated in the case as well as those espoused by group members. We have a saying that "nothing is sacred" in a case discussion, not even the activities that teachers hold dearest or the recommendations of the latest reform effort. Through the case discussion inquiry, teachers are "enabled to assume responsibility for their own learning rather than simply being instructed" (Harrington & Garrison, 1992, p. 721).

Content of Case Discussions. As Ball (1997) notes, both knowledge of subject matter and knowledge of children and their mathematical thinking are crucial to effective teaching. In an introductory seminar, teachers come to understand that a productive discussion has a strong emphasis on understanding the mathematics from both the students' and teacher's points of view. We believe that many teachers rely too much on external authority for their teaching decisions in mathematics, principally because of their limited pedagogical content knowledge. Excerpts from a case discussion by Lisa's group are provided later in this chapter to illustrate how a focus on content during case discussions relates to growth in teacher autonomy.

Facilitator Role and Norms of the Case Discussion Process. The role of facilitator varies among users of the case discussion approach (Christensen, Garvin, & Sweet, 1991; Silverman & Welty, 1996; Wasserman, 1993). One variant is the amount of authority and status the facilitator assumes in the discussion group. Although the facilitator attends to the flow of the discussion, it is the participants who frame the issues to be discussed, decide where the discussion should start, and assess the process and content of the discussion. Thus, the responsibility for the direction and quality of the discussion is shared between the facilitator and the participants.

Both facilitators and discussants attend a 1- to 2-day seminar to learn their roles in a discussion. The seminar stresses that both the facilitator and discussants are responsible for the quality of the discussion. During the seminar they learn to use specific tools to help them assess that quality for themselves.

One of the tools is a short questionnaire given at the end of a discussion, in which each participant rates different aspects of the discussion and makes comments anonymously. The forms are then collected and read back to the group, as feedback for future discussions. If a serious problem is detected, the group discusses what action they should take to improve the situation. The Reflection Guide is another tool the group uses to assess and improve the quality of their discussions. This tool is more detailed and provides specific guidance to assess how issues were examined and linked to other issues, how alternative points of view were treated, how ideas were presented, and so on. This instrument is relatively new, but is considered to be a valuable tool by teachers who are using it.

Discussions are lead by a facilitator, whose role is to ask teachers to clarify and elaborate their ideas, justify their positions, and critically examine alternative perspectives. The facilitator attempts not to take on the role of expert, leading participants to particular conclusions or points of view. If the group becomes entrenched in a particular way of thinking, or is overlooking an important alternative, the facilitator may present an alternative idea that the group is not considering. In this role, the facilitator may or may not agree with position he or she is arguing. The introductory seminar makes it clear to the group that this form of deliberation can be expected and why it is important.

Framework of the Program.   Since its inception, the Mathematics Case Methods Project has relied on teachers' involvement in decision-making and input into the overall direction of the program. They serve as advisory board members; help coordinate and plan the logistics of the program; write, edit, and revise cases based on field-test results; and contribute to the design of the research. They not only take leadership roles by facilitating case discussions, they also conduct seminars to help others learn to discuss and facilitate case discussions. Our goal in developing the structure of the case discussions and the design of the program itself is to support the shift in teachers' perceptions of authority from external sources to internal and collective sources, thus promoting autonomy.

EXAMPLES OF INDIVIDUAL AND COLLECTIVE AUTONOMY DEMONSTRATED BY THE CASE DISCUSSION TEACHERS

In the following sections, we discuss how we perceive autonomy to be exhibited by the case discussion teachers. We have sorted the examples into three categories. Examples that demonstrate autonomy through (a) the strengthening of content and pedagogical content knowledge bases, (b) the realization that capability and wisdom exists within the group, and (c) the development of a critical stance toward teaching decisions. Although each factor is discussed separately in the sections that follow, they are interrelated.

Content and Pedagogical Content Knowledge. To illustrate how case discussions could support the development of teacher autonomy, we return to the group of teachers described earlier. The following excerpts were drawn from a transcript of one of their case discussions. We attempted to summarize and condense the discussion with care so as not to misrepresent the conversation among teachers.

The seven teachers in this particular discussion group spent from 15 to 45 hours discussing cases. All were from the same school. They were a diverse group, representing a range of teaching experience (from 2 to more than 20 years), professional development exposure (from none to extensive), and grade levels (from Grades 4 through 6). This was the group's fifth case discussion.

This particular case discussion was selected because it illustrates the fervor with which teachers discuss mathematical content and pedagogy, and it contains several vivid examples that illustrate the ideas presented in the sections that follow.

SIX HOURS ISN'T ONE SIXTH OF A DAY: EXCERPTS AND COMMENTARY FROM A CASE DISCUSSION

In this case the teacher-author writes about a lesson in which she asked her students to make circle graphs representing the amount of time they spend on activities during a day. The circles given to the students were divided into 24 parts, one part for each hour of the day. The case included a circle graph that one of her students drew (see Fig. 3.1). The teacher asked the students to name the fractional part of the graph that was spent conducting each activity.

In the case discussion various issues were raised. It was discussed why students in the case had difficulty seeing that the section of the graph representing time spent in "school" was one fourth of a day. Sue, a member of the group, argued that it is "much more visible" to start with a circle divided into fourths and then figure how out many twenty-fourths it represents, than to see one-fourth imbedded in a circle "presubdivided" into twenty-fourths. (*Presubdivided* was a term coined by this group and used frequently in their case discussions.) After some discussion, most teachers agreed with Sue, even though the idea seemed counterintuitive at first.

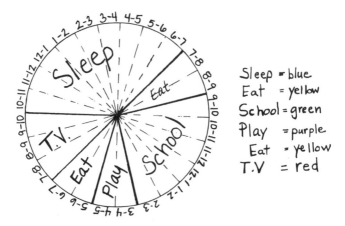

FIG. 3.1 Student's activity circle graph.

The participants also speculated that maybe students could not name the one fourth because they were accustomed to the textbook rule of counting the number of *equal* parts to determine the denominator, and the number of shaded parts to determine the numerator of a fraction. If students focused on the *unequal* parts representing time spent on the different activities, they would be unable to name the fraction based on the textbook rule that they had learned.

This prompted Sue to question whether unequal parts could even represent fractions. According to a definition she had been using, the parts had to be equal or it wasn't a fraction. This began a serious debate. Sue went to her classroom to get some examples from a resource book she had been using with her students.

Returning to the group, Sue described how she had shown her students different drawings and asked them use the book definition to determine if the drawing represented a fraction and what fraction it represented. The drawings were not the usual textbook drawings of circles and rectangles. One drawing in particular (Fig. 3.2) stimulated a spirited debate among her students (Transcript 2/12/92, pp. 7–8).

Sue reported that some students claimed the drawing represented three fourths, some that it represented three-thirds, and others that it wasn't a fraction at all, but instead was a whole. Sue indicated that she had accepted all of these answers because the students were able to defend their answers based on the three-part definition that she had presented earlier to the class.

In response to Sue's "classroom case," Nancy and Jim discussed whether or not Sue should "allow" her students to consider this drawing to be a

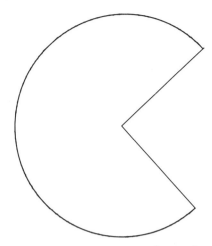

FIG. 3.2. "Whole PacMan" shape drawing.

whole, even though her students had justified their assertion saying that it was a "whole PacMan."

Nancy: I'd let them go ahead and see it as a whole with a part missing, but I would be really happy when they saw the PacMan shape as the whole. Therefore, they're getting themselves out of that rut saying the whole has to be the circle.

Jim: I have a problem with the directions of this thing and maybe it's because I'm simple-minded, but I want my students to get something firmly fixed in their mind, which is this visual sense of what fractions might be. What I'm afraid of is if I've led them through this, their original visual sense that this represents three-quarters of something is going to be confused by a lot of these things that will leave them less intuitively able to solve problems than they were beforehand.

Facilitator: So what would you recommend?

Jim: Well I would recommend staying away from irregular shapes, giving them a variety of regular shapes divided into fractions or relatively regular numbers, not giving them these ambiguous things.

Sue: But somehow we want them to get the concept of the one, and that's all my discussion was.

Jim: But I would not show students [irregular shapes] at this point, except for a handful.

Sue: Maybe it does depend upon the level of the student, but I feel that at some point it's good to get them out of that thinking that the one square is the whole, the one circle is the whole, or the one long strip.

Lisa: Maybe they're not ready for [irregular shapes]. Maybe if we worked to get fourth graders to understand the parts, then by the time we get to sixth grade we could take them farther. I see what Jim is saying. ... But they need to have some kind of understanding, and if they don't have that basic understanding, then how can they know what one-fourth is? Why is that a quarter? Because I'm the teacher?

The deliberation over what represents a whole and what represents a fraction continued. The group debated examples from Sue's resource book and referred back to examples from earlier cases. Although there was no clear consensus about the teaching implications, there was an awareness that something that looks like a part might be considered a whole, depending on the situation, it is important to define the whole up front. For some teachers, using ambiguous examples with students was desirable; for others, it's value was questionable.

Sue was clearly unsettled by this discussion. She was questioning the role of a definition, her uncritical use of the resource book, her colleagues' opinions, and her own understanding of fractions. Near the close, she reflected back on the case discussion.

Sue: I don't know how many times I've heard people say things, and I go—Wait a minute! I looked at this and I said, oh boy, and I didn't look at it with a discerning eye. I questioned the circle [graph] myself, and it doesn't fit the definition. And I was telling Elena I'm the kind of person who has to plow through it [the resource book]. I accept it when it's written, and that's the way I'm going to go with it. But right now I am getting a little anxiety. I'm pushed and pulled about it.

During a case discussion, the teachers openly discuss, question, and revise their thinking about mathematical concepts. Sue, for example, related that she had asked her students to learn a definition for naming fractions that asserted that the "whole" needed to be divided into equal parts. She explained to her students that if the whole wasn't divided into equal parts, it wasn't a fraction. When she brought this up in the discussion with her colleagues, they had to confront their own understandings of what defined a fraction and how a definition differs from a rule for naming a fraction.

The debate was even more passionate about what constitutes a whole. Could (or should) you call a PacMan shape a whole when it has (as some viewed it) a piece missing? This debate, along with subsequent discussions, helped teachers realize the ambiguity of the whole, and how many different ways it can be represented. In some situations (such as the PacMan shape) they realized that the whole might have the appearance of a part. In other case discussions they discovered that one has to temporarily consider the whole to be whole and a part (when finding one half of two and a half). By reassessing mathematical issues in different contexts from case to case, teachers' understanding of the mathematics appears to become gradually more complex and connected.

This conclusion is further supported by data gathered from assessments of teachers' understanding of rational numbers, a questionnaire addressing teachers' attitudes and beliefs, and transcripts of interviews and case discussions. Detailed reports of our findings are provided in other papers (Barnett, 1998; Gordon, Heller, & Lee, 1995; Heller, 1995). However, we give a brief overview of some of our findings here.

Two separate studies (see Gordon, Heller, & Lee, 1995) examined the impact of case discussions on knowledge of mathematics. Each study involved approximately 30 teachers who were administered pre- and post-discussion tests of their understanding of rational numbers. No control group was used for either study. The assessment instrument was adapted from one developed by Post and Harel to assess teacher knowledge in a nationally recognized professional development project. This assessment, composed of 40 free-response items, elicited not only numerical solutions but also explanations of the solution process, made up of either words or drawings. It was administered in each of the two separate studies. In both studies, the teachers involved in case discussions during a single school year experienced a statistically significant growth in their knowledge of rational numbers (see Gordon, Heller, & Lee, 1995).

In this section we attempted to describe how knowledge of mathematics content might develop through case discussions, and we provide a glimpse of the findings from our ongoing series of studies. We believe that an outgrowth of this enhanced content knowledge is an increased ability to operate as autonomous professionals in mathematics education.

Capability and Wisdom Within the Group. Our cases embed problems for teachers to work on jointly. As can be seen in the discussion excerpts just presented, often teachers struggle together to understand mathematical representations from the student's point of view. They challenge each other's values and deliberate on the teaching strategies portrayed in the case and generated by the group. Although the case is not authored by a member or the group, the members project their own experiences to the dilemma so that, in a sense, it becomes their own.

Little (1990) contends that is through joint work that teachers must "open their intentions and practices to public examination" by their colleagues (p. 16). In turn, members of the group can be "credited for their knowledge, skill, and judgment" (p. 17). These characteristics of joint work, which collectively build autonomy, and in turn guide individual and group teaching decisions, are among the most important aspects of case discussions. A second-year teacher said it this way:

> We're all these individuals bouncing ideas off each other and going, "wow," some of these things I thought of. It was reassuring. [But then] I'm thinking to myself, "oh, my God, I could be a lot better. I could do that, and I could probably get better results with my students." So in one way it was reassuring and the other way it was startling. (Interview transcript 6/23/94, pp. 13–14)

As teachers work together on the problems captured in cases or on the issues they generated, they begin to develop common understandings, shared values, and a common language for talking about their practice. For example, in the excerpts from the discussion reported above, teachers had coined the term *presubdivided*. Through the discussions, they discovered that many manipulatives are constructed in such a way that the thinking required by a child is minimized. For example, if students use fraction materials with premade equal subdivisions, they may not pay attention to the fact that the parts are equal, or they may not learn how to make equal parts themselves. Also, if the manipulative is partitioned in only one way, students may not realize that it can be divided into equal parts in many different ways unless they do the dividing themselves. The significance of these ideas arose in case after case and was one of many common ideas that teachers developed as part of their mutually shared knowledge base.

In many of our interviews, teachers express an appreciation for this mutually generated wisdom. "You learn a lot from everybody," asserts Sue from the above case discussion. She continues,

> There's so many varying ideas out there, and honoring [each other's] thinking and looking at things in a different way than you had before, and understanding math a little bit more. I think I understand ... I'm able to do a little bit more about my presentations to kids. You just get a real high out of discussing. (interview transcript 6/18/94, p. 22)

Given the structure of the case discussions and the less authoritative role of the facilitator, these references to a mutually generated wisdom are not surprising. It is understood that both the facilitator and the group are responsible for the quality of the discussion. Explicit instruction is given to teach group members how to discuss issues so that all views and alternatives (even those that are held by the minority) are examined for both benefits and drawbacks.

Furthermore, we have evidence that when discussions are held among teachers from the same site, the mutually generated wisdom is frequently called on in making classroom decisions. Because the teachers have daily access to members of the case discussion group, the issues that emerged from the cases remain part of their everyday conversations. For example, it was common for teachers to consult with each other about the units they were planning. They would talk about how to adapt lessons to compensate for perceived weaknesses and deliberate about the strengths and weaknesses of particular manipulatives. The lunchroom became energized with conversation about what students were doing and thinking in their classes. One of our primary goals is to break down teacher isolation and to encourage the exchange ideas around specific mathematics content. Although we did not ask the teachers to draw on the expertise of their peers outside of the case discussion group, we feel that we created the conditions and habits to evoke this ongoing dialogue.

Developing a Critical Stance.   One goal of the case discussion method is to engage participants in thoughtful analyses of mathematical ideas and teaching strategies, so that they develop a critical eye toward teaching decisions and techniques. The facilitator challenges teachers—and, in time, the teachers challenge each other—to justify their responses, to examine both the desirable and undesirable consequences of recommendations, and to identify the constraints and limitations of different ideas. At times the facilitator or a participant may even play devil's advocate by presenting an argument with which she or he may not necessarily agree. In doing so, the facilitator gives voice to perspectives that would not otherwise be examined. The facilitator also attempts to encourage participants to articulate their own views either in support of, or in distinction to, the one being presented. By articulating and hearing multiple sides of the issues, teachers begin to develop a critical stance and are able to articulate their reasons for adopting one idea over another. Ultimately, they become more confident—and competent—to make judgments for themselves instead of deferring to an authority.

In the beginning, it is primarily the facilitator that probes for critical analyses and presentation of different perspectives. Through the course of the discussions, however, teachers begin to offer critical analysis of the cases, of each other's comments, and of their own teaching. One teacher states,

> I felt [it] was very good for me to hear disagreements. I mean disagreements with my own viewpoints whether I expressed mine and people were disagreeing with me or not was not really important, but things that were contrary to what I believe. I need to be reminded that there are other ways of thinking [about] how to teach and it then can help to reinforce what I am feeling, or it can help to sway me the other way.

> For example, in one case discussion a participant said she didn't feel there should be any wrong answers put on the board because it would confuse the students. She didn't want any responsibility for the students leaving something wrong on the board or hearing a wrong answer. I disagree with that. I think being able to hear it was a revelation to me. I didn't realize that people could feel that way. But, that's wonderful for me because I can really ask myself, why do I feel this, or do I really. Is there a part of me that might agree with her? This time I decided that I did not agree. I think there's really a valid place for wrong answers. But hearing opposing viewpoints, and in a professional kind of way, in a respectful way, has been very valid. (Interview transcript 6/12/91, p. 2)

By articulating their own views and comparing them to the views of their peers, teachers are able to develop their own criteria for judging the merits and demerits of various ideas. One criterion that case discussion teachers applied to curricula, teaching strategies, and assessment items is the extent to which they represent important nuances of mathematical ideas. For example, after labeling the distinction between "presubdivided" and "non-presubdivided" materials, the teachers analyzed how fractions were represented in their texts and manipulatives. They became critical of materials that didn't allow students to make subdivisions of the whole themselves, and adapted their materials to provide more of this experience.

In general, the teachers developed a stronger critical eye as to whether materials accurately represent the mathematics from the viewpoint of the students. They examined things such as manipulatives, drawings in curricula, assessment items, and teaching strategies, all with the student vantage point in mind. They would ask themselves, "What do the students need to know, think or do to answer a particular problem or question?" They would ask if the student could get an answer simply by counting fraction pieces instead of seeing the part–whole relationship or the relative magnitude that is so fundamental to the understanding of fractions. This is how one teacher talked about it in an interview:

[The discussions] made me question a lot before I started any unit. Instead of going through the math book, I was trying to think what really makes sense to the kids. What's irrelevant, what's relevant and what should I use or not use. … I think that it really made me think and also start planning for next year. (Interview transcript 6/8/91, p. 1)

Another teacher put it like this:

I think the biggest thing that came out of this seminar as far as my teaching ability, was to become … more critical of how I'm presenting things, more critical about "Is it really in a logical sequence?" More critical about students' understanding, their ability levels, and their maturity level as far as which concepts they are grasping. (Interview transcript 6/9/91, p. 1)

Some teachers stopped looking for the one right material and decided that a diverse set of materials would be the best approach, as each has its strengths and weaknesses. The teachers demonstrated a type of contingency thinking in which one material would be used for one purpose and another would be used to represent a different idea. One teacher said that when she taught fractions she blended the use of her textbook, fraction kits, and three other reputable curricula. She describes how involvement in case discussions prompted her to seek out and analyze new materials:

[The case discussions] created this sense of wanting to go out and do more and new different things. But it has also led to a lot of frustration in the fact that materials aren't readily available, so you're always searching and analyzing materials more than you ever did before. And not just the textbook. It's even [curricula created by a nationally acclaimed mathematics educator]. I would look at a lesson and say, "But is this really the best thing that I could do? What's the drawback of this particular thing? Should I really be making fraction kits?" On and on and on like that … it's questioning, questioning, questioning what [the materials are] doing. (Interview 6/9/94, pp. 21–22)

In another demonstration of their autonomy, the teachers in one group challenged their district-approved curriculum for the various grades. They asserted that according to the scope and sequence, the same topics were to be taught, with roughly the same amount of attention each year, in the elementary grades. They determined how to emphasize particular math topics in each grade so that there was less redundancy, and developed a plan to present their ideas to other teachers in their school at a faculty meeting.

CONCLUSIONS AND IMPLICATIONS

The language used to discuss professional development, reform, or teacher empowerment often holds an implicit assumption that the developing, reforming, and empowering is done by someone other than teachers themselves. At one extreme, professional development programs may actually predicate their goals on the belief that teachers are resistant to change and must be prompted by orders from above, holding them accountable. Other programs may recognize teachers as professionals, but still require them to implement reforms that others think are best for them. Change itself is often viewed as something imposed on teachers—as Richardson (1990) points out, a critical feature in the literature on teacher change is that change, research-based or otherwise, is defined as "teachers doing something that others are suggesting they do" (p. 11). We propose that programs based on these assumptions may have unintended, and possibly undesirable, consequences. That is, they may be disempowering for teachers, simply because they provide an external source of legitimation for change.

Case discussions appear to hold particular promise for motivating change in classrooms. We have argued that this is partly due to their potential to build autonomy, where the knowledge and wisdom within the group is respected, yet all ideas are open to critique. We must keep in mind, however, that not every case is constructed, nor every case discussion conducted, in such a way that it will live up to this potential.

For example, it is possible to have case discussions that are merely "sharing groups" where the case and the discussion only serve to reinforce the ideas and beliefs brought to the table (Little, 1990). On the other hand, cases and discussions can be designed to lead participants toward a particular point of view, so that genuine critique and problem-solving is minimized or even discouraged. Harrington and Garrison (1992) warn that cases like this can become mock problems with little impact.

If cases are to have an impact in classrooms, they must be designed and used so that teachers grapple with their beliefs, values, and goals; critically evaluate their teaching practices; construct new knowledge; and develop the motivation to learn more. As Little (1990) emphasizes, "the beliefs teachers hold and their substantive knowledge of subject and student" (p. 20), is what becomes consequential in classrooms. If we want to see an impact on classrooms, the content and purpose of case discussions is critical.

It is important that teachers develop a critical stance and their own internal sources of authority. As Wilcox, Lanier, Schram, and Lappan (1992) emphasize, "One of our biggest challenges may lie in how to develop in teachers a disposition to ask critical questions—about curriculum, instructional practices, educational policies, testing, their own learning and that of others." In our view, the development of professional judgment and teacher empowerment may depend on creating environments where teachers learn to become their own authorities, holding themselves mutually accountable and responsible for what occurs in their classrooms.

Comments on "Case Methods and Teacher Change: Shifting Authority to Build Autonomy"

Nel Noddings
Stanford University

Although I have some concerns about the concept of *autonomy*, I am impressed with the account given here of case methods and teacher discussion groups. It seems clear that teachers who participate in these groups become more reflective, acquire an increased tolerance for ambiguity, and gain in their confidence to teach mathematics. These are quite remarkable achievements whether we include them as aspects of autonomy or not.

As a philosopher, I have difficulty with any concept that is ill-defined or that is asked to bear too much weight. Autonomy suffers from both problems. For most educational purposes, it might be more fruitful and accurate to speak of "intelligent heteronomy." This label captures both the intellectual interdependence and the critical stance encouraged by the discussion sessions reported here. It isn't so much that teachers come to depend on themselves as authorities as that they know better where to turn and whom to consult. Notice how one teacher describes her search for more and better materials, and she now brings a critical eye to the selection of those materials.

Teachers become more critical and reflective through both the choice and discussion of cases. It is impressive to hear teachers admit "I never thought of that" and to acknowledge that it is sometimes better to recognize and live with ambiguity than to seek one right answer. The teachers' expressed surprise at the views held by their colleagues is powerful testimony to the traditional seclusion of teachers from their professional peers. Greater openness to opposing positions is one positive result of the case discussions.

It seems, too, that teachers gain in their confidence to teach mathematics as they share struggles and successes. My own sense is that at least some of the increased confidence is well grounded in enhanced mathematical competence, but this is an issue that should be studied further. Perversely, confidence can grow from a realization that everyone else is also struggling. How much mathematics do teachers learn from one another? If we were to adopt a Vygotskian stance, we would want to be sure that someone in each group is fully competent to handle the material at issue. Perhaps all of the teachers are fully competent and need only a recognition of their competence and an opportunity to display it. But Barnett and Tyson are careful to mention that some case discussions can deteriorate to mere "sharing" or lead to somewhat dogmatic instruction. In both cases, "genuine critique and problem solving are minimized or even discouraged." Many of us will look forward to follow-up studies on the question of increased mathematical competence.

I fully agree with Barnett and Tyson that cases for teacher discussion must be well designed and that one important purpose should be to induce critical evaluation, another to develop the motivation to learn more. To gain new knowledge, however, it may be necessary to augment discussion sessions with workshops or, at least, lists of possible resources. Teachers are enormously busy, and they cannot be expected to search out all of the materials that might prove useful for them. Like learners of every age, they too can profit from some direct instruction, but they should be encouraged to choose it and not coerced into enduring it. Teachers who participate in discussion of case studies generated in their own experience may well choose to study more deeply and systematically.

4

Researching Case Pedagogies to Inform Our Teaching

Elizabeth B. Moje
University of Michigan
Janine T. Remillard
University of Pennsylvania
Sherry Southerland
Suzanne E. Wade[*]
University of Utah

As this volume attests, there is a growing body of research on case pedagogies, investigating what students learn from various types of cases and studying how discussions, the facilitator, or particular written assignments contribute to teacher learning (see also Harrington, 1995, 1996; Levin, 1995; Lundeberg & Fawver, 1994). Less attention has been given to what teacher-educators can learn about their own pedagogy by conducting research on case methods in their courses, nor has much been written about how research findings can shape and reshape their teaching. In this chapter, we describe the processes and findings of our research on cases that we used in four different teacher education courses. Our aim, however, is not to re-

---

[*]The authors are equal contributors and are listed in alphabetical order.

port research results but to examine what they might teach us about our goals and practices as teacher-educators.[1] We follow Lave's (1996) assertion that "if we intend to be thorough [in our research on teaching], and we presume teaching has some impact on learners, then such research would include the effects of teaching on teachers as learners as well" (p. 158).

Each of us represents a different area in teacher education—specifically, literacy, mathematics education, science education, and general teacher education. We also represent different research paradigms, including sociocultural, poststructural, conceptual change, and socioconstructivist perspectives. Over the last several years, we have worked together as a research group to share case pedagogies and to study the results. By looking across our findings and interpretations, we were able to compare our students' responses to cases at different points in their development as teachers. This pooling of findings also allowed us to analyze and interpret the findings at a theoretical level.

Despite differences in our use of cases and in our theoretical perspectives, our findings are similar in that they shed light on aspects of teacher thinking and learning that have serious implications for our practices. In particular, we found that our students[2] (both preservice and inservice teachers) had strong ideas about and images of teaching and learning that figure into their interpretations of the cases and that remain unchallenged through the case discussions. These findings have led us to examine the assumptions about teaching and learning that we, as course instructors, brought into the classroom. Our examinations illuminated significant issues in teacher education, prompting us to rethink and refine our teaching goals. As a result, we are intent on complicating our ideas about and images of what case pedagogies can achieve, and we continue to develop new pedagogical practices that reflect our learning.

In the pages that follow, we describe our goals as teacher-educators and how our initial assumptions about case pedagogies fit with those goals. We discuss what we learned about our students as learners and how our findings changed our teaching. We then describe how our case pedagogies changed when we engaged in systematic research of our teaching. We also discuss the limitations of our research and offer suggestions for other teacher-educators interested in conducting research on their own practice using cases. We conclude by arguing that inquiry into our own teaching is an essential, iterative,

---

[1]Individual chapters describing our curriculum and research findings will be published in Wade (in press).

[2]In order to differentiate between our students and children and adolescents in schools, we use students to refer to the university students in our courses and learners or pupils to refer to the children in our students' classrooms.

and dialectical part of teaching. Although we believe that we would change our practice even if we did not study it systematically, we argue that viewing teaching as a learning process and that engaging in systematic inquiry is critical to moving beyond a reliance on methods—including case methods—as panaceas, toward the development of thoughtful, critical pedagogies and practices. Thus, much like we expected from our students, we have attempted to immerse ourselves in critical, reflective practice via this pedagogy-based research initiative. As a result, we do not offer specific "solutions" to the issues we encountered; rather, we problematize case teaching by emphasizing the tensions in teaching and learning that our research has raised for us and we discuss how we are grappling with these tensions.

OUR GOALS IN USING CASE PEDAGOGIES IN TEACHER EDUCATION

When we sat down together to write this chapter, we had little trouble agreeing on our goals for using cases in our courses, despite the differences in course content, in our theoretical perspectives, in the cases and pedagogies we chose to use, in our data collection methods, and in the different questions we asked of that data. We all agreed that we wanted to create communities of learners in our classrooms, to engage students in the social construction of knowledge, and to foster highly engaging dialogue in which students applied theory as tools to understand practice (Carter, 1990; Christensen, 1991a; J. Shulman, 1992b; L. Shulman, 1992; Sykes & Bird, 1992). We wanted students to develop what some scholars call "pedagogical thinking" (Feiman-Nemser & Buchmann, 1986; Wilson, Shulman, & Richert, 1987)—that is, the ability to use knowledge of learners, content, context, pedagogy, and educational aims to transform subject matter knowledge into instructional activities. We wanted our students to develop new perspectives and understandings that would allow them to scrutinize ordinary practices (including their own teaching goals and actions) for unjust or undesired outcomes. We also wanted them to consider and design alternative teaching practices.

Perhaps most importantly, we viewed case pedagogies as ways to foster our goal of critical reflective thinking (Grossman, 1992; Harrington, 1995; Harrington & Garrison, 1992; Harrington, Quinn-Leering, & Hodson, 1996; Merseth, 1991a; L. Shulman, 1992; Sykes & Bird, 1992). Although we each had a theoretical conception of what it means to think critically and reflectively, and we each engaged in various kinds of critical work ourselves, when we analyzed our data we realized that we had some work to do in terms of encouraging critical thinking in our students. This realization is one of our primary focuses in this chapter. In the following, we describe what we mean by critical reflective thinking, which serves as a framework for studying our own teaching. To clarify our perspective on critical reflective thinking, we compare it to what is often referred to as "technical, rational thinking" (Apple, 1990; Schon, 1983; Zeichner & Liston, 1996).

Drawing on the work of Dewey (1910/1991), Schon (1983, 1987), Gore and Zeichner (1991), Zeichner and Liston (1996), and others, we view critical reflective thinking as involving both openmindedness and critical inquiry, problem framing and reframing, and an approach to problem-solving that considers a variety of consequences. Dewey (1910/1991) described reflective thought as deliberately seeking the basis of a belief and examining the adequacy of its support. This involves two elements: The first is a willingness to experience perplexity, hesitation, and doubt—to suspend belief and live with confusion for a time. The second is to search for information that will corroborate or refute the belief, which he views as the act of inquiry. "To maintain the state of doubt and to carry on systematic and protracted inquiry—these are the essentials of thinking" (p. 13).

These two orientations toward beliefs and knowledge (as well as toward participants in a dialogue) have been similarly contrasted by others as "inclusive" and "critical" orientations (Burbules, 1993), as the "believing game" and the "doubting game" (Elbow, 1973, 1986), and as "connected knowing" and "separate knowing" (Belenky, Clinchy, Goldberger, & Tarule, 1986). The first describes a willingness to consider, at least initially, the plausibility of what another person is saying by listening and thereby attempting to understand the beliefs, experiences, and emotions of the other (Burbules, 1993). By feeling empathy (which comes from experience), people can attempt to share the experience that has led a person to embrace an idea—realizing, however, that such knowledge can only be an approximation (Belenky et al., 1986). The words Elbow (1973) uses to describe the believing game reflect his desire to give this stance legitimacy—for example: involvement, commitment, willingness to explore what is new, opening, flexible, nonaggressive, supportive, cooperative, listening, silence, and agreeing (pp. 178–179).

In contrast, the doubting, critical stance is skeptical, questioning, distanced, and evaluative, testing interpretations and beliefs against evidence, logic, and consistency (Burbules, 1993). Dewey describes this as "the close study into facts, of scrutiny and revision of evidence, of working out the implications of various hypotheses, and of comparing these theoretical results with one another and with known facts" (pp. 5–6). To Elbow (1973), this is the doubting game—seeking Truth by "seeking error" through the use of evidence and logic (p. 148). Belenky et al.'s conception of "separate knowing" is similar, equated as it is with being tough-minded and skeptical, assuming that everyone, including oneself, might be wrong. While these two stances may appear to conflict, both are necessary and complementary. For example, in a case discussion, participants need not hold to one attitude or the other exclusively but instead change their stance depending on the context, subject matter, or course of the dialogue (Burbules, 1993). Yet, these characterizations of thinking suggest a dichotomy that may be unnatural and unhelpful in a case discussion. Perhaps a term such as *benign criticism* best captures the ideal (Pat Alexander, personal communication).

At the heart of Schon's conception of reflective thinking is problem setting, or framing, which involves defining the decision to be made, the ends to be achieved, and the possible means that may be chosen. To Schon (1983), "problem setting is a process in which, interactively, we *name* the things to which we will attend and *frame* the context in which we will attend to them" (p. 40). This is a difficult process, he argues, because problems are unique and do not present themselves as givens, but rather must be constructed from what is known. He further argues that problems can be framed in many different ways, suggesting ends that may conflict. Thus, practice is seen as complex, uncertain, and value-laden, requiring a kind of inquiry that includes experience, trial and error, and intuition. Schon calls this "an epistemology of practice implicit in the artistic, intuitive processes" (p. 49), which involves reflection-in-action (in the midst of an experience) and reflection-on-action (a thinking back on an experience).

Because reflection-on-action is most relevant to case pedagogies, we have concentrated on this aspect of Schon's work. This involves thinking back on a situation that has occurred and critically examining the way the problem has been framed, the "theory" developed to understand it, the course of the action adopted, and the role of the practitioner within the larger institutional context. While reflecting on the situation and her own assumptions, beliefs, and understandings, the practitioner allows herself to experience confusion and puzzlement. Then, the practitioner experiments—whether actually or hypothetically (as in a case discussion)—becoming the researcher in the context of practice.

Such reflection is not necessarily considered critical, however. Critical reflection examines problems and events in the larger institutional, social, ethical, and political context (Gore & Zeichner, 1991; Zeichner & Liston, 1996). Framing problems in a critical, reflective mode leads to problem-solving that is oriented toward systemic curricular and pedagogical change. This approach to problem solving also involves consideration of the personal, academic, and sociopolitical consequences of a teacher's actions on students, using the criteria of equity, social justice, and caring to evaluate teaching decisions and actions.

In contrast to critical reflective thinking, technical rational thinking has been described as instrumental problem solving through the application of scientific principles (standardized knowledge) and method (cf. Schon, 1983). In a hierarchical fashion, researchers supply the scientific principles (theory) that practitioners use for the purposes of diagnosis and problem-solving, which culminates in the delivery of services. It is "an exclusive concern with measurement, prediction, control, efficiency, and governance by experts in addressing all human problems" (Bullough, Goldstein, & Holt, 1984, p. 7). One problem with this way of thinking, according to Schon, is that practice is seen exclusively in terms of *problem-solving*, conceived of as an instrumental question: What is the best solution, or means, to achieve certain ends? Instead of seeing the uniqueness and complexity of practice, embedded as it is with conflicting values, the question of how one ought to act becomes a scientific and instrumental one of efficiency and effectiveness. As a result, beliefs and goals are never questioned and problems are narrowly framed, usually focusing in education on changing students while ignoring the context of the classroom and students' interactions within that context. Technical rationality also does not question the values and consequences of the solutions that are adopted—ones that might "fix" students and maintain control but not change the classroom context (Zeichner & Liston, 1996).

For example, a teacher might hold unexamined beliefs that students who fail in school are lazy (thus locating the problem in the student), that ability is a fixed entity rather than a malleable trait, that certain kinds of knowledge are foundational and should be privileged, that there are "best practices" that can be applied to any situation without regard for context, and that the essence of teaching is organizing and controlling behaviors and knowledge. A technical–rational approach to problem-solving would be most concerned with organizing the curriculum to find the most efficient way to disseminate it and to maintain classroom control without changing the conditions—both local and systemic—that may have contributed to the problem or considering moral and ethical criteria for evaluating solutions and their consequences.

Critical–reflective and technical–rational approaches have usually been contrasted in the literature in a dichotomous manner. However, we found that the dialogues we studied did not fall neatly into one or the other of these two categories. That is, teachers' thinking often revealed characteristics of each of these stances. In our later work (cf. Wade & Moje, 1997), we adopted the heuristic of "blended voices"—what Bakhtin (1981) called "heteroglossia"—to suggest that thoughts and utterances are socially constructed and historical, "overpopulated" with the voices of others—reflecting both critical reflective thinking and technical rational thinking.

OUR RESEARCH QUESTIONS

The research presented here represents an amalgam of each of our individual teaching and research efforts. Although we were engaged in different studies, we met as a group to examine and share what our research findings meant for our thinking about case pedagogies and our own teaching. From the outset we shared some similar research questions. These included:

1. How do prospective and practicing teachers respond to cases and case teaching? Do they consider them a valuable teaching approach? How do they think case methods contribute to their own professional growth?
2. What tools (e.g., theory, experience as students and as teachers, other cases) do teachers use to make sense of the cases under study and what is the nature of their sense making processes?
3. What images of teaching and learning do teachers use in case discussions?
4. Did our use of cases move teachers toward the goal of critical/reflective thinking about their students and about classroom practice?

Our findings related to these research questions led us to ask similar questions related to our own teaching. These questions framed our self-study and are central to this chapter:

1. What are our own assumptions of what it means to become a critical, reflective practitioner? What would this look like in a teacher education setting? What is a realistic time frame for such change to occur?
2. What are our teaching goals for the use of cases? How do we know when these goals have been achieved?

Data Sources

Because the research presented here represents an amalgam of individual efforts, the data sources used were wide in scope. In general, we each wanted to examine the content of the interactions during the case discussions. Therefore, we audiotaped and transcribed these sessions. These transcripts were essential to our analyses, as they allowed us to uncover the ideas and images that students brought to the case discussions and the tools they used to make sense of them. To more fully understand students' responses to the cases, we also held debriefing sessions during which we asked students to discuss the impact that the case pedagogies had on them. Some of us also asked students to reflect on their learning from cases during individual or group interviews after the completion of the course. In addition to providing us with details on students' thoughts about the cases, our analyses of transcripts of these sessions also provided insights into students' beliefs about teaching, learning, and learning to teach. Other classroom artifacts such as students' journal entries, written assignments, and written evaluations of the case activities provided us with additional information about students' thinking. Finally, we collected data that allowed us to analyze our own beliefs and practices, including transcriptions of debriefing sessions with observers or colleagues, researchers' field notes, and our own plans and reflections.

Data Analysis

Each of us analyzed our data using methods of within-case and cross-case inductive analysis (Patton, 1990). We first looked for patterns within the data from each case, and then analyzed the patterns we recognized across cases. This was a recursive process and these initial patterns guided further teaching, data collection and analysis, thus modifying the progression of each of the studies. Although we did not predetermine categories for analysis, the categories and patterns constructed from the data were based on our own beliefs, perceptions, and experiences as researchers and teachers. Thus, we understand that these patterns did not emerge from the data, but came from our own particular social, cultural, political, and historical perspectives on knowledge, learning, and teaching.

WHAT OUR RESEARCH REVEALED
ABOUT STUDENTS' LEARNING FROM CASES

Our analyses of interviews, course evaluations, and students' comments during debriefing sessions suggested that our students enjoyed reading and discussing the cases and found them helpful in their thinking about teaching. These responses fit with our initial assessment of the case discussions—students were actively involved, treated the issues seriously, and seemed to engage in an appropriate level of analysis. Our analyses also revealed that to some extent the case discussions did help students consider issues that might emerge in their teaching, as well as ways to address these issues. We found that many students' ideas about the activities of teaching became more complex. For example, Moje and Wade found that students discussed the influence of teacher accountability, parents' demands, and students' different abilities when they discussed a case teacher's decision to lecture to students rather than to adopt a different pedagogical approach.

Remillard found that students became aware of the multiple factors, particularly those related to the structures of schools, that influence teachers' decisions. Gess-Newsome and Southerland found that students began to articulate concerns regarding patterns of differential student participation in the classroom.

Nevertheless, systematic analyses of the interactions during the case discussions and follow-up interviews raised questions for us about the extent to which the rich discussions were indicative of meaningful learning. There was little evidence to suggest that this increased awareness of the complexity of teaching prompted students to examine or transform their fundamental ideas about teaching. Nor did the cases prompt them to develop critical reflective thinking abilities or tools that might guide their decision-making. Analyses of the interactions during the case discussions revealed that the images of knowledge, learning, and teaching students brought into our classes influenced how they made sense of the case discussions. These ideas and images served both to focus and inhibit what students were willing to examine critically (Gess-Newsome & Southerland, in press; Moje & Wade, 1997; Remillard, 1996).

Four particular images or ideas related to teaching were prominent in our varying groups of students. These include (a) knowledge as fixed and neutral, (b) teaching as technical, (c) teaching as individualized, and (d) students as individualized and their abilities as fixed. These ideas are interrelated and together compose an image of teaching as idiosyncratic and technical. We discuss each idea here and how our students used it to make sense of the cases.

An image of knowledge as fixed and neutral was prevalent among students in each of our classes. This view was evident in the ways that students tended to take for granted curriculum and the teaching goals discussed in the cases. Their analyses of the teaching in the cases tended to focus on *how* teachers taught, rather than *what* was taught. Moje and Wade (1997), for example, found in a content literacy course that students' responses to problems in the cases tended to focus on interesting or alternative ways to get students to learn some taken-for-granted knowledge or skills, without questioning the value of the goals themselves. Gess-Newsome and Southerland (in press) referred to this view as a "positivistic" view of knowledge.

This positivistic view influenced the ways our students interpreted and analyzed the situations in the cases. They tended to locate the problems either in the teachers and their pedagogies, or in the pupils and their parents or culture, suggesting changes in teaching methods rather than revisions in pedagogical or curricular goals. Even when the cases emphasized particular curricular or learning goals, our students tended to interpret the problem as questions about pedagogical strategies. For example, Remillard (in press) found that students viewed teachers' emphases on mathematical discourse as a strategy to help students learn mathematics, rather than a component of mathematics itself. The students' views of mathematical knowledge as limited to computational skills made it difficult for them to recognize a case teacher's goal for all the children in her classroom to learn to participate in a mathematical community.

Our students also held strong views about learners and learning, which they used to make sense of the cases. They viewed pupils as individualized and learning as an individual activity. When analyzing pupils' behaviors or needs, they tended to look at each child in isolation, claiming that each child's learning was determined by her own style and abilities. Moreover, they seemed to view these individual abilities and styles as fixed and innate rather than learned or changeable. For example, students viewed a child's reading difficulties as reflecting only cognitive ability and a child's preference to work alone or to follow procedural rules as indicative of particular learning styles. Because they assumed these needs were unchangeable, they viewed the teacher's role as one who accommodates such needs. For example, students suggested that teachers should provide props and reduce or modify assignments, rather than change the curriculum or pedagogy in ways that might make accommodations unnecessary.

One particular characteristic of learners that students seemed to view as fixed was intellectual capacity. Our students tended to accept and use categories such as "high" and "low" ability to describe pupils. They were disinclined to question the nature or use of these labels, and—like learning styles—they saw such terms as accurate and permanent descriptors of learners. These classifications had definitive meanings and implications for teaching that students brought to bear on the case discussions. Remillard (1996), for example, observed that students tended to criticize case teachers' attempts to adjust their teaching situations in order to accomplish their goals. One case described a fifth-grade teacher's struggles to teach "low-ability" students to use math journals. Although the teacher in the case wondered whether a "mixed-ability" class would facilitate this activity, students in class argued that the teacher's expectations were inappropriate. "Her program that she's got now isn't working with these kids. They can't do their journals the way that she's expecting them to," one student argued. Another added, "I think that she needs to think about how she can reach all of her students instead of changing the situation so that it will work" (p. 20). Although the case teacher hoped to question whether a different arrangement might enhance pupils' abilities and learning, the students viewed the "low-ability" pupils as incapable of participating in particular activities. The students were not willing to acknowledge the possibility that contextual arrangements could influence pupils' classroom behaviors.

In addition to their views of knowledge and learners, our students had strong ideas about and images of the activities of teaching and the role of the teacher. An image of teaching as technical permeated each of our case discussions. Our students viewed teaching as the act of applying correct techniques in the appropriate circumstances, and they believed that good teachers had well-stocked, up-to-date collections of such tools. In fact, many expected to accumulate more techniques through their course work.

This image was evident in their writings and conversations about teaching. It was particularly apparent in the solution-oriented approach they took to the case discussions; students were often quick to recommend management strategies, alternative methods, or arrangements that the teachers in the cases might employ to assuage the challenges they encountered. Even though we structured our discussions to focus on analysis of related issues prior to considering solutions, students often moved directly to offering solutions or pointing out tactical errors made by the teachers. In short, the preservice and inservice teachers in our courses tended to view the cases as problems to solve, rather than contexts to examine issues or alternative perspectives.

A final image that played a prominent role in the preservice teachers' interpretations of the cases was that of teaching as an individualized endeavor. Students explained that each teacher has a style or approach that is her own and has its own merits. This image was apparent in the case discussions that called on students to assess the merits of particular pedagogical approaches. Even though the cases prompted students to clarify or articulate their own teaching philosophies, many were reluctant to draw on external or nonrelative ideals in their assessments. Instead, they used relative and somewhat idiosyncratic criteria to assess teaching, arguing that the best choice depended on the situation, the students, and the teacher. This image of teaching was also evident in follow-up interviews during which students described their learning from the case discussions. Other than listing techniques that they might try in their classrooms, students believed that the cases did not contribute significantly to their learning but rather helped them to articulate, strengthen, or clarify their existing ideas. Our analyses suggest that students interpreted the open-ended nature of the case discussions as reinforcement of their image of teaching as individualized and idiosyncratic. This image discouraged students from pursuing critical analyses of teachers' assumptions or actions.

Our students' tendencies to view knowledge and pupils' abilities as individual and fixed, and teaching as technical and highly individualized, figured into their reading of the cases and learning from the case discussions. Despite sound theoretical arguments for the use of cases in teacher education and development, we found that the opportunities for learning provided by the cases were mediated by the experiences, ideas, and images that students brought with them to the courses. Thus, it appeared that cases did not necessarily facilitate learning or change as much as they provided tools for supporting students' already-developed assumptions about teaching. It was our hope that reading and discussing cases would prompt students to learn to examine teaching practices from critical perspectives. Although this level of analysis initially appeared to be part of the case discussions, our findings reveal its superficiality. Moreover, we also have realized that the student analyses we observed during the discussions did not necessarily translate into significant transformations of the ideas and images that underlie their decision-making. These findings have encouraged us to examine our assumptions about teaching and learning, which we discuss in the next section.

WHAT WE LEARNED ABOUT OUR ASSUMPTIONS OF TEACHING AND LEARNING

One of the features of cases that initially aroused our enthusiasm as teachers was their potential for student engagement. As discussed by Moje and Wade (1997), because students approached cases using the tool of past classroom experience (as teachers and as students), often case discussions allowed for a great deal of emotional involvement with the topic. In our experience, student interactions during case discussion were very dynamic. These discussions were fast-paced and the level of emotional investment, evident through their voices and body language, was high. In cursory reviews of the class sessions, case discussions seemed rich as students drew on a number of resources to make sense of the situations portrayed.

Based on the high degree of engagement and enthusiasm displayed, and the multiple images and issues raised by students, each of us felt that the teaching cases were useful in prompting students to grapple with the complexities of the classroom. Implicit in our assessment was an assumption that engagement with multiple perspectives translates into critical reflection and reconstructed conceptions of teaching. Had our assessment of our use of cases stopped here, that assumption would have remained unchallenged. However, more rigorous analysis of classroom transcripts and student work (described in the previous section) led us to question the extent to which our students had learned to think critically about their teaching. We noted that although many images and issues were raised, several students might have offered the same idea repeatedly, apparently unmoved by the discussion swirling around them. Indeed, many of our students' concepts of teaching and learning appeared to remain unchanged despite our assumptions of fruitful case discussions. For example, Moje (in press) documents how one student in a literacy course assessed a particularly intense case discussion: "[The discussion] was somewhat tedious because we spent all this time discussing just so we could come to the conclusion that what I thought was the problem at the beginning—teacher resistance—was the problem." Such a response particularly illustrates the non-dialogic nature of the students' discussion because, in fact, many alternative explanations of the issues in the case had been raised by other students. This student, nevertheless, maintained her explanation and dismissed the others as "tedious."

This example raises the question: What did we assume to be a rich and fruitful discussion? The analysis of the facilitator's behavior in two case discussions that occurred in Remillard's (in press) study of the mathematics methods course revealed that most of her effort was devoted to promoting student involvement in the discussion. She devoted a much smaller percentage of her effort to actually directing the content of the discussion. It seems, then, that while facilitating case discussions, we operated from a tacit assumption that lively discussions, in which multiple students speak and offer contrasting images, are rich and fruitful, thus promoting and reflecting conceptual movement. However, based on the outcome of our research, we can no longer equate high student engagement and the discussion of multiple ideas and images alone with meaningful learning. We have learned that although discussions were animated and even complex, they were not necessarily dialogical or critical.

A second assumption that we brought to our teaching was that students' use of terms reflects their underlying understanding of those terms. As described in the analysis of case pedagogy in a science methods course, Gess-Newsome and Southerland (in press) found that students began to use the term *inclusive science teaching* in class discussions. As instructors, Sherry and Julie interpreted this use to signify that students had accommodated the definition stressed in class, a definition that attempted to address the diversity not only in traditional terms of academic ability and behavior, but also in terms of gender, ethnicity, experiential background, and socioeconomic status. However, students' lessons and unit plans for the science course reflected a different perception. Analysis of these classroom artifacts demonstrated that students continued to address issues related to inclusion only in terms of different academic abilities and behavior patterns. It became evident that their use of a term did not reflect a conceptual shift in the term's meaning. Based on this tentative idea, Sherry and Julie again reviewed case discussion transcripts, which allowed them to recognize that instructors and students were "talking past" one another, using different concepts and definitions but assuming a shared meaning.

Talking past, or appropriation of language without an underlying understanding, can be understood in terms of conceptual change. Some conceptual change theorists describe the incremental development of conceptions as occurring through learner's appropriation of terms into pre-existing explanations. After this initial rather uninformed appropriation, the meaning a learner assigns to a term is subtly and gradually modified (Demastes-Southerland, Good, & Peebles, 1996; Metz, 1991). Seen in this light, we now recognize that students in the science methods course had just begun to understand inclusive science teaching in the broader sense.

A related explanation of this phenomenon of talking past comes from work on discursive practices embedded in particular activity networks. As Moje and Wade (1997) suggest, all of our students are working hard to adopt the discursive practices of the university activity network in which they find themselves as preservice teachers, while also attempting to learn the discourse of schools and classrooms. Elizabeth and Suzanne found that as university students, preservice teachers tended to adopt language and ways of thinking that reflected the educational theories they had learned in other education courses. For example, the preservice teachers often referred to behaviorism and constructivism. After a rigorous analysis of their transcripts, Elizabeth and Suzanne realized that, much like Julie and Sherry, they were interpreting students' uses of the theoretical labels according to their own understandings of those perspectives. In contrast, the students interpreted constructivism, for example, merely as "active learning," rather than as a theory of how people actually make sense of experiences and construct understandings. Thus, in both situations, students were attempting to engage in a theoretical discourse without the underlying thematic development necessary to fully understand and incorporate the concepts into their thinking (see Lemke, 1990).

Our research also prompted us to question our pedagogical goals. As mentioned previously, at the outset of our teaching we viewed cases as tools for engaging our students in examining the issues embedded in the act of teaching. Our goals for our use of cases were to enable students to assess teaching practices using theoretically informed images of pedagogically sound teaching and to reflect critically on their own assumptions about teaching and learning. Although these were our goals for case discussions, analysis of our teaching revealed that we may have approached these goals with a certain amount of naiveté. We discovered that while we initially held critical reflection as a goal, we had little idea of what such reflection would look like in discussions or students' subsequent efforts. We began to wonder how far toward the nebulous goal of critical reflection could we expect students to move? In what ways would an informed assessment of classroom practice unfold? Is it fair to assume that students could forgo the traditional, individualistic, solution-based approach to teaching for use of a set of images informed by educational theory and social justice? And how much conceptual restructuring could we realistically expect in the span of one course?

THE COMPLICATED NATURE OF TEACHING
AND TEACHER EDUCATION

What did we learn from our research on cases and how did our learning inform—and complicate—our teaching? In many ways, we did not learn anything that we did not already know. We knew, for example, that both prospective and practicing teachers are generally conservative in their views of teaching and learning (cf. Lortie, 1975), and that teaching is often considered an individualized and idiosyncratic practice, without a well-structured domain of support. In fact, the argument that teaching represents an "ill-structured domain" and that knowledge of teaching is located in stories of practice (Spiro, Vispoel, Schmitz, Samarapungavan, & Boerger, 1987, p. 2), is often used to support case methods.

We also knew that views of knowledge as technical, fixed, and immutable are not uncommon among teachers and members of the larger society (cf. Apple, 1990) and that ability is similarly seen as fixed, stable, and unchanging. Indeed, most artifacts of schooling—testing, grading, and tracking, to name a few—indicate such views of knowledge and ability. Why, then, were we so surprised by our students' expression and maintenance of these views throughout case discussions? Had we fallen victim to the assumption that case methods would serve as a cure-all for these views of teaching and learning? Did we fail to examine our own assumptions and ideologies of teaching and learning as we prepared for the case discussions? Why do these fairly commonplace findings complicate our teaching?

As we analyzed our own case discussions and met to discuss our findings with one another, we have become aware—painfully so—of the fact that although we had clear objectives for our use of case methods, we had not carefully examined our larger goals for and our own images of teaching, learning, methods courses, and teacher education in relation to our students' images. We have begun to wonder whether our own course-specific goals matched our images of learning to teach and of teaching. We have had to ask ourselves what we can realistically expect from our students in one teacher education course. We have struggled with what it means to "change." And we have wondered what kind of change we expect in teachers. Are we assuming that teachers should adopt *our* images? Are our analyses of the case discussions "biased" by our images of teaching and learning?

All four of us expected students to engage in reflection via the case readings, discussions, and role-playing activities. We expected that these reflections would be at a critical rather than technical level because that type of reflection matches the kind of activity in which we—as theorists, researchers, and teacher-educators—desire to engage on a regular basis (see Lave, 1996). And yet, in most instances, we chose cases that would present problematic situations that we hoped would lead to a discussion of constructive, theoretically grounded practices. In other words, we may have expected critical reflection while only establishing the grounds for translating theory to practice. Thus, we were engaging in a type of transmission model—one that required students to be involved in the activity but that expected particular kinds of changed understandings as a result of the activity. Despite our belief that theories of teaching must be considered in relation to specific contexts, we may have wanted students to use cases to see that *our* theories and perspectives were valuable, that they could use them to address to a number of classroom problems.

Did our approach inadvertently discourage critical reflection? Were we really asking students to challenge their assumptions? Or were we asking them to use our theories, our research, our knowledge base to make sense of the real world of classroom practice? We must emphasize that none of us subscribes to a philosophy of generalizable theory good for all teaching practice. It is also important to emphasize that each of us carefully planned our case pedagogies—usually with a teaching peer—to yield rich, fruitful, engaged discussions. We consulted one another and talked through our work. We drew on a variety of methods including small group work, debates, role plays, whole-class discussions, and follow-up research activities. Nevertheless, we may have failed to fully examine our images, our assumptions, our ideologies of teaching, learning, and teacher education as we engaged in these case pedagogies. Perhaps more important, our subsequent examination of our own images, assumptions, and ideologies about teaching and learning has yielded difficult questions for which we have no simple solutions.

When Are Case-Based Methods Appropriate?

Each of us has found that our research informs our local and particular acts of teaching in different ways. We taught in four very different types of courses, each of which is taken by students at differing points in their teacher education programs and has different goals for student learning, although we would all agree that critical reflection on practice is an overarching goal. Gess-Newsome and Southerland (in press) have had to grapple with whether case methods have a place in a course in which the need for teaching pedagogical methods must be weighed against the demands of teaching science content and methods of scientific inquiry to teachers who fear science. In such a course, are case methods too time-consuming? If cases are used, should we expect (and accept) that discussion and plans of action will be more technical in nature? Perhaps it is appropriate for cases to be used to illustrate practical applications of theoretical and empirical studies of elementary science pedagogy. Perhaps asking for critical reflection in the face of so many other demands on teachers—especially prospective teachers—is asking too much (cf. Kagan, 1992). But, as many have argued (cf. Calderhead & Gates, 1993; Grossman, 1992; Harrington & Garrison, 1995), we should not separate the moral and ethical demands of teaching from the technical and practical. Can science content be taught without critical reflection on the implications of such content? And if, as Gess-Newsome and Southerland point out, prospective teachers view science knowledge as rigid and immutable and sort students on the basis of their "abilities" to learn science, what happens when such teachers develop strong scientific understandings? If their use of these understandings is potentially oppressive, will the development of a degree of comfort with science and its teaching help or hinder their approach to inclusive science teaching and thus the learning of all of their pupils?

Sherry and Julie continue to struggle with these questions, trying to achieve a balance between engaging students in critical reflection and teaching much-needed science content and habits of mind. Toward these ends, they have reduced the number of case discussions, but they have expanded discussion of each case to include the appropriateness of a particular pedagogical approaches as well as a reflection on the type of science knowledge addressed, always being mindful of the context described in the case. Thus, in all case discussions, students reflect on what kinds of learners are reached by a particular instance of teaching, as well as a reflection on what kinds of learners are left in the margins. In a related fashion, students are encouraged to review local and national curricula to determine if the science content described is fruitful for the learners in their own classrooms. Thus, in case discussions and their own preparation for teaching, students are helped to reflect on the utility of the knowledge produced through science for their particular communities.

The Tension Between Teaching and Learning as Contextualized and Idiosyncratic

Remillard's (in press) findings, which indicate that teachers view mathematics teaching as an individualized and idiosyncratic practice, also complicate our notions of teacher education. On one hand, we use cases to encourage teachers to think about the contextualized, local, and particular nature of teaching and learning. We argue that generalized solutions do not work for everyone because teaching and learning always happen in particular contexts. On the other hand, we are frustrated when teachers suggest that teaching is a matter of individual experience, values, and knowledge, and as a result dismiss theoretically grounded pedagogies. We want to believe that there are better ways to teach and learn; that we have learned something valuable about teaching and learning from years of research and theorizing. And we want prospective and inservice teachers to recognize that a conception of teaching and learning as based in local and particular contexts is different from a conception of teaching and learning as individualized, in which "anything goes."

But we must ask what it means to say that teaching is not individualized and yet is always situated in particular contexts. We need to work through ways to help students deconstruct a notion of individualization, challenging them to think about how even particular contexts are embedded in and shaped by social interactions. An image of teaching as individualized and idiosyncratic tends to allow the teacher to make any decision she deems necessary, according to *her* sociocultural background and ideologies, rather than to emphasize that as a teacher one is responsible for considering the needs, experiences, and interests of others in the community of learners. For Janine, these findings have led her to investigate her own role in the case discussions. As a result, she has begun to experiment with different ways of facilitating discussions that include taking a more directive role in the discussions in a way that allows her to redirect questions of individualization, to challenge teachers' thinking and future practice. In particular, she has made an examination of underlying assumptions and goals an explicit part of each case discussion. She devotes a significant amount of each discussion to unpacking and analyzing the beliefs about teaching, learning, and mathematical goals implicit is the students' remarks. Janine's intent is to raise students' awareness of the tacit beliefs that guide their decision-making. Her hope is that they make explicit and critically examine the personal theories underlying their own preferences and styles.

Moje and Wade's findings (1997) have helped us become more aware of the deeply held beliefs about knowledge and ability that we must challenge if we hope to encourage teachers to engage in critical reflection and, ultimately, more democratic and critical pedagogy. As a result, Elizabeth has begun to introduce explicit discussions about knowledge and ability into her courses, whether using case or other pedagogies. Discussions in her courses range from what it means to categorize someone as "high" or "low" ability to questions about how knowledge is constructed, learned, and shared. In addition, as a result of findings that suggested that students saw teaching strategies merely as isolated "props" for accommodating—not developing—students' abilities (Moje & Wade, 1997), Elizabeth has begun to ask students to discuss both pedagogical (not strategic) and curricular changes that could address the concerns raised in case discussions. This move is designed in part to help students think beyond simply "dealing with" learners and controlling their behaviors. Elizabeth is interested in helping students come to understand learners as people with backgrounds and experiences from which pedagogy and curriculum can be built. She hopes that such discussions will help to challenge conceptions of knowledge and ability as fixed, and will push students to look for ways to challenge the knowledge that is privileged in the curriculum or in their pedagogy. Moreover, such discussions help students think about how teaching "methods" need to be knit together into pedagogical practice, rather than being used idiosyncratically or randomly. The discussions focus on pedagogy and curriculum as philosophical and epistemological constructions instead of sets of teaching and learning tools. And finally, Elizabeth has introduced cases and case discussions that make issues of race, class, and gender explicit and central. To accompany these case discussions, students read and discuss articles that exemplify a variety of critical, feminist, and poststructural pedagogies.

Suzanne has also restructured case pedagogies to foster greater critical reflection in a teacher education course that is primarily case-based. First, restructuring has involved providing students with more tools for making sense of the cases—that is, careful analysis in class of pertinent readings on race, culture, gender, and language that can be used across cases. Second, case discussions have been restructured, first, to begin with in-depth discussion of issues in ways that press students to examine beliefs and assumptions about students—their own beliefs and those expressed in the cases (similar to what Janine described earlier). Then, she works with students in explicit ways to help them frame and reframe problems, with each framing analyzed as to how it leads to certain kinds of solutions with different consequences at the personal, academic, and social, and political levels. For example, this might involve explicitly asking students to think of the ways that different protagonists in a case had framed the problem, and contrasting the results in terms of their underlying assumptions, goals, and possible consequences. Third, after role plays and case discussions, more attention is given to debriefing, which gives students an opportunity to distance themselves from the case and reflect on it analytically. During debriefing, students are also asked to evaluate the purpose and value of the case-related activities they are engaging in. Finally, students have more practice discussing the cases in newsgroups on the Internet and in formal written case analyses and action research projects. Recent research on these various case-related activities has revealed evidence of a good deal of critical reflective thinking among many preservice teachers, although there is still evidence of technical rational thinking as well (Wade & Moje, 1997; Wade, Niederhauser, Cannon, & Long, 1997).

What Are We Looking For?

It is this notion of "evidence," however, that we find complicated. When we see evidence that at least some students have engaged in critical dialogue, what effect does that have on students' thinking? When they hear their peers question and challenge assumptions, or when they participate in discussions of equity and social justice, do they begin to question their own assumptions and broaden their views? Are we creating conditions in which students are challenged to think differently, or are we creating situations in which we are transmitting a particular conception of good teaching practice? How is this different from a transmission model in which we *tell* students that they should engage in critically reflective practice?

We believe that our practice is now different in many ways: We are beginning to create conditions in which students engage in a dialogue with one another. This dialogue—in which students struggle with moral and ethical issues of teaching while also examining techniques of practice—requires that teachers think differently, yet it does not require a specific outcome for their thinking. Nevertheless, how do we evaluate these discussions? If the dialogical nature of the discussions is rich, but the students' beliefs are not changed, have we failed? And what does it mean to say that someone's thinking is or is not critical? Finally, we must ask whether our goal is to change students' beliefs—perhaps an unreasonable goal in one course or even in a teacher education program—or is it simply to challenge them? And, how do we assess our work? Have we been successful only if our students adopt the critical perspectives that *we* hold?

Challenges of Studying Our Own Practice

Despite the number of different data sources that we collected, we must admit that it is difficult to conduct research on case pedagogy and methods. In addition to the questions posed above, there are many more we need to grapple with. What, for example, counts as evidence of learning in case pedagogies? If we observe our students eagerly reading the cases, participating in discussions, and challenging ideas, then have they learned? If our students tell us that they "didn't learn" from the case discussions, but only refined their ideas and thought about issues differently, then how do we interpret their claims? Moreover, how do we assess whether what appears to be learning at the time of the case discussion extends to any meaningful change in students' pedagogical thinking and practice at a later date? Can students apply what they learned in case discussions in a university setting to the activity networks of their schools and classrooms?

Further, despite multiple measures to analyze case discussions, we recognize the possibility that not all the voices of our students were heard. Some participants may resist speaking their images and raising issues of teaching and learning they consider important, especially if their views contradict the general flow of the discussion or would be considered unpopular. Further, we have examined only some aspects of the case discussions and missed others. As Gee, Michaels, and O'Connor (1992) noted, "our ability to say what a text means is always partial and incomplete" (p. 233). Texts—including the transcripts of the case discussions we studied—are always produced in social settings that involve far more than language. The things we have not captured in our transcripts include actions, gestures, aspects of the physical environment, glances, attitudes, unspoken thoughts, and values. These reflect and can influence what a text means—what sense participants were making as the text was being created and what sense we make of it as researchers. In addition, turning an oral text into a transcript inevitably means losing much of the texture of the talk, the voice quality, inflection, and rhythm. These qualities as well as the way we format the text on a page influences what we notice and how we interpret it. Further, our interpretive framework focused our attention on some features and not others. Thus, the text as a written document, our theoretical framework, and our research questions and tools all influenced what we saw and how we understood it.

CONCLUSIONS: TEACHING
AND RESEARCHING AS LEARNING

Our research goal in this project was not to assess the effectiveness of case pedagogies. Instead, we wanted to examine our students' thinking and learning as well as our own thinking and learning as we engaged in case pedagogies. Indeed, we want to argue that too often researchers study methods and pedagogical approaches as if the methods themselves lead to change. What we found in our research—research that focused on our teaching rather than on case methods—pushed us to restructure our pedagogies and to examine and re-examine our goals for teacher education, our images of teaching and learning, and our ideological commitments in relation to teaching and teacher education. Like Schon's (1983) practitioner-researcher (and as we ask our students to do), we have had to construct new theories for each situation, to frame and reframe problems that we discover from systematic inquiry, to reconstruct our goals, and to experiment with different means of achieving those goals. All of this has occurred interactively, in the context of practice. As practitioner-researchers, we aspire to the ideal described by Schon: "The inquirer is willing to step into the problematic situation, to impose a frame on it, to follow the implications of the discipline thus established, and yet to remain open to the situation's back talk" (p. 269).

Our research has not led us to simple solutions; indeed, it has complicated our practice. We believe, however, that these complications have led us to ask new questions that will ultimately improve our work as teacher-educators. We also believe that these complications help us rethink what it means to be a teacher-educator. As Lave (1996) argues, we believe that we must reconceptualize teaching as an act of learning. She writes that, "teachers are probably recognized as 'great' when they are intensely involved in communities of practice in which their identities are changing with respect to (other) learners through their interdependent activities (p. 158). Our identities as teacher-educators (and as theorists and researchers of teaching and learning) have changed in relation to the other learners—our students and our teacher education colleagues—in our communities of practice. We hope to continue to learn as we explore case pedagogies.

Commentary on "Researching Case Pedagogies"

Kenneth M. Zeichner
University of Wisconsin—Madison

T his candid self-study by four university teacher-educators of their use of case methods in their university courses is noteworthy for several reasons. First, it represents an unusual situation where teacher-educators have gone beyond asking the questions of what research about their own practices tells them about what their students have learned, to also consider what they might learn about their own teaching goals and practices from self-study. Most often the self-studies of teacher-educators have merely focused on how well a particular teaching method or strategy has led to prospective teachers' and teachers' internalization of a certain set of ideas and the ability to practice in ways consistent with those ideas, but has not problematized the goals and practices themselves. In this case, we have a group of teacher-educators who have taken on the difficult task of rethinking and redefining their teaching goals and practices when confronted with data from their systematic examination of their practices that showed that their students were not performing in ways that they had envisioned. In viewing their own teaching as a focus for study, these teacher-educators are modeling the very kind of critical and reflective practice in which they seek to have their students engage. This study is also unusual because the diversity of disciplinary and theoretical perspectives represented within the group of teacher-educators researchers enabled them to challenge their own goals and practices through dialogues across the diverse perspectives within their own group. Too frequently, there is a failure by teacher-educators to step outside of their own favored paradigms to engage in a dialogue with those who do not share their perspectives.

The findings of their research showing that prospective teachers and teachers interpreted the cases through their existing conceptions of teaching, learning, and knowledge are consistent with much of the recent literature on teacher learning. The discovery of the dominance and persistence of technical and individualist views of teaching and learning, of the lack of attention to curriculum content, and of the limited expectations for the learning of some pupils is strikingly similar to the picture painted in recent portraits of U.S. teacher education.

Much literature in teacher education focuses on the alleged benefits of employing various instructional strategies. In addition to case studies, action research, teacher portfolios, journals, peer coaching, and so on are often viewed as panaceas for the development of thoughtful and critical teaching. The researchers in the current study go beyond the uncritical glorification of teacher education methods and closely examine the consequences of using case studies. Instead of accepting the high level of student enthusiasm for the cases as evidence of a transformation in teacher thinking, these researchers looked closely enough to see that what on the surface appeared to be highly fruitful discussions of the cases did not lead to reexamination of the conceptions of teaching and learning that students brought to the experience.

Instead of blaming their students for the less-than-hoped-for outcomes or concluding that critical reflection is an unreachable goal in teacher education programs as many others have done, these researchers turn their attention to critiquing the ways in which their own assumptions and actions as teacher-educators may have contributed to the situation in which they find themselves. They then seek to change their expectations for their teaching in ways that will help move them closer to the accomplishment of their ideals. While correctly acknowledging the limitations of what can be achieved in any teacher education course, the authors also ask some tough questions of themselves about the ways in which they may have been unthinkingly creating a situation that undermined their goals. It is very refreshing to see teacher-educators questioning whether their professed desire to promote critical reflection is really perceived by students as a requirement to adopt particular conceptions of good teaching favored by their instructors—an act of indoctrination as opposed to a genuine exchange of different perspectives.

This research serves as a model for the kind of close and detailed analysis that teacher-educators need to conduct to reveal the inevitable contradictions between their professed aims and the reality of their practice. The use of case studies in teacher education by itself will not necessarily accomplish any particular goals related to teacher development. It is only through the close study of the content and construction of cases (and those whose perspectives are represented in them) and of how case study discussions are directed that teacher-educators will be able to develop case study work in teacher education programs into a pedagogical practice that contributes toward the preparation of critically reflective teachers. Teacher education is very difficult and complex work even under the best of conditions. Things are as complicated at the conclusion of this research as at the beginning. This is as it should be.

PART II

STRUCTURING THE LEARNING ENVIRONMENT WITH CASES

5

The Role of the Facilitator in Case Discussions

Barbara B. Levin
University of North Carolina at Greensboro

Mastering the skills of questioning, listening, and response is a lifelong process for discussion teachers, but the gains are enduring and substantial. If we teachers deepen our knowledge and systematize our practice of these skills—if we find better ways to communicate the "what" and "why" of our practice to others—we will serve both our colleagues and ourselves.
—Christensen, Garvin, and Sweet (1991, p. 155)

Case-based teaching includes a variety of ways of using cases and case discussions. In professions such as law, business, medicine, and teacher education, cases are one of the tools that can be used to help novices develop ways of thinking like professionals do about the problems, issues, and dilemmas that confront those experienced in these fields. The use of case methods in teacher education offers opportunities for beginning teachers to develop perspective, make connections between theory and practice, and learn to apply problem-solving skills to teaching and learning. For experienced teachers, cases can offer opportunities to reflect on and change their practice, develop authority, become more autonomous, and to think metacognitively—at least these are some of the claims made for the value of using case-based instruction in educational settings.

With the goal of explicating what we know empirically about learning from and teaching with cases, this chapter focuses on the role of the facilitator in teacher education settings where the use of case-based instruction is a part or the central focus of the curriculum. Unfortunately, there is little research available that focuses explicitly on the role the facilitator plays in case discussions, with some notable exceptions (Barnett & Tyson, 1993a; Levin, 1993, 1995; Lundeberg, 1993a, 1993b, 1997; Morine-Dershimer, 1991, 1996a, 1996b). However, several educators have written about the facilitator's goals and style of interaction when using cases. This is helpful in understanding the goals of discussion-based teaching (e.g., Christensen et al., 1991; Christensen & Hansen, 1987; Colbert, Trimble & Desberg, 1996; McAninch, 1993; Miller & Kantrov, 1998; Wasserman, 1993; Welty, 1989), even though there is relatively little empirical evidence focusing strictly on the role of the discussion leader in case-based teaching. Research that addresses this topic is summarized in this chapter and evaluated as it corresponds to the claims made about the value of case methods.

While acknowledging the importance of the role of the facilitator in what teachers may learn from cases, Merseth (1996) cautions us about the synergy between the content of the case and case-discussion methods used and reminds us that *what* is discussed is as important as *how* it is discussed. However, she also writes: "In the large-group case discussion, the discussion leader plays a very important role—guiding, probing, directing, giving feedback, or sometimes simply observing the exchanges and contributions among the class members" (Merseth, 1996, p. 727). Therefore, whether cases are used to help educators link theory with practice, serve as examples or exemplars of practice, or to develop problem-solving and perspective-taking as heuristics for thinking about teaching and learning, the role the facilitator takes as the case-discussion leader is as important to study as what is learned by the participants.

In an effort to clarify and elaborate on the roles of the facilitator using case-based pedagogy, this chapter addresses claims made about the role of the case facilitator in the literature to date, research available on the role of the facilitator in case-based teaching including methods used to collect and analyze information about the case facilitator, and directions researchers might take in the future to help us better understand the impact of the facilitator on case-based pedagogy.

WHY STUDY THE CASE FACILITATOR?

"Cases, even with commentaries, do not teach themselves" (J. Shulman, 1996, p. 155). First, the facilitator plays a significant role, beginning with selecting the case and convening the discussion. Second, the facilitator's actions can influence the purpose for which a case is used, what is learned during the discussion of a case, and how the learning community develops (Barnett & Tyson, 1993; Christensen et al., 1991; Levin, 1993, 1995; Merseth, 1996; Miller & Kantrov, 1998; Morine-Dershimer, 1991, 1993). Third, the person facilitating a case discussion has the power to influence the discussion through questions asked and comments made, as well as by the way the discussion is structured (Garvin, 1991; Miller & Kantrov, 1998; Morine-Dershimer, 1991, 1993). For these reasons it is important to study case facilitation when attempting to understand what the research says about case-based pedagogy.

Originally, comparing my own style of case facilitation with anecdotal evidence I gathered from talking with and observing others facilitate case discussions over the past several years led me to believe that leading case discussions may be a very idiosyncratic process. However, I also wondered if research would bear this out. Arguably, a large part of what occurs during case discussions rests on the teaching and leadership style of the case facilitator. This style has much to do with the instructional goals of the facilitators and their purposes for choosing particular cases as pedagogical tools (Christensen et al., 1991; Merseth, 1996), but there are other factors that also play into a facilitator's style.

As Wasserman (1994) asserted, the role of the case facilitator and the style he or she develops are influenced by individual beliefs about teaching and learning and individual psychological need, including needs for power and control. For example, an instructor who believes that knowledge is certain, that there is a body of information that needs to be conveyed to students, that students must learn facts and know correct answers, and that the instructor's role is to deliver information for students to absorb, would probably not be comfortable using case-based teaching methods (Wasserman, 1994). However, if an instructor is comfortable with ambiguity and uncertainty, believes that knowledge is constructed by the learner, favors knowledge application, doesn't require single correct answers, and feels okay about not getting closure on difficult questions, then case-based teaching methods may be a more useful tool for this instructor.

From the previous description, it may sound as if there are only two kinds of case facilitators, Type A or Type B (Silverman, personal communication, July 1997). However, the act of case facilitation and the decisions a facilitator makes before and during a case discussion are as complicated as people's beliefs about teaching and learning. The point is that the epistemological and pedagogical beliefs of instructors who use cases will influence why they use them and how they facilitate discussions. Furthermore, cases and case discussions may have a place in the pedagogical toolbox of many different kinds of instructors and be used for many different purposes.

As Morine-Dershimer (1993) concluded from her study, which compared three different instructors who facilitated the same case, "it seems clear that 'a case is a case is a case is a case' is NOT the case" (1993, p. 38). Certain factors, such as the degree of structure, amount of teacher direction, selection of specific questions, and time allotted for discussion of certain topics all have an impact on the problems and issues participants identify as important. So, although an individual's style of case facilitation may fit their purposes for using cases, there is a lot of variability across individuals who use case-based teaching methods. Furthermore, there is probably as much variability within the field of education in how cases are used and facilitated as there is across various other disciplines that use case-based teaching methods.

WHAT CLAIMS ARE MADE ABOUT THE FACILITATION OF CASE DISCUSSIONS?

In recent years, authors of casebooks have made many claims about the value of using cases and case methods. They claim that studying cases can help teachers identify the major concepts in their discipline, offer direct involvement in learning about teaching, improve thinking skills, develop problem solving skills, and help tie together theory and practice. Silverman, Welty, and Lyon (1992), for example, assert that using case methods helps teachers learn how to use theories to identify, analyze, and solve classroom problems.

Among the most thorough discussions about the role of the facilitator in discussion teaching are two books by Wasserman, *Introduction to Case Method Teaching* (1994) and *Getting Down to Cases* (1993), and two books that Christensen has co-edited with colleagues from the Harvard School of Business, *Education for Judgment* (1991) and *The Art of Discussion Leadership* (1987). These books present firsthand accounts of the authors' experiences with case-based teaching, the first two in educational settings, and latter two in business school settings.

Christensen, the guru of case-based teaching at the Harvard School of Business, has been using discussion-based teaching as the primary pedagogical tool in his courses since 1947. His analysis of his own case-method teaching over the years has led him to conclude that both the discussion leader and the participants spend the vast majority of their time asking questions, listening to answers, and making some sort of response. Therefore, these are the most important aspects the case leader must address and facilitate. Furthermore, Christensen believes that attempts to master the skills of questioning, listening, and responding will also increase the discussion leader's ability to influence the mood, tone, pace, abstraction level, and the culture of the classroom. However, Christensen also notes that while the discussion leader sets the agenda, the participants in the discussion affect the sequence and the timing as they take up or diverge from the facilitator's plans. As Christensen states (1987): "Given these circumstances, discussion teachers do not, like lecturers, set the agenda; they manage its emergence, direction, and evolution" (p. 107). Ultimately, for Christensen each case teaching opportunity is as much a learning experience as it is a teaching experience.

Like Christensen, Wasserman (1993) also discusses the complexity of the interactions during discussion-based teaching and the importance of the role of the facilitator. For her, case teaching was a logical extension of her earlier work on teaching for thinking, because she saw case-based teaching as a way to "engage students in higher order mental processing, requiring their reflection on substantive issues in the curriculum" (p. ix). Nevertheless, she cautions that case methods, like any "new" teaching methodology, are not a panacea for education or a formula for successful teaching; they are not for every instructor, and educators will be subject to disappointment if they don't make a commitment to long-term professional development and to the study of the complexity of classroom interactions around case-based teaching. However, Wasserman is interested in helping teachers develop their own style of teaching with cases, beginning with helping them identify their epistemological beliefs and psychological needs as instructors, in order to determine if case-based teaching suits them.

Like Christensen, Wasserman's descriptions of the facilitator's role are based on years of personal experience teaching, writing cases herself, and working with inservice and preservice teachers who are learning to use cases (rather than conducting focused research analyzing the role or influence of the facilitator). Despite what we can learn from experienced case teachers, we also need empirical studies about the role of case facilitators.

WHAT DOES THE RESEARCH SAY ABOUT THE ROLE OF THE FACILITATOR?

The empirical evidence available from those who have studied the role of the case facilitator offers an opportunity to consider this aspect of case-based pedagogy. For example, in one study Morine-Dershimer (1993) compared "teacher-directed" versus "student-centered" case discussions based on her analysis of videotapes of three different instructors teaching the same case with four different classes. In this study "teacher-directed" meant that the case discussions were facilitated by a graduate assistant leading the whole class, whereas the "student-centered" discussions were not led by a facilitator; rather, the students discussed the case in small groups. Both the videotapes and written output from these case discussions with post-baccalaureate preservice teachers were data sources. Morine-Dershimer's analysis showed that teachers in student-centered case discussions displayed more active involvement, more attention, and more complex understanding of case content than participants in instructor-led discussions.

However, the size of the groups may be a confounding variable in this study, because the instructor-directed case discussions were large, whole-class discussions and the student-centered discussions were held in smaller groups. This raises questions for future researchers, who might consider unpacking teacher-directed versus student-centered variables from the small-group versus large-group factors to see how group size and the leadership roles of the case instructor influence learning from cases. Nevertheless, videotaping or audiotaping case discussions and studying what students write about cases before and after case discussions are two very useful methods to study case facilitation.

Levin (1993) analyzed the discourse in the case discussions that were conducted as part of her dissertation about the role of discussion and experience in learning from cases. In the small-group case discussions she facilitated, Levin found that the pattern of discourse differed dramatically from typical classroom discourse as described by Cazden (1986). In the 1993 study, the case facilitator spoke less than 20% of the time, compared to the 66% of time that most teachers talk in typical classrooms. Furthermore, the pattern of the discourse did not follow the typical Interrogatory–Response–Evaluate (IRE) pattern that Cazden (1986) describes as occurring in most classrooms. Instead, the pattern was an IRRRR–IRRRR–IRRRR pattern, indicating that the facilitator asked fewer questions, which were followed by several responses from a variety of participants without intervening evaluative comments before other questions were posed. In addition, about half of the questions proposed by the facilitator were taken up for discussion by the group, which corresponds to Christensen's (1991a) experience with case discussions in large-group, instructor-led case discussions in business settings.

Saunders (1992) also found that the percentage of time that she talked as facilitator was much less than during typical classroom discourse. Her careful analysis of the transcript of a case discussion with undergraduate students interested in a teaching career showed that she talked 33% of the time, half the normal percentage of teacher talk noted in studies of classroom discourse. Furthermore, Saunders also found that the participants sometimes took the case discussion in their own direction and away from her purpose for discussing the case. This made Saunders question how researchers should assess "active engagement" in a case discussion and prompted her to raise questions for future research about the extent to which participants' engagement with and learning from discussion varies with their control over the issues discussed, the effect of the physical arrangement of the room, and the familiarity of the participants with the facilitator.

In another study, Levin (1996) found that the content and tone of anonymous case discussions held simultaneously on computers using "groupware" software with undergraduate preservice teachers was very different from typical face-to-face discussions led by a facilitator. The anonymous, computer-based discussions were found to be more superficial and more negative when no one facilitated the discussion—hence, no one to ask for clarification or to probe further into participants' thinking. Probably due to the anonymity of the participants' comments on computer screens and the controversial nature of some of the issues in the cases, there were "flaming" and hateful comments, including blatantly biased and racist remarks, which were harmful to any sense of community developed earlier with this group. In contrast, during face-to-face facilitated discussions of the same cases, the participants displayed more depth, made many more serious and thoughtful comments about the controversial topics in the cases, and preserved the dignity of all participants.

In this study (Levin, 1996), preservice elementary-grade teachers in computer-based discussions keyed in their responses to each question and wrote them unchallenged and without anyone probing for clarification, or asking for elaboration—typical roles the facilitator of a case discussion would and should take as the leader. The issue of leaderless case discussions raises concerns similar to those raised by Feiman-Nemser and Buchmann (1983) and Zeichner and Liston (1987) about the potentially miseducative consequences of certain kinds of field experiences in teacher education. I believe this study also raises similar concerns about potentially miseducative consequences of leaderless and anonymous computer-based case discussions. Given this context—with inexperienced preservice teachers in an undergraduate teacher education program—case discussions that include issues of race and bias should not be conducted either anonymously or without a facilitator.

Richardson (1991) came to similar conclusions about leaderless case discussions and cautioned that teacher education students should not read and interpret cases without guidance, lest they develop (mis)interpretations of the cases that might be detrimental to their own teaching later on. Based on her analysis of eight cases written by inservice teachers about student motivation, Richardson called for the active involvement of the teacher-educator in guiding students through the interpretation of cases and in helping them to apply theory and judge alternative solutions. She also emphasized the potential added value of the case method as a way of making theories in textbooks come to life through the contextualized nature of the cases, stressing the importance of the role of the instructor: "The teacher educator can help students supply theory to some situations, and help students judge alternative solutions. ... Thus, it would be the teacher educator's responsibility to guide students in the interpretations and to ensure that the cases do not bias students against particular groups of students" (Richardson, 1991, p. 9).

The teacher-educator who facilitates a case discussion with preservice teachers may be the most experienced person in the room and therefore has the responsibility of guiding the case discussion to prevent miseducative interpretations. However, the role of the facilitator in inservice settings may be somewhat different. For example, Barnett and Tyson (1993a) claim that the role of the case facilitator varies with regard to the degree of authority and the status assumed (chap. 3, this volume). Their research shows that when the facilitator promotes greater autonomy in case discussions, this will eventually lead to shifts in authority, as this quote illustrates:

> [T]he facilitator does not take on the role of expert or lead participants to a particular conclusion or point of view. Participants frame the issues to be discussed, decide where the discussion should start, and assess the process and content of the discussion. The responsibility for the direction and quality of the discussion is shared between the facilitator and the participants. (Barnett & Tyson, 1993a, p. 7)

In ongoing case discussions with inservice teachers on mathematics teaching (particularly rational numbers), Barnett and her colleagues found that inservice teachers' understanding of the mathematics in the cases improves along with their ability to operate as autonomous professionals. Barnett also found that when she structured case discussions so that the authority shifted away from the facilitator and toward the group, teachers were able to take a critical stance on the content and the issues in the cases. They also began to make judgments for themselves about curricula, materials, examples, teaching strategies, and assessment instead of deferring to an authority. "In the beginning, it is primarily the facilitator that probes for critical analyses and presentation of different perspectives. Through the course of the discussions, however, teachers develop an increasing predilection to offer critical analysis of the cases, of each other's comments, and of their own teaching" (Barnett & Tyson, 1993a, p. 17).

In another study that focused on the facilitator's influence, Lundeberg (1993b) analyzed her interactions with males and females, both traditional and nontraditional college-age students, in two case discussions held during an educational psychology class. Overall, the contributions of males and females to the discussion were relatively equal during both discussions. However, Lundeberg's analysis of videotaped data indicated that her verbal interactions as the facilitator in the first discussion favored the nontraditional females and excluded the traditional males. In the second case discussion with the same group her interactions with the nontraditional females were all nonverbal and she favored the non-traditional males over the traditional males. Lundeberg ends this study with a caution about ignoring male students during class discussion. She also cautions against overcompensating for historical inequities in instructor–student interactions in classrooms that have traditionally favored men in an effort to include more women in class discussions. Lundeberg suggests that future researchers who study gender interactions in classrooms and during case discussions measure both verbal and nonverbal interactions when studying the role of the facilitator. Future research would benefit from focusing a video camera on the instructor, or by having several video cameras strategically placed around the room, to record both verbal and nonverbal interactions during case discussions.

In another study, Morine-Dershimer (1996b) found that gender interactions (and particularly, the gender of the case facilitators) may have an impact on the outcomes of case discussions. In this study, Morine-Dershimer noticed that the categories and patterns of written responses from two small groups, who discussed the same case but were led by instructors of different sexes, were different even though every effort was made to balance the membership of the groups with regard to age, ethnicity, and area of specialization within elementary education. Based on a content analysis of reaction papers written following these case discussions, one group exhibited more generalizations from the case to principles of practice, made more connections to their field experiences, focused more on the effects of teachers' behaviors on their students, and displayed more changes in attitudes following the case discussion than the other group. The other group placed more emphasis on possible causes for the problems in the cases, did not generalize from the case to principles of practice or to their field experiences, and did not make connections to their experiences or show much change in attitude. Given that the case discussions were planned and structured in the same way using a predetermined format, Morine-Dershimer concluded that the only apparent difference between groups was the gender of the pair of graduate students who served as case facilitators: the first group described was led by two female case facilitators and the second group was led by two males.

Lundeberg (1997) also conducted a study to test a "pedagogical assumption that [the facilitator] standing and recording discussion ideas on the blackboard as they emerge in case discussions leads to more [student] learning than sitting, carefully listening, and verbally summarizing students' ideas" (p. 6). In this study, Lundeberg stood and used the chalkboard to track issues and ideas with one class and sat with the students in a circle in a less structured format without using the chalkboard with a second class. She reversed her position in the classes during a second case discussion with the same group of undergraduate students. Based on the written reflections of the students after the second discussion, Lundeberg found that where she was did not impact the number of important ideas that they identified about the cases. However, these ideas tended to be expressed in fewer words when written after the more formal case discussions, with the facilitator standing and using the blackboard. When the students were in the less structured environment, they tended to write longer explanations. Furthermore, 68% of the students reported preferring the less structured discussion, noting that they liked the more relaxed and open atmosphere, that more people participated, and seemed to explore ideas more in depth, and that they experienced a feeling of sharing rather than the professor being "above" the students. They also believed that the relaxed format established more of a sense of community. However, the 27% of students who preferred the more structured discussion liked having the chalkboard to use as a visual aid, and found it helpful in taking notes and as an aid to remembering issues. Lundeberg (1997) obtained similar results when this study was repeated with graduate students.

Lundeberg's (1997) study is one of the first to report systematic manipulation of some of the structural and organizational factors that can be employed when planning to use case-based teaching. It provides us with a useful research design and models how future research on these kinds of factors might be conducted. In addition, Morine-Dershimer's research questions in her 1996 study—(a) Can common procedures for case discussions promote common outcomes across sections? and (b) What factors, other than discussion procedures, might account for differences in outcomes between sections?—are two questions that researchers interested in case-based teaching should continue to ask about their own practice.

HOW SHOULD WE STUDY THE ROLE
OF THE FACILITATOR IN CASE DISCUSSIONS?

Studying case-discussion structures and procedures as well as other factors that affect the outcomes of case-based teaching is important because, if every case discussion is unique and idiosyncratic, then what can we say to instructors who might be interested in learning more about how to use these methods effectively? Are there any principles of practice when using cases and case methods? What does this mean for selecting cases as well as for planning how to use them? Are there such things as "exemplary" cases, cases that can be identified as being "classics" for learning about handling particular issues in teaching and learning because the learning outcomes of these discussions are always similar? Or do cases lend themselves to a variety of learning opportunities, depending on the participants' experiences, knowledge-base, background, context, or place in their teaching career? All these points are sources for future research both within one's own courses and also in looking across a case-based curriculum where multiple instructors use cases with inservice and preservice teachers.

Both J. Shulman (1992b) and Morine-Dershimer (1996b) call for systematic research on the multiple factors that influence case teaching. In addition, Morine-Dershimer (1996b) emphasizes that

> discussion necessarily means that each person, leader and student alike, will bring their own experiences, values, and perspectives to the topic being discussed. If any student or instructor input is allowed, then no amount of planning can insure a pre-determined effect (McAnnich, 1993) or uniformity of responses between sections of the same course. Insuring active student involvement and reflection also insures diversity and unique combinations for each class. (p. 15)

If this is true—and I expect that it is—then it will be difficult to determine if the "how" of learning from cases can be accurately repeated. However, we can still focus on "who learns what" from cases, which is what most of the research on cases and case methods to date provides us.

HOW DOES THE RESEARCH ON THE FACILITATION OF CASES AND CASE PEDAGOGY COMPARE WITH THE CLAIMS MADE?

The research that attends to the role of the facilitator appears to focus on two areas: First, much of the research hinges on identifying outcomes of case discussions and on explicating what is learned from cases by the participants. Second, many of the manipulations in the research on case methods have to do with structural and procedural features of case discussions such as (a) the size of the discussion groups (small groups vs. whole classes), (b) student-centered vs. teacher-directed discussions, (c) facilitated versus unfacilitated discussions (e.g., on computers vs. face-to-face), (d) the use of the board for recording comments versus more a informal role for the case leader, and (e) the influence of the gender of the case facilitator. Studies that focus on identifying student learning from cases are valuable because they provide us with information that attempts to answer some of the claims made about the value and efficacy of using case methods. Studies that manipulate the structure of the discussions and include analysis of the role of the facilitator also provide us insights about how the ways we structure case discussions may affect potential outcomes. The two are closely related and often studied together.

What have we learned from these studies? With regard to student outcomes and what is learned from cases, we have some recurring evidence that case discussions held in small groups followed by processing in the larger group may mean more active involvement and more attention by the participants than cases read but never discussed, or discussed without a facilitator. We also have evidence that case discussions in smaller groups can yield more complex understandings of the case content than large-group or whole-class, instructor-led case discussions (Morine-Dershimer, 1993). However, we also know that facilitated (instructor-led), face-to-face case discussions can also lead to deeper, more serious, and more thoughtful thinking about the issues in the cases than unfacilitated case discussions (Levin, 1996; Richardson, 1991).

These findings raise questions for future research, however, because they contradict each other in some ways: For example, what would be the outcome if the small-group discussions were facilitated, or if they were not followed by a facilitator processing what occurred with the whole class? What if the facilitation were provided for students by proxy, almost vicariously, through specific instructor-designed questions and activities for the groups to accomplish? What would the learning outcomes be if these small-group discussions were left completely unstructured and unfacilitated? In addition, although we know that reading, writing about, and discussing cases is more beneficial for understanding the issues in cases than just reading and writing about case without any discussion (Levin, 1995), we don't know very much about what kind of writing is productive for what kinds of outcomes. We also don't know very much about what kinds of questions are most useful for the facilitator to ask (or provide) in either small or large groups.

For example, the Levin (1995) study showed that anonymous, computer-based case discussions had a negative impact on the sense of community already developed in the group. Christensen (1991) claimed that a sense of community is important to foster during case discussions. The anonymous, on-line case discussions in the Levin (1996) study were very divisive for that group of preservice teachers, whereas the face-to-face discussions were friendly, supportive, and respectful. In addition, Lundeberg's (1997) study, which examined the impact of the facilitator's position (standing at the board vs. sitting among the group) and actions (writing on the board vs. facilitating from within the group), indicated that sitting without writing had a positive influence on the sense of community during case discussions. Studies such as these, which examined a variety of methods of conducting case discussions, need to be repeated. Furthermore, the focus needs to be on student learning from the cases and on assessing the facilitators' success in achieving their goals in the first place. That is, if community-building is an important goal, then perhaps less structured and more student-centered case discussions are in order. However, if being sure that participants don't come away from a case discussion with misinterpretations of the case is an important goal, then perhaps more directive case facilitation is in order. Future research studies need to look at assumptions and purposes for using case-based teaching methods and focus the research questions on analyzing outcomes in relation to these originating goals and purposes.

In addition, we have some preliminary evidence that the gender of the facilitator can influence the focus of the case discussion, hence the outcomes. Both the Lundeberg (1993a, 1993b) and the Morine-Dershimer (1996a, 1996b) studies show us that communication styles of males and females may impact facilitation of case discussions. Furthermore, the interaction of gender and the age and experience of the participants in the discussions may also influence communication styles, even when the facilitator is aware of these potential pitfalls (Lundeberg, 1993a, 1993b). Although case facilitators cannot change their gender, they may be able to learn different facilitation styles, and use different structures and procedures for case discussions with different purposes in mind. In addition, case facilitators can certainly study their own practices, paying careful attention to their interactions with both genders, to the kinds of questions asked of males and females, to the amount and kind of feedback and follow-up, and to the influence of male and female participants on each other as well as on the case leader during the discussion. Rich descriptions of the discourse during case discussions and attention to the discourse styles of males and females would be very informative and perhaps lend some insight about what and how males and females learn from cases.

For example, in her study, Levin (1993) noted that the interaction and communication style of the males in her case discussion groups differed from that of the females. That is, the males tended to raise the level of abstraction in the discussion, preferring to comment about the more far-reaching societal implications of the issues in the case under discussion than the females. On the other hand, the females kept the discussion on more concrete issues, making personal connections to the issues in the cases, not discussing the case in the abstract but keeping the discussion focused on the presenting problems in the cases. This finding was not expected, but may be explained by work from sociolinguists such as Tannen (1990) about the differing communication and interaction styles of men and women. Future research in this area, however, is needed to help us uncover the implications of these findings.

However, in the contexts available to the researcher, given the real world of course structures in teacher education programs, it may be more practical to study our own teaching of cases than to study others. As a matter of fact, the concept of "teacher as researcher" could be applied to several of these studies, where the case facilitator was also the researcher engaged in studying her own practice (e.g., Levin, 1993, 1996; Lundeberg, 1993a, 1993b, 1997; Morine-Dershimer, 1991, 1996b). There was some effort to employ quasi-experimental designs, with test—retest situations using groups of students who analyzed cases at the beginning and end of a course, or where several case analyses were compared over time. For example, Morine-Dershimer (1991, 1993, 1996b) employed mainly qualitative methods but also reported simple quantitative data (proportional frequencies) in several of her studies. She conducted a content analysis to identify key ideas that focused on determining the substance of the responses she received to the question and to identify the relationship of these responses to the facilitator's instructional process. However, she then converted these data to proportional frequencies so that comparisons could be made across groups. Additional categories of what participants heard others say during the case discussion were also counted, based on the source.

WHAT ARE SOME FUTURE DIRECTIONS FOR RESEARCH ON CASE FACILITATION?

In addition to paying particular attention to explicating details about the purposes of and planning for case-based teaching, the procedures used during case discussions, and the rules for transcription (see Levin, chap. 7, this volume), it would be very instructive for those engaged in case-based teaching to begin analyzing their own practices, particularly their discourse patterns as case facilitators. The ultimate goal would be to see if one's purposes for using cases match the outcomes. That is, if the purpose for using cases is to help students connect theory with practice, how does the facilitator do this? If the purpose for using cases is to develop perspective in beginning teachers or to promote the use of problem-solving as a heuristic process for thinking about teaching, then how does the case facilitator do this, how well, and what are the criteria that are used to judge growth toward these ends that can be tied to the use of cases? If case discussions are unique forms of discourse, how can we show this and explain the role or roles of case facilitators?

CONCLUSIONS

In the continuing effort to study what is learned from the use of cases and the variety of case methods in teacher education, it is important to understand the nature of what is learned from cases, how this learning occurs, and by whom (Harrington, 1995; Merseth, 1996). Therefore, it is also important to understand the goals and purposes of the case facilitator, whose position as instructor and class leader influences what is learned from the discussion of cases. Toward these ends, I have tried to present the claims made for the role and influence of the case facilitator, the empirical evidence available from studies that explicitly focused on case facilitation, and how these data match the claims made and questions asked about case facilitation. Many of the inferences I draw from these data remain preliminary and await additional study. More research is certainly needed to study the role of the facilitator in case discussions as well as what is learned by the participants in these discussions. I also summarized the data collection and data analysis procedures used to date in these studies and suggested areas for future research. In general, I think all of us interested in case-based teaching should study our own practices, be clear about our goals and purposes for using cases, and analyze the outcomes of our own case discussions. Self-analysis of our individual "styles" of case discussion leadership may lead to some very productive research and findings about "who learns what from cases and how?"

Commentary on "The Role of the Facilitator in Case Discussions"

Rita Silverman
Pace University

Levin's chapter on the role of the facilitator approaches, in a thoughtful and thorough manner, an aspect of case discussion that has not received a lot of attention. As Levin acknowledges, this lack of attention may be a function of the difficulty of studying the role of the facilitator separate from studying the pedagogical role cases might play in pre-professional and professional preparation, and studying the role of the facilitator separately from the process, and from the impact of case-based instruction on the participants. Levin faces this difficulty herself in her review of the literature for this chapter.

An additional quandary in the study of facilitation style is how to measure and compare the personal styles of case leaders. One has only to look at the work of three distinguished case teachers to begin to understand this. The preeminent authority on case teaching in this country, C. Roland Christensen, professor emeritus at Harvard, teaches business cases to graduate students in groups of 75 to 90, in a U-shaped room of raked rows with swivel chairs—a "dedicated" case classroom. Christensen uses the same opening for each discussion he leads: He asks one student to tell the group about the case, and he asks a second student to act as back-up, filling in important information the first student has not included. Once these two students have finished, Christensen, sitting perched at the edge of a table in the center of the open area of the classroom, asks a follow-up question, nodding almost imperceptibly at the student he wants to respond. As the discussion continues, Christensen remains in his spot, his voice soft, quietly orchestrating a discussion that observers and students alike describe as electric, rich, and complex.

Selma Wasserman, professor of education at Simon Fraser University in British Columbia, points to Christensen as her model, and Wasserman's style is as soft and respectful as is his. But Wasserman uses cases in classes of 20 to 25 students, in traditional university classrooms, and with a style quite different from Christensen's. Wasserman begins the case by assigning discussion questions to small groups of students. After students have had time to prepare responses to the questions, Wasserman asks for each group's report. While the first group is sharing their responses, Wasserman listens carefully, asking questions to clarify and to make sure she understands their ideas. Before she moves on to the next group, she confirms with each member of the first group of respondents that all of their ideas have been presented. Wasserman does not use the chalkboard to record students' ideas, nor does she take comments from anyone other than the students in the target group. By the end of the class, each group will have received Wasserman's close attention, and everyone will have had an opportunity to speak. Although students report that her discussions are also rich and complex, they are quite different from Christensen's in organization, facilitation style, and role of the facilitator and the participants.

Bill Welty, professor of management at Pace University, credits Christensen with teaching him how to think about teaching with cases, and, like Wasserman, names Christensen as his case teaching mentor. But Welty's case facilitation style offers yet another picture of what it means to teach with cases, contrasting sharply with both Christensen and Wasserman. Similar to Christensen and Wasserman, he is considered a master discussion teacher by students and colleagues who have watched him lead a case, but his style is more active, clamorous, and involved than either Christensen's or Wasserman's. Welty teaches groups of up to 35 students in traditional university classrooms. The students sit at tables arranged to form a deep U, and Welty incorporates the space inside the U into his facilitation style. He moves close to the student who is speaking, listening carefully, and often walks backward, still facing the speaking student, to "carry" that student's ideas to another part of the room. He has been known to run from a far end of the U to get an idea onto the chalkboard, where he records the discussion, fitting the students' ideas, in their own words, into a board outline he has planned in advance of the discussion. He also begins each case with a different opening question, chosen from the discussion outline he prepared for the case. Students in his classes talk about the excitement he generates in a classroom, the complexity of the discussions, his ability to listen, and his humor.

I've watched each of these outstanding teachers lead case discussions, and, on reflection, it seems to me that while the facilitation style of each case leader (use of the board, movement in the room, size of discussion group, etc.) could be emulated, the personal style of each is not transport-able—others may attempt to copy one of their styles, but they may not achieve the same results. The enthusiastic reports of the students of these three experts (and those of other successful case facilitators) result, in all likelihood, from an interaction between the actual facilitation style and the personal magnetism of the leader. Others could mimic exactly what these three case teachers do but achieve different results as a function of the inter-action between their facilitation styles and their unique personalities. Studying case facilitation as a way to guide future case teachers by measur-ing facilitation style and student outcomes, without regard for the powerful role of personal style, may be a thankless task. Rather, it seems to me, that Levin's call for case facilitators to study their own teaching, manipulating some of the variables that current research suggests might influence student outcomes, is a way to take into account the idiosyncratic nature of personal style as well as the immutable differences among populations being used for the outcome measures.

Encouraging faculty in teacher education, particularly, to use their own university classrooms for action research will yield payoffs both in the im-provement of college teaching and in our ability to model for our students the power of classroom research to improve teaching at all levels.

6

Learning From Videocases

Virginia Richardson
University of Michigan
Robert S. Kile
University of Nevada, Las Vegas

The use of cases in teacher education has been advocated by many as one answer to the problem of working with students whose cognitive schema regarding teaching is underdeveloped or inappropriately tied to their experiences as students. A major problem of teacher education has been described by Katz, Raths, Mohanty, Kurachi, and Irving (1981) as "anticipatory socialization":

> All preservice training can be characterized as anticipatory socialization which inevitably involves giving students answers to questions not yet asked, and not likely to be asked until students are in the thick of actual service. This aspect of socialization can be called the feed-forward problem. It includes resistance from the student at the time of exposure to given learnings and, later, protestations that the same learnings had not been provided, should have been provided, or should have been provided in stronger doses. (p. 21)

Another way of framing this problem is to suggest that preservice teachers, as long as they are still students and not teachers, do not have the cognitive schema or practical knowledge that are acquired from teaching experience to be able to ask appropriate questions and reconstruct their own sense of

121

theory and practice. For them, most teacher education class readings and discussions of teaching practice counts as theory, and practice is what goes on in their internship classrooms in the schools. For the teacher-educator, however, class discussions of teaching are often accompanied by images of classroom practice that they carry with them from observation and their own practice. They work hard to introduce more practice into the discussion, but it is still usually seen by the teacher education students as theory.

The question then becomes: how may we effectively immerse preservice teachers in issues, problems, and solutions of teaching practice before they have the experience of being first-year teachers, fully responsible for their own classrooms? Or how may we help preservice teachers develop the cognitive schema, a "need to know," and practical knowledge such that they benefit from discussions of and readings about teaching?

One possibility is the use of cases. Cases of teachers, students and classrooms may bring preservice students closer to the dilemmas of classrooms, to the lives of "real" students and teachers and to the varying contexts and the effects of these contexts on the methods teachers use to approach these dilemmas (Carter, 1989; Colbert, Trimble, & Desberg, 1995; Merseth, 1991a, 1996; L. Shulman, 1992). Cases are advocated by many as a way to help students begin to "think like teachers" (see Sykes & Bird, 1992, for descriptions of the various conceptual frameworks for case-use advocacy).

One argument for the use of cases is face validity—that is, "if people read the case and it seems realistic, then the case can be said to exhibit high face validity" (Kent, Herbert, & McNergney, 1995, p. 140). If the case has high face validity, it may no longer be viewed by the preservice teacher as just another academic exercise. One would hypothesize, therefore, that videocases have the potential to be high in face validity, because they project a moving picture of a classroom context. The purpose of this chapter is to examine videocases, their use in teacher education, and research on the use of videocases.

WHAT ARE VIDEOCASES?

Videocases are multimedia presentations of classroom actions and analyses that include moving pictures (usually on videocassette) of classroom action. In addition to the videos, videocases may include written or videotaped analyses; interpretations and/or explanations of the classroom action by the teachers, students, principals, parents, and/or others such as experts in the field; and other materials such as the teachers' instructional plans. Examples of such videocases follow (see also Sykes & Bird, 1992; and Desberg & Fisher, 1996, for descriptions of videocases).

The multicultural videocases developed at the University of Virginia consist of videotapes of short classroom action segments, each of which is followed by the teacher in the scene discussing the actions (Herbert & McNergney, 1995). A number of these videocases take place in U.S. schools with diverse student populations; multicultural education is stressed. In addition, videocases have been developed from materials collected in England, Denmark, India, Singapore, and South Africa. There are also a series of written analyses of the videocases by people from different perspectives—teachers, researchers, and teacher educators. These videocases accompany a foundations of education text (McNergney & Herbert, 1995).

The cases developed at the Cognition and Technology Group at Vanderbilt University (CTGV) combine media for the purposes of creating anchored instruction or situated instruction in an information-rich videodisc environment (CTGV, 1990). The group began their work with material for students in elementary schools (*The Young Sherlock Holmes Project,* CTGV, 1990), and then moved to the development of videocases for pre- and inservice teacher education. The cases provide videodisc and computer access to data gathered in a number of classrooms. The data include videotapes of classroom activity, data on each student's background and progress, the curriculum, student products, information on the school, and other artifacts such as letters to parents and report cards.

Lampert and Ball (1998) also produced cases that may be accessed through computers. Each was videotaped as she taught mathematics in an elementary school classroom (third and fifth grade). The videotapes were put together with planning documents, student work, and interviews with students and parents, and this material was transferred to hypermedia technology such that it could be accessed by computer. Lampert and Ball's goal was to engage their preservice students in inquiries concerning teaching. They also made the materials available to their teacher education colleagues.

Bliss and Mazur (1995) developed a set of "common thread" cases that are on CD-Roms. These CDs attempt to tie teaching standards to cases of teaching that demonstrate the standards. The cases include photography, video clips, audio narration, original music, and graphics. The program has E-mail and Internet capabilities, so that it may be used for distance education.

We used videotapes of Grade 4, 5, and 6 classroom teachers of reading comprehension in several southwestern schools, in combination with written documents that were extracted from interviews with the teachers about their teaching (Richardson & Kile, 1992). The written cases provide the teachers' own descriptions and explanations of context and practices as depicted on the videotape. The videocases are used in teacher education classes.

In Japan, Sato (1991, 1992) works with written cases developed by practitioners in conjunction with professional quality videotapes taken in the teachers' classrooms. He feels that these videocases represent teachers' practical wisdom, and are extremely valuable in developing theory through practice.

DO THEY WORK?

Unfortunately, there is very little research on the outcomes of the use of videocases. In fact, there is little solid empirical work on case use in education. The literature about the use of cases in teacher education is primarily analytic, speculative, and, at times, promotional. As Merseth (1996) points out: "The extent to which individual writers assert the benefits of cases and case methods far outweighs the actual empirical work that confirms these benefits" (p. 728). This, she suggests, is particularly the case in teacher education, where the interest in case use is quite recent. Only recently have we begun to accumulate a sense of how cases are being used in teacher education and their effects on the students. For example, an issue of *Journal of Teacher Education* focused on case use in teacher education with some anecdotal descriptions of the use of cases and potential problems. And J. Shulman's (1992a) book presents reflections on the use of cases in teacher education by a number of students, practitioners, and researchers. Although the research literature is beginning to grow on written case use (e.g., Barnett & Tyson, 1994; Harrington, 1994a; Kleinfeld, 1991a), there is very little on the use of videocases.

At the same time, a number of authors have questioned current views of the potency of cases for beginning teacher education students (e.g., Sykes, 1989). In a powerful essay that questions cases for use in teacher education, Sacken (1992) suggests that there is no analytic scheme "that knits teaching or educational practice together" (p. 11) such as there is in the law. As he suggests, "to think like a lawyer implies a process that is explicit and transferable; it is in fact the central gift of legal education" (p. 10). Because cases do not have a fixed meaning, "a case-based curriculum will take teacher education toward an asystematic universe of teacher preparation classrooms dominated by the particular ideologies of the resident professor" (p. 12), or toward a "kitchen sink" approach to multiple meanings and analyses.

Although Sacken's commentary is primarily related to the larger knowledge base of teaching, there still should be some concern about the effects of the use of videocases in teacher education. Videocases are expensive to develop (Goldman & Barron, 1990), and classrooms must be organized somewhat differently in order to use them. They should, therefore, provide for different experiences and learning opportunities than written cases. We describe three examples of empirical study around the use of videocases, discuss the methodological issues involved in such research, and propose additional research. The first example consists of a series of studies around the CTGV videocases, the second presents the authors' study of the use of videocases in their teacher education classroom, and the third summarizes the work of Lampert and Ball (1998).

The Cognition and Technology Group at Vanderbilt

Aligning their work with the theoretical construct of situated cognition (see Brown, Collins, & Duguid, 1989), the CTGV researchers argue that their anchored instruction offers students a vehicle to explore everyday cognition, authentic tasks, and in-context apprenticeship training (CTGV, 1990, 1993). Through the use of case-based videodiscs, students are offered opportunities and advantages that text-based instruction does not allow. The videodisc cases, according to the CTGV (1990), create "macrocontexts" for the students that "enable the exploration of a problem space for extended periods of time from many perspectives" (p. 3). These macrocontexts anchor the instruction in complex problem spaces, as opposed to microcontexts, which typically address specific subsets of larger problems. Thus, the students have a common focal point from which to begin their discussions and explorations of problems.

CTGV (1990, 1993) offers several reasons for their macrocontexts to be visual rather than textual and videodisc rather than videotape. First, the visual format does not offer the writer's interpretation and cognitive patterning; the visual medium allows the student to develop their own pattern recognition skills. Furthermore, the videodisc offers to students a more dynamic, visual, and spatial representation that may allow students to form "rich mental models of the problem situations" (CTGV, 1990, p. 3). Finally, CTGV's preference for the videodisc system of delivery is that it has random-access capabilities that allow a teacher instant information in problem situation. HyperCard technology in conjunction with the videodiscs was developed for these studies, which allows the researchers and students to use the "rapid, random access and freeze-frame capabilities of videodisc technology" (Risko, Yount, & McAllister, 1992, p. 39). This allows the professor and students to quickly access and then reexamine different scenes and cases to discuss and analyze information that is difficult to describe in written or verbal accounts.

Risko et al. (1992) explored the use of video-based case instruction methods in an undergraduate teacher education course. Three videocases were recorded on videodiscs and used throughout the fall semester. The study offers an analysis of the "communication patterns among class members during the implementation of [our] instruction" (p. 38).

The study was conducted in a Remedial Reading and Practicum course that is required for elementary and secondary education majors. The course included 7 weeks of classes and 5 weeks of practicum observations. Following the last week of observations the preservice teacher participants returned to the university to share information about a low-achieving reading student that they had observed and analyzed using a case study format. Twelve preservice students participated in the study.

The videocases were used to offer to the preservice teachers an opportunity to "explore authentic classroom and Chapter 1 situations" (Risko et al., 1992, p. 39). The researchers argue that the videocases via the videodisc format offer the preservice teachers the capability to reexamine scenes and cases for different reasons that are difficult to explore using verbal or written formats. Furthermore, the HyperCard computer program allowed the participants to access multiple sources of information contained in the videocases (Risko et al., 1992).

Data collection for the study included field notes of the participants' daily discourse during the class sessions. The data were analyzed using interpretive qualitative techniques to identify themes and patterns of the participants' discourse.

Risko et al. (1992) found four patterns emerging from the data. The researchers found that the participants' discourse patterns demonstrated "active engagement and generative learning" (p. 40). For example, during the first showing and analyses of the videodisc, 8 of the 12 participants were highly engaged in conversations about the videocase. The participants also demonstrated spontaneous connections between the cases and prior experiences. The researchers contend that those connections were not linear connections as might be found during a lecture format designed to transmit information. Furthermore, the participants' discourse revealed a metacognitive awareness of the importance of specific information without being told of those connections by an expert.

A second theme to emerge from the data was the participants' discourse that demonstrated that mediated learning has multiple textures. That is, "the students and the professor guided one another's learning by initiating questions, by summarizing, and by elaborating" about the videocases (p. 44). Furthermore, the students often referred to their readings to support their ideas and enhance the discussions. The students also demonstrated this mediation of learning by introducing vocabulary and concepts that became part of the classroom discourse. For example, the term "icky" became part of the classroom jargon when referring to poorly written stories. Through the use of multiple perspectives, a common vocabulary, and generative learning, the researchers believe that the students' classroom experiences "enable our students to understand problems that experts [teachers] encounter and the knowledge these experts use as tools for problem solving" (p. 47).

Risko et al.'s (1992) third theme demonstrated that learning situated in rich, complex contexts invites in-depth analysis by the preservice students, as well as higher order thinking. The videocases about students experiencing reading difficulties offered the preservice students opportunities to observe and analyze "multiple classroom events involving the student and several interviews with the parent, teacher, and student," which "illustrated the complexity of factors surrounding a teacher's decision making about a pupil's reading instruction" (p. 45). As such, the study found that the preservice teachers were invited to synthesize case information, examine interrelated issues, and "generate reasonable interpretations, analogies, and conclusions" (p. 45).

The finding discussed here led the researchers to the last theme to emerge from the study: that there is a need to offer authentic case studies, as opposed to a sequenced or predetermined order of instruction. The researchers contend that their students' spontaneous use of information and experiences enhance and strengthen the students' levels of analysis and higher order thinking when framed within the videocase studies. The study concludes that "such experiences may help preservice teachers acquire mental models of authentic classes, enabling them to think flexibly and to understand the meaning of classroom events, so that they are better prepared for actual decision making when it is needed in the classroom" (Risko et al., 1992, p. 48). The study's findings furthered the researchers' beliefs that anchored instruction offers authentic experiences and a common ground for the preservice teachers to explore.

Risko, McAllister, Peter, and Bigeho (1994) conducted a study exploring the influence of videodisc-based instruction on preservice teachers in a remedial reading methodology course. Similar to the previous work discussed, this study furthered the investigation into the impact and effectiveness of anchored instruction—that is, situating the learning in interesting and realistic classroom situations and encouraging active construction of knowledge. The cases in this study "were narratives, as opposed to lectures" and were "designed to create contextual learning to help preservice teachers and the college instructor mediate each others' learning while examining the cases from multiple perspectives" (Risko et al., 1994, p. 156).

The study had 17 preservice teacher participants, enrolled in a course entitled *Remedial Reading and Practicum*. Two sets of data were collected, which included interviews and pre/post videocase analyses. Three formal 15-minute interviews were administered at three points in the semester: one interview each at the beginning of the course, one in the middle of the semester and prior to the practicum, and a final interview at the end of the semester. Prior to the first interview the preservice teachers were to respond in writing to a series of questions that probed for their understanding and theories of literacy teaching. During the interviews the students were asked to elaborate upon their written responses and notes were recorded.

The videocase analyses occurred in two stages. The participants analyzed one videocase at the beginning of the first day of class and a second at the end, of the class sessions, but prior to their practicum. The written analysis of the two cases by the participants were then compared by the participants at the end of the semester using a set of questions to guide their comparisons and analysis of the previous responses. The data analysis by the researchers was conducted within the tradition of qualitative research that employs an interpretative stance to guide the analysis (Risko et al., 1994).

The study found four consistent patterns emerging from the data analysis. The patterns described the preservice students' progress in "developing flexible and alternative interpretations to problems, learning how to situate facts and procedures in meaningful contexts, learning how to know and understand, and learning the importance of knowing" (Risko et al., 1994, p. 159). In essence, the findings indicated that the students were thinking about how to use the course content to guide their instructional decision-making. Furthermore, the students demonstrated that they had gained substantial knowledge about how their learning influenced their beliefs and how their beliefs developed and changed during the course (Risko et al., 1994).

Richardson and Kile

We worked with 21 preservice students (5 males and 16 females) who were taking one of five Classroom Processes and Instruction sections (Richardson & Kile, 1992). Richardson was the major professor and Kile, then a graduate student, was responsible for the laboratory activities and school placements. The students were both elementary and secondary majors, and 7 of them were nontraditional—that is, they had not followed a linear and continual school track (Crow, Levine, & Nager, 1990). Field experiences were held in one secondary and two elementary schools, and videocases were used extensively in the course.

The videocases were developed from the Reading Instruction Study (Richardson, 1994), and each consisted of a videotape of a teacher's lesson, accompanied by a written statement using the teacher's own words as extracted from extensive interviews. These videocases were developed by Barbara Morgan-Flemming, now an assistant professor at Texas Tech University.

Our questions about the use of videocases were as follows:

1. How did the written elements of the cases add to the students' interpretations of the videotapes?
2. Were there signs of theories of reading expressed in students' descriptions of the videocases? Did these change over the course of the semester?
3. What analytic categories were emphasized in the students' descriptions of the videotapes?
4. Were particular types of videocases more or less conducive to student analyses?

The videocase exercise was presented three times during the course of the first semester. Toward the beginning (September 5) and the end (December 5) of the semester, students were asked to go to the computer lab and pick one of five videotapes to view. They were asked to keep a written record of their observations while watching the tape. They were then asked to read the written case, and answer the additional questions. The assignment was as follows:

1. View at least 30 minutes of the tape, and maintain running notes concerning what is going on in the classroom.
2. Read the notes from the teacher. Did the teacher's notes add to or change your understanding of what was going on in the classroom? How?
3. Did the teacher's notes change your judgments about how the teacher was doing? How?
4. On the basis of both videotape and notes, list good and poor aspects of the lesson.
5. What advice would you give the teacher?

Toward the middle of the semester, the students viewed a videotape of one of the teachers and were asked to discuss the case in their groups, and then read the written case and fill in the form. The group discussions were audiotaped.

In terms of the first question, concerning the degree to which the written elements of the videocase contribute to students' understandings, we found that twice as many students replied that the text changed or strengthened their analysis of the videotape as students who responded that it either confirmed or did not change their analysis. The changes seemed to lead to greater understanding of the teacher's actions and softening of harsh judgments.

Although we expected to find differences between the elementary and secondary students, the differences were even greater between the traditional and nontraditional student groups. We found that none of the elementary nontraditional students responded that they had changed their analyses, whereas six out of eight of the traditional students stated that they had changed. This difference was not found in the secondary traditional and nontraditional students. However, as described here, the nontraditional students wrote much deeper analyses of the tapes than the traditional students; thus, they may have felt, on reading the cases, that they had interpreted the teacher's actions correctly.

Descriptions of teaching in the first assignment were teacher-directed, featuring the teacher as knowledge giver and student as passive recipient. This was evident in the extreme concern for classroom management (e.g., "I wouldn't have let the students wander around the room"; "the noise level is too high"; "the students shouldn't be able to sign out to go to the bathroom") and in the many negative judgments of the teachers (e.g., "The teacher is not in touch with the student interests;" "the teacher's reaction to Jose's absences are harsh"). In all, the students' responses presented a teacher-deficit model.

The theories of teaching had altered considerably in the third assignment. Fewer negative judgments were expressed about the teachers, and management concerns were considerably reduced. The student role seemed to be redefined as active participant rather than passive recipient of information (e.g., "open discussion, tried to involve various students, encouraged various answers"; "good use of wait-time allows for 'some' discussion").

The terms used by the students in describing the first videotape were quite general in terms of description and judgment (e.g., *enthusiastic, teacher explains assignment, teacher listens to students*). However, by the third videotape, the students used terms and concepts that had been covered in the course. These included such terms as *wait time, transitions, lesson flow, gender issues, cooperative learning, engaged time, effective planning, follow-up questions,* and *inference-level questions*.

The descriptions also changed considerably from the first to the third assignments—from behavioral descriptions to functional descriptions of the teachers' actions; and from a student's to a teacher's perspective. Examples of these descriptions and perspectives are provided here:

- Behavioral description of teacher's actions: *teacher using map; explaining to class; constant questioning; teacher led discussion.*
- Functional descriptions of teacher's actions: *explains distinctions in words and meaning; teacher ties old to new by questioning students' prior knowledge;* [teacher] *discussed tactics to find meaning in context.*

- Student's perspective on the assessment of teacher's actions: *open discussion; letting students discuss openly is fun; students engaged with examples and story; most children involved.*
- Teacher's perspective on the assessment of the teacher's actions: [teacher] *showed students they can understand story and not know all the words; particularly good wait-time during discussions and good transitions; short geography and language lesson.*

Further, the descriptions given an action were richer and deeper in the third assignment as compared to the first.

The major shifts in these categories occurred with the traditional students, as the nontraditional students' descriptions on the first assignment were already more functional and teacher-focused. In fact, the nontraditional students' descriptions were deeper and displayed considerably more complexity than the traditional students. A possible explanation is that the nontraditional students, who have had life experiences in adult roles such as parenting or working in another job, understand that professional actions are functional. Therefore, they identify with the adult in the classroom rather than the student, and focus on the function of the action rather than simply the behavior.

Two of the tapes were not conducive to analysis. The first was the tape in which the students were quite disruptive. The responses focused on the students' inappropriate behavior, and very little on the teacher's instruction. It would appear that the use of disruptive classrooms in videocases is more problematic than in written cases. Student misbehavior on the videotape seemed to pull the students' attention away from other issues within the classroom.

Videocase examples of mediocre and excellent teaching produced good analytic responses. However, another tape that evoked very little writing, but considerable interest, was a tape of one lesson within a large and complex unit. On this tape, students were working at independent and group activity, and the teacher was floating around the classroom and checking up on group work. There was little that the preservice teacher could analyze that could be described as active teaching. A considerable amount of background information on the unit was presented in the written case, but the written responses from the students were positive but few in number. This suggests that the videocases should mix and combine activities, so the students may use a number of concepts that they are learning about in their analyses.

To summarize the findings, we found considerable change between the first and third assignments in the following areas: increased use of concepts and language covered in class; a large decrease in negative judgments about the teacher and student behaviors; a change in the theory of teaching from a teacher-centered approach to one in which students take an active part in their learning; a change in language from behavioral to functional descriptions of the teacher's actions, and from a student perspective in assessing the teacher to a teacher perspective; and a change in the descriptions of a given action from simple to rich and deep. There were also differences on the first assignment between traditional and nontraditional students that indicated that the latter group of students applied some of their life experiences to the task of analyzing videotapes of teaching. By and large, students felt that the written elements of the cases contributed considerably to their understanding of the videotapes.

Lampert and Ball

The research conducted by Lampert and Ball (1998) revolved around the inquiries conducted by their students in seven sections of a mathematics methods course in the elementary school programs at the University of Michigan and Michigan State University. The students were asked to work in small groups or individually and formulate questions that could be addressed with the hypermedia materials. For example, a group of students might address a question: "What did Deborah (the teacher on the tape) do if a student gives the wrong answer?" The students used the hypermedia and other materials, such as readings, to respond to the question. They developed multimedia presentations to respond to the question and gave public presentations. Lampert and Ball then analyzed 68 of these investigations.

They found that two thirds of the projects focused on teaching or the teacher, seven on specific students, and several on the intersection of teaching and external policy factors, such as the NCTM standards. Of the 68 projects, 42 concluded with answers and 26 concluded with revised questions. From their analysis, they found five patterns:

1. There was great variation across classes in the quality of the projects.
2. The initial assumptions reflected strong normative assumptions, such as notions about good classrooms, and so on.
3. The students seemed willing to change their minds about empirical matters once they examined the data.
4. The relationships between the particulars and generalizations were tenuous.
5. The investigations focused little on mathematics.

Following this investigation, Lampert decided to provide somewhat more structured tasks for the students, in addition to more open-ended inquiry tasks. One task, in particular, asked students to investigate classroom culture in the hypermedia materials. A case study of one student who, along with a partner, investigated this issue was then developed and described. Lampert and Ball then address what the student may have learned in this class in which the multimedia materials are used extensively. They provide conjectures about the student's stance toward understanding classroom action—that she has become more tentative and developed a deeper understanding of the nature of mathematics, and a sense of the complexity of teaching. They do not suggest that the student learned more in their classes than she would have in a more conventional methods course, but suggest that she certainly learned differently.

METHODOLOGICAL ISSUES

There are two sets of methodological issues related to the use of videocases in teacher education. The first set concerns to the use of videotapes in capturing classroom action and using them for purposes of teacher education (preservice or inservice). Tochon (in press) suggests that there are four critiques of the practice of using videos in teacher education.

1. To some extent, the use of the camera alters the naturalness of the professional activity. If the teacher is aware of the video camera, it may affect his or her instructional practice.
2. When preservice teachers or inservice students come together to review a videotape—particularly one that is taken in one of the participant's classrooms—the somewhat artificial setting diminishes the value of the conversation.
3. By necessity, the videotape reduces the complexity of the classroom, thereby preventing full professional learning.
4. Competencies cannot be exercised in isolation from one another.

Thus the question, "what is this a videocase of?" is ever-present. Tochon presents some examples of these critiques; but representation of reality is by definition inauthentic and less complex than reality. Videocases are probably the best representation of any of the other materials used in the classroom, except a live video hookup that would affect the class being watched.

There are also methodological issues related to conducting research on the use of videotapes in teacher education. A question, for example, concerns the measurement of change in preservice or inservice teachers who are participants in the teacher education or staff development processes in which the videocases are being used. A basic assumption is that the students will, undoubtedly, learn something. As Lanier (1986) pointed out in her teacher education article in the *Handbook of Research on Teaching*, people usually change when they are trained to do something. There are many studies that suggest this. However, videocases are designed to change participants' beliefs and deep understandings as well as actions. This is difficult to capture (see Richardson & Anders, 1994, for a description of issues related to conducting research on teacher change). Further, because the use of videocases in the classroom is a complex venture and may entail a reorganization of the curriculum as well as the physical space, it would be helpful to know whether videocases work better than written cases, or better than a class that operates around discussion of a textbook. Is it possible to conduct research that compares different media? Of course, comparative, experimental designs may be developed; however, it is not clear that all of the variables may be accounted for in any such design. After all, the instruction entails considerably more than the use of the videocases. And what, exactly, does "use of videocases" mean, and how can such use be standardized across classroom? For Lampert and Ball (1998), the materials were meant to be used in student investigations. However, they could be used in many different ways in teacher education classrooms.

We believe that although comparative experimental designs may shed some light on the question of what teacher education students learn with videocases as compared with textbooks or written cases, so too do comparative case studies. Teachers and (we assume) teacher-educators adapt new practices when the assumptions that underlie the practice are seen to match those of the teacher (Richardson, 1996). Case studies of practice provide teachers with information on context, assumptions, practices, and curriculum that allow them to make more informed judgments about the practices used in their own classrooms. Thus, although these cases are not "comparative," they do provide necessary information to teachers in their considerations as to whether to implement a practice in their classrooms.

CONCLUSIONS

It would appear from the research described here that the use of multimedia cases significantly impacts preservice teachers' cognitions. The rationale used most often in explaining the results is that the cases have the potential to bring theory and practice together by presenting a visual, moving picture of teaching in a real-life classroom, along with the teacher's thoughts that accompanied the classroom action. It has been suggested that this activity may begin the development of practical knowledge and reflection on practice. However, whether the changes represented in this research are long-lasting, or may be affected by other, perhaps less costly teacher education pedagogical approaches is not known. Nonetheless, even with a very small literature base with which to work, the following suggestions may be considered and explored further.

Videocases by themselves will not transform the teacher education classroom. The teacher-educator is the agent of reform and should his or her beliefs and understanding differ from the assumptions that underlie the cases, the results will probably be somewhat disappointing. For example, Saunders (1992) studied the use of videocases in a class of undergraduate teacher education students. Saunders found that the teacher-educator had different goals for using the cases than the developers, and therefore there were quite different results than anticipated. Another example is Lampert and Ball's (1998) hypermedia cases, and their expectations for using them in classrooms in which the emphasis is on inquiry into teaching and learning. Should the teacher-educator not accept this understanding of his or her role, the results of their use will be very different from Lampert and Ball's results.

In their review of the literature on students who enter teacher education programs, Brookhart and Freeman (1992) emphasize the need to look at subpopulations of students. The results of our earlier study (Richardson and Kile, 1992) supports this assertion. In this study, the traditional and non-traditional students appeared to have considerably different analytic skills and perspectives on teaching and learning at the beginning of the course. It would be a mistake to assume that students in our preservice programs are a homogeneous group with respect to their perspectives on classroom activities.

The media form is extremely important. Unless one is viewing a complete videotape, videotapes are difficult to use in a teacher education classroom. As suggested by Goldman and Barron (1990), "the tapes were awkward for the instructor to use, and the linear sequence of video scenes made the planned class activities somewhat inflexible" (p. 24). Further, videotapes focus on just one aspect of classroom action at a time. There is too much going on for one camera to capture. The use of several media was helpful in our study, in which we used videotapes and written cases; however, this too could be awkward. Hypermedia has transformed the possibilities for the use of cases in teacher education. It allows actions to be categorized and found quickly, and also brings in other data easily and quickly.

Strong arguments have been made for the use of authentic cases (Risko et al., 1994). At the same time, the permission process for videotaping in classrooms has become significantly more difficult in recent years, making authentic cases even more difficult to develop. Thus, there is a question as to whether simulated cases would be a useful alternative in the teacher education classroom. We would argue in favor of making every effort to use authentic cases.[1] As Risko et al. (1994) pointed out, the authentic case allows the whole group—including the teacher educator—to inquire into the nature of teaching and learning with an authentic case. This would be more difficult to accomplish with a simulated case that has been designed to demonstrate a specific aspect of teaching. However, a study of the use of simulated and authentic cases would be a useful addition to the research base.

Given the issues and conclusions discussed above, it would appear that comparative case studies of the use of videocases and other methods of teacher education would be useful. Videocases are expensive and difficult to produce. They require a different organization of the teacher education classroom, and a different role for the teacher-educator. At the same time, the empirical research that exists does indicate that videocases help preservice teacher education students begin to develop deep and meaningful understandings of the complexities of the classroom and the ability to use useful constructs in approaching the dilemmas that they will face when they begin to teach. It would certainly be worth exploring further the potential of this approach to teacher education.

---

[1]Of course, as Tochon (in press) pointed out, a videocase is not "authentic." Choices are made as to what to include and what to leave out. In fact, any representation of reality is unauthentic. However, a simulated case is more removed from reality than a videocase and is developed for a particular purpose. The authentic videocase is much more open-ended.

Commentary on
"Learning From Videocases"

Gary A. Griffin
Teachers College, Columbia University

Richardson and Kile's chapter causes me to think more seriously than I have about the interaction of the following two questions related to case use in teacher education: In what ways do cases move teacher candidates into close engagement with the practice of teaching? What should videocase research focus on?

I believe strongly that teaching and schooling are, at heart, about relationships—creating, strengthening, and sustaining them, and, at times, altering their character. If school- and classroom-embedded relationships form the core of working in schools, it seems logical to assume that almost everything teacher candidates encounter in their preservice programs should provide opportunities for enacting and capitalizing on the role of relationships in teaching. Except in cases of personal romantic relationships, it is intuitively appealing to believe that a relationship depends on and is always in search of something to relate *about*. We have come to believe that the focus of "something to relate about" is school subject matter. I believe it is also necessary for teacher–student relationships to move beyond content to issues of civility, predictability, concern and caring, competence, justice, democracy, and others.

How can cases assist teacher education students as they come to value important features of relationships in schools and classrooms? Cases can demonstrate relational aspects of a "thinking community," can illustrate how members of such communities are connected to one another for good or ill, and can provide opportunities for safe and neutral explorations of the consequences of teachers' and students' ways of being with one another. My own use of cases has demonstrated to my satisfaction that this is a powerful way to move teacher candidates' thinking from that of student to the perspective of teacher, a serious intention of teacher education.

At the same time, however, I wonder if once again we may not be substituting representations for context immersion in many of the same ways that we have in the past. We have asked students to read texts, examine transcripts, interview experienced teachers, and other once, twice, or even several times removed expressions of teaching practice. We may find that cases enrich students' ability to represent teaching and even enhance their cognitively based understanding of teaching strategies. Do they, however, influence teaching in subsequent practice? Does engagement with videocases help to develop the habit of "seeing oneself at a distance," an attribute of the reflective teacher? Do group discussions of cases contribute to explorations of underlying values and assumptions about what worthy teaching is and is not?

These questions, emerging out of a preoccupation with teaching as relational, help me to focus on research in relation to cases. Obviously, one could (as others have) aim inquiry at knowledge and behavioral issues—for example, what did students learn about teaching, and can they do what is included in the case? However, Richardson and Kile have caused me to consider issues of value, belief, and disposition. They remind me that our inquiry into case use is fragmented and fragile, and that enthusiasm for case use in teacher education comes primarily from advocacy. They help me to overlay my own expectations for teaching onto existing and emerging conceptions of how learning to teach takes place. And they stimulate me to imagine research that cuts through the several richly textured layers of these conceptions, expectations, and strategies. To paraphrase a line from their chapter, they bring to consciousness the question, "What is case *research* a case of?"

7

The Role of Discussion in Case Pedagogy: Who Learns What? And How?

Barbara B. Levin
University of North Carolina at Greensboro

There is a way to energize your classrooms, to excite a much higher percentage of your students, and to add more value to their education. You can get out from behind your lectern and still communicate content and theory—do so better, in fact. But to do this you will have to pay far more attention than you have in the past to teaching process *questions, to the teaching* methods *you are using.*

—Welty (1989, p. 41)

The use of case-based teaching methods with preservice and inservice teachers appears to have great potential for fostering knowledge and creating the right disposition that teachers need to function successfully in today's complex world of teaching. Case-based teaching methods have received renewed interest in the past decade and the research available on using the case method for teacher education continues to be fruitful. Cases seem to be a viable form of pedagogy—especially if one believes that knowledge is constructed individually and in groups, and that teaching and learning to teach is problematic, contextualized, and highly complex. The research presented in this chapter bolsters the need to continue studying what is learned by participants in case discussions. The more we know about the factors that influence teachers' understanding of and thinking about cases, what can be learned from cases, and how to conduct case discussions effectively, the better able we will be to determine when, with whom, and how to best use this potentially powerful pedagogical tool for teacher education.

Just as case-based teaching takes a variety of forms and occurs in a variety of contexts, there are also many kinds of cases available for use. There are narrative, text-based cases (both short ones and long ones), videocases, multimedia cases, and cases taken from literary works. The content of cases also varies widely. For example, cases can focus on curriculum content and delivery, pedagogical concerns, multicultural education, other diversity issues, classroom management, motivation, families, children with special needs, school governance, and so on. However, in all of these instances the case provides a common source, a story, for teachers to discuss.

No critique will be made in this chapter of what form cases take or of their content. Rather, the focus here is on what is learned from the discussion of cases in a variety of teacher education settings, who learns, and how this occurs. After a brief overview of research on case-based teaching, I focus in more detail on studies that look at the role of discussion in learning from cases. I review the research on case discussions undertaken with preservice teachers and then present the few empirical studies conducted to date in inservice settings. Following that I discuss some of the promising data collection and data analysis methods used by researchers in this field. Finally, I focus on where we must go with future research on case methods, especially with regard to research on the role of the case discussion in teacher education settings. I conclude with some of the questions that remain to be studied regarding who learns what from case discussions, and how.

OVERVIEW

There are several theories as to why case-based instruction is an effective pedagogical tool for teacher education. For example, because cases are richly detailed and contextualized narrative accounts of teaching and learning, they represent the complex problems, dilemmas, and issues that surround teaching in today's world. The narrative quality of cases also suggests that they may be valuable tools for teacher development because they address ways of knowing that are valued by educators (Bruner, 1986, 1990; Carter, 1993; Doyle, 1990). Furthermore, cases can be used to help teachers understand and make connections between principles of practice and theoretical concepts, grapple with moral and ethical questions in teaching, and promote strategies, dispositions, and habits of mind needed by teachers (L.

Shulman, 1992). They may also stimulate paradigmatic ways of knowing also valued by teachers (Bruner, 1986, 1990). And because cases are by their very nature highly contextualized, case-based learning may promote the situated nature of teachers' thinking that is influenced by their prior beliefs, knowledge base, and cultured thinking (Brown, Collins, & Duguid, 1989; Lave, 1988; Levin & Powell, 1997). These theoretical reasons lead us to believe that using cases and case-based teaching methods should be a viable vehicle for teaching both inservice and preservice teachers (Merseth, 1996).

In addition, current research tells us that both novice and experienced teachers benefit in many ways from grappling with the issues embedded in cases. For example, there is evidence that preservice teachers prefer using cases (James, 1990; Lundeberg, Matthews & Scheurman, 1996; Van Zoest, 1995) over other more traditional or didactic methods of instruction. They can also learn about classroom management (James, 1991; Stoiber, 1991), motivational issues (Richardson, 1991), cultural diversity (Kleinfeld, 1990; Noordhoff & Kleinfeld, 1991; Shulman, 1991), teaching mathematics (Barnett, 1991; Barnett & Sather, 1992; Barnett & Tyson, 1993a), and teaching other content areas (Kleinfeld, 1992a; Lundeberg et al., 1996) using cases and various case methods. We also have evidence that using case-based teaching methods can help preservice teachers learn to frame problems (Harrington, Quinn-Leering, & Hodson, 1996; Kleinfeld, 1991a; Lundeberg et al., 1996), foster reasoning (Harrington, 1995), make connections between theory and practice (Lundeberg et al., 1996), take multiple perspectives, (Levin, 1996; Lundeberg et al., 1996), and generate a range of problem solutions (Kleinfeld, 1991b).

Although the body of research surrounding cases and case methods is growing annually, there are still many unanswered questions and untested claims about case-based pedagogy. My own case teaching experiences and research in this area lead me to believe that *discussion*, whether in small or large groups, is a crucial variable in learning from cases. However, as a source for understanding what is learned during case discussions, case writing (both writing about cases and developing one's own case from personal experiences) provides us with important insights and what Harrington (chap. 2, this volume) calls "performance of thought." Written responses to cases give us a window into understanding what and how teachers are thinking about the problems, dilemmas, and issues embedded in cases (see chap. 2, this volume). In fact, written analyses of cases elicited before and after discussion are valuable research tools for finding out what teachers are thinking. Therefore, written responses to cases provide the source of much of the data presented in this chapter (e.g., Harrington, 1995, 1996; Levin, 1995, 1996, 1997; Lundeberg et al., 1996).

RECENT RESEARCH ON LEARNING
FROM CASE DISCUSSIONS

Unfortunately, there are few published studies to date about the specific effects of the discussion of cases on preservice teachers' learning and thinking. However, we do know that discussion is an important factor in case-based teaching methods because it affects teachers' thinking in ways that advance understanding about the problems and issues embedded in cases (e.g., Barnett & Tyson, 1993a; Harrington, 1995; Levin, 1995; Lundeberg & Fawver, 1994; Lundeberg et al., 1996; Richardson, 1991).

Case discussions appear to be especially valuable for student teachers and beginning teachers because they serve as a catalyst for cognitive conflict that encourages perspective and leads to clearer, more elaborated understanding of the issues in cases (Kleinfeld, 1991; Levin, 1995; Lundeberg & Fawver, 1994). However, case discussions also appear to have the potential to foster reflection, promote metacognitive thinking, develop critical thinking, and encourage a sense of autonomy and authority in experienced teachers (Barnett & Tyson, 1993a; Harrington, 1995; Harrington & Hodson, 1993; Levin, 1995; Lundeberg et al., 1996).

Preservice Teachers.   Studies of preservice teachers indicate that the discussion of cases can contribute to the development of important ways of "thinking like a teacher" and also aid in the development of knowledge about content and pedagogy that is likely to transfer to similar situations in the real world. Preservice teachers learn to clarify their thinking, become more critically reflective, consider other viewpoints, apply theoretical concepts, and process more complex information in case discussions settings. These outcomes appear to be the result of the opportunity for peer interactions during the case discussion, which often lead to shifts in beliefs and changes in thinking, and also to increased willingness to take responsibility for proposed actions.

For example, in reviewing Kleinfeld's article Hutchinson (1996) reported the following:

> Kleinfeld (1991b) taught preservice teachers in a weekly lecture, and then randomly assigned them to weekly meetings taught by the method of case discussions or by the discussion of readings. On the mid-term the case discussion group recognized more problematic situations, analyzed dilemmas in more sophisticated ways, and identified more alternatives for action. In this study case methods were deemed more effective for younger undergraduate candidates versus older, more experienced candidates. (Hutchinson, 1996, p. 5)

However, caution is warranted in considering what can be learned from this study: Other researchers have noted that experienced inservice teachers also learn from case discussions (see, e.g., Barnett & Tyson, chap 3, this volume).

In her studies, Levin (1995, 1997) found that social interactions during case discussions appeared to be the source of changes, both assimilations and accommodations, in the preservice teachers' thinking in these case discussions. These findings were gleaned from comparing the content of participants' pre- and postdiscussion writing about the case with a detailed discourse analysis of the audio transcripts of the case discussions. Because of this level of detail in the analysis, Levin discerned that participants' social interactions were not always direct, verbal interactions—the thinking of the teachers in these studies was affected even when their participation was more listener than talker. However, the content and the context of the case discussion apparently served as a catalyst for internal cognitive conflict, which acted as a trigger for potential change when individuals reflected in writing about ideas or perspectives that clashed with their original thinking. In other words, participants were influenced by the ideas and perspectives of others in the group, which caused them to rethink their own understandings about issues in the case. Of course, the participants' previous understandings and experiences, personal background, and their individual interests also served as a filter for what they understood about a case and the discussion of it (Levin & Powell, 1997).

In another study Levin (1997) found that almost half of the undergraduate elementary education majors in her study changed their minds about what to do and set new courses of action following the discussion of the Elaine Adams case, concerning "helping" during standardized testing (Silverman, Welty, & Lyon, 1992). Based on a comparison of pre- and post-discussion responses to similar questions, all 27 participants clarified their thinking about the issues in this case following the discussion, and learned from others in the group: half moved from uncertainty about the issues in the case to more confidence about the appropriate actions to take. However, very few elaborated about why they selected the particular course of action addressed in their postdiscussion writing. There was also evidence of a shift in their postdiscussion writing toward more critical reflection, and a willingness to take responsibility for their own ideas. This was evident in responses to a question asking what the protagonist in the case should do. Participants in this study shifted from saying in their pre-discussion writing what "she" should do (referring to the student teacher in the case), to using the pronoun "I" to indicate what they would do personally. Comparing the transcript of the discussion with participants' writing about the case indicated that the social interactions among peers during a case discussion, the exchange of ideas and problem solutions, and the sharing of personal experiences and stories related to the issues in the case influenced participants' thinking about the case. These interactions led to shifts in thinking as preservice teachers in this study came to understand the ethics of administering standardized tests based on discussing this case.

In her dissertation, Van Zoest (1996) used videocases of high school mathematics teaching to learn how opportunities to participate in discussions based on common observations of instruction in classrooms would influence the robustness of these observations and preservice teachers' reflections on what they observed in the videocases. The participants were 12 prospective secondary mathematics teachers in the early stages of their teacher education program. Van Zoest's findings, based on the participants' pre- and posttreatment written reflections and individual interviews, were that small-group discussions are an effective way of increasing the quantity of reflections. However, this increase was mainly in general reflective statements or reflective statements without justification, which are considered to be less robust forms of reflection than reflections justified by experience or by logical reasoning (Van Zoest, 1996).

An additional finding of interest in the Van Zoest study, based on postdiscussion interviews, were participants' reasons for expressing a preference for discussing the videocases with their peers over just writing about the observations or viewing more of them without benefit of any discussion. These participants suggested the following reasons for preferring group case discussions: (a) more interesting, (b) get ideas from others, (c) reinforce what was observed, (d) pay more attention to the lesson, (e) notice things that might have otherwise been missed, and (f) finding out what others think is important. Participants in the Lundeberg, Matthews, and Scheurman (1996) study discussed here stated similar benefits of case discussions along with others.

In a study of case discussions held with preservice teachers, Morine-Dershimer (1996a) reported that the degree of structure and teacher direction during case discussions has an impact on the complexity of information processed by the participants in the discussion. She found there was more active student involvement, sustained student attention, and complex processing of the information in cases when case discussions were smaller and more student-centered (small group discussions without a facilitator) over case discussions that were teacher-directed (larger, whole-class discussions led by a facilitator). Also, based on her analysis of preservice teachers' written remarks about the key ideas and salient issues expressed during the discussion of cases, Morine-Dershimer (1996b) concluded that the social exchanges among participants in small case discussion groups were influenced by their initial ideas about the case, associated with the kinds of discussions held in small groups, reflected in ideas expressed during follow-up large group discussions, and were incorporated into their final written reflections. In addition, Morine-Dershimer also noted that the ascribed status of individuals in the case discussions influenced others in larger group discussions. In a finding similar to the Levin (1997) study discussed earlier, Morine-Dershimer also noted a shift in the use from the pronoun "they" to "we" in participants' pre- and postdiscussion writing about the cases and concluded that

> by examining the social exchanges selected for attention by participants in these discussion groups, we can see the advances in individuals' ways of thinking, in this instance by tracing the gradual transformation of novice teachers' interpretations of a case as they engage in collaborative analysis. (Morine-Dershimer, 1996b, p. 19)

Morine-Dershimer's detailed analysis of written comments from this study yielded three different interaction patterns: (a) generative discussions (teacher responsibility was initially identified as the central issue, which led to the group's development of ideas that went beyond any individual member's original ideas about the case), (b) interactive discussions (initially problems were identified that were out of the teacher's control, which limited the development of ideas beyond those originally suggested), and (c) influential discussions (original ideas suggested by one member of the group were adopted by others in the group). Furthermore, Morine-Dershimer noted that the impact of peers' comments in the discussions was related to their area of certification: secondary, elementary, or special education.

In a study of the contributions of males and females during two case discussions held in a five-credit educational psychology course required of secondary teacher education majors during their sophomore year, Lundeberg (1993) noted no difference in the mean number of contributions by gender. Instead, what she did find were a disproportionate number of contributions during the discussion that favored the nontraditional students (both males and females) over the traditional, college-age students. Lundeberg's interpretation of these findings is that case discussions may allow more mature women to engage in the kind of conversations Belenky, Clinchy, Goldberger, and Tarule (1986) call "connected knowing," or that the more mature men and women prefer these kinds of discussions because they offer opportunities to exert power and status as described in studies of communication patterns and participation rates in organizational settings. Lundeberg (1993b) states that, "Perhaps the academic task of analyzing cases gives more power to nontraditional students because it allows them to utilize life experiences in the classroom, and they have more experiences to draw from (thus more power) than do the traditional students" (p. 164).

In a study by Lundeberg and Fawver (1994), conducted with a similar population of students during an educational psychology course, preservice teachers who participated in multiple case discussions became more constructivist in their beliefs during the course of the semester. For example, these prospective teachers noted how their beliefs had shifted by comparing their own written case analyses at the beginning and end of the course. By the end of the course, which included several different types of cases and case discussions, these students changed their beliefs indicating that (a) they now thought that knowledge is constructed and not received, (b) the role of the teacher is to encourage and facilitate thinking rather than impart knowledge, (c) their awareness of sexism and other diversity issues increased, and (d) they developed more flexible thinking, including changing from dichotomous ways of thinking to the appreciation of more conditional ways of thinking. The authors of this study corroborated these findings with their own qualitative and quantitative analyses of the participants' written data and concluded that it may be "the challenging quality of case discussions that promotes changes in beliefs and reflectivity" and that "perhaps the narrative nature of cases and controversial discussions somehow touches the story-like nature of students' beliefs" (Lundeberg & Fawver, 1994, p. 295).

In addition to the suggestion that the narrative nature of cases may contribute to shifts in beliefs following case discussions, Lundeberg and Fawver (1994) also suggest another explanation of learning from case discussion, based on the research on conceptual change. That is, unless individuals become dissatisfied with existing beliefs and consider the utility of alternative or new beliefs, there may be no change in thinking. However, case discussions may provide the opportunity for participants to confront previously held beliefs and come to understand plausible alternative ideas, which might in turn be the catalyst for a shift in beliefs and understanding about particular issues in cases. Other research on case discussions (Levin, 1995, 1997; Morine-Dershimer, 1996a, 1996b) and the data from preservice teachers' own comparative analysis of their written case analyses seems to confirm this interpretation in the Lundeberg and Fawver study (1994).

In another report on the quantitative data from this study, Lundeberg (1993b) also noted some age and gender differences. That is, older, nontraditional students identified twice as many issues and made twice as many decisions as the traditional, younger students in the course. Furthermore, the women generated significantly more decisions about the issues in the case than the men, based on examination of pre and post means. These data contrast with earlier studies (Kleinfeld, 1991b, 1992a; Richardson, 1992) that suggested either no differences between traditional and nontraditional students, or greater benefits for traditional, college-age students using case methods. However, they confirm other studies that show different benefits for more and less experienced teachers who participate in case discussions (Levin, 1995).

On the other hand, Levin (1996) found that unmoderated case discussions held anonymously, simultaneously, and on-line using computer software known as "groupware," can be miseducative and even harmful to the sense of community already established by the participants. In this study Levin compared the results of discussing two cases in the typical, face-to-face mode, with the guidance of a facilitator to discussions of the same cases on computers, where the on-line "discussion" was both anonymous and unfacilitated. The face-to-face discussion appeared to be more beneficial to the development of teachers' thinking about the issues in the cases than the anonymous computer-based discussion, even when the latter context allowed everyone to contribute equally to the discussion. Apparently the social interactions and the opportunities for clarification and elaboration during the oral discussion of a case impacted the thinking of those who participated in the discussion in a constructive manner. The opportunity to probe for understanding and to clarify statements so that others can better understand their meaning was highly valued by and beneficial to participants in face-to-face case discussions and missing from the computer-based discussion. Levin concluded that anonymous or unfacilitated discussions may be miseducative for preservice teachers, especially when the content of the case included potentially controversial issues such as racial prejudice and bias.

Feiman-Nemser and Buchmann (1983) and Zeichner and Liston (1987) discuss the potentially miseducative consequences of certain kinds of field experiences in teacher education, and the Levin (1996) study raises similar concerns about potentially miseducative consequences of certain forms of case discussions. In this situation with undergraduate preservice teachers, case discussions about controversial issues should probably not be conducted without a facilitator and without the benefit of face-to-face interaction. The potential for unmediated, destructive comments to create discord and animosity within a group was costly to the cohesion and sense of community of the group. Furthermore, because one of Levin's stated purposes for using cases and the case method as a pedagogical tool for teacher education is to develop perspective, allowing people to make comments that go unchallenged in anonymous situations where people are not held accountable for their thoughts and actions did not promote students' taking a wider perspective. Growth in preservice teachers' ability to see other points of view does, however, occur when participants have opportunities to engage in face-to-face case discussion where they can probe and question one another as they try to understand another perspective or express and elaborate on their own position.

Richardson (1991) reached similar conclusions about leaderless case discussions, and cautioned that teacher education students should not read and interpret cases without guidance, lest they develop interpretations of the cases that might be detrimental to their own teaching later on. In her paper, Richardson called for the active involvement of the teacher educator in guiding students through the interpretation of cases and in helping them to apply theory and judge alternative solutions.

Lundeberg, Matthews, and Scheurman (1996) also found that the "discussion of complex cases containing classroom dilemmas enabled preservice teachers to find problems, rethink their ideas, consider others' viewpoints, and embed theoretical concepts in a relevant situation" (p. 2) in a study about the interaction between participants' current knowledge base and what is learned from cases and case discussions. In addition to concluding that a case can be used effectively more than once, serving as an anchor for instruction and for applying new knowledge, Lundeberg et al. (1996) also concluded that "engaging in case discussion is a form of social construction of knowledge that strengthens both previous conceptual understandings as well as knowledge currently being used" (p. 17). In fact, 85% of the secondary education majors participating in this study believed that they learned more from discussing a case in class than they did from either working with a partner to analyze a case or from writing an analysis of a case on their own. Furthermore, 70% of the participants indicated that the class discussion was valuable because it exposed them to different viewpoints, while 33% said that the case discussion increased their understanding because they had to learn to defend or alter their viewpoints.

Citing the work of the Vanderbilt group (e.g., Bransford, Sherwood, Haselbring, Kinzer, and Williams, 1990; Bransford & Vye, 1989) on situated cognition and anchored instruction and the work of Spiro and his colleagues (e.g., Jacobson & Spiro, 1995; Spiro & Jehng, 1990) on cognitive flexibility theory, Lundeberg and her colleagues (1996) argue that using a case more than once allows students to experience situations embedded in cases that are located in real-world contexts. The verisimilitude of cases helps make related theories useful and relevant, decreases the danger of participants developing inert knowledge, and increases the probability of that knowledge will transfer to similar situations in the future. "According to the students, while the case itself may have served as the anchor for them to develop situated knowledge, it was the discussions in large groups which encouraged preservice teachers to develop new perspectives" (Lundeberg et al., 1996, p. 18).

In findings similar to the Lundeberg et al. (1996) study of the importance of knowledge in learning from cases and case discussions, Kleinfeld (1992a) also discovered that prospective high school teachers with prior knowledge of a subject benefited significantly more from a case about teaching Shakespeare's *Hamlet* than those without such background knowledge. Kleinfeld's analysis revealed statistically significant differences in the scores of English majors versus non-English majors after reading, writing about, and discussing an exemplary case about teaching *Hamlet* including improved understanding of students' problems in reading Shakespeare, more knowledge of alternative teaching strategies and materials, and increased awareness of the purposes and issues in teaching such literary classics. In addition, most of these students were able to transfer their knowledge from the *Hamlet* case to the teaching of another Shakespeare play and about half were able to apply their new pedagogical content knowledge to teaching a poem. Labeling this the "Matthew effect" in cases about pedagogical content knowledge ("For the man who has will always be given more, till he has enough and to spare"—Matthew 25:29), Kleinfeld also noted that "cases of pedagogical content knowledge might be quite successful with practicing teachers, who have some knowledge of content but whose knowledge needs to be deepened, as Barnett (1991) has done in California and Sato (1991) in Japan" (Kleinfeld, 1992a, p. 16).

Inservice Teachers.   Although several good studies have been conducted in recent years involving preservice teachers and case discussions, there are far fewer studies that focus on what inservice teachers learn from cases and case methods. However, studies conducted with experienced teachers suggest several contributions that case-based discussions play in the professional development of such teachers. For example, experienced teachers' pedagogical knowledge, sense of authority and autonomy, and content knowledge are fostered through the discussion of cases. In addition, case discussions provide inservice teachers with the opportunity to discuss issues relevant to them within a community of peers. The studies described next provide evidence for how these outcomes of case discussions occur.

In their work with inservice teachers discussing printed mathematics cases developed by classroom teachers, Barnett and her colleagues (Barnett, 1991; Barnett & Sather, 1992; Barnett & Tyson, 1993b) found that "discussing a collection of cases in a relatively narrow domain of mathematics learning, such as rational numbers, enhances both teachers' content and associated pedagogical content knowledge bases" (Barnett & Tyson, 1993b, p. 10). In addition, Barnett and Tyson report shifts in "locus of authority" and the development of both individual and group autonomy, based on their continuing work with inservice teachers engaged in case discussions (see Barnett & Tyson, chap. 3, this volume). The conditions for the development of a sense of authority and autonomy occurred as the teachers in their case discussion groups realized that the members of the case discussion group were capable and wise, having much to teach each other; that developing a critical stance meant learning to question the content of the cases, critique each other's comments, and critically analyze their own teaching; and that their understanding of mathematical content and pedagogical content knowledge increased over time.

However, these changes reported by Barnett and Tyson were not immediate. They developed as the group members came to trust each other, overcame their predilection to be "politically correct" and learned to take on more authoritative roles as they developed more ownership of their own professional development as teachers of mathematics. The subtler aspects of case discussions that led to these shifts in teachers' thinking and content knowledge are discussed in detail in chapter 3 by Barnett and Tyson.

In a study conducted with experienced inservice teachers in a professional development school (PDS) setting, Levin and Irwin (1995) studied whether any discussion can promote learning, or if there is a difference in what is learned from case discussions with experienced teachers versus discussions of their own professional issues. In other words, what can be learn from alternately discussing cases and teachers' personal and professional concerns? Levin and Irwin (1995) concluded that although both kinds of discussions are valuable for teachers to experience, the case discussions, were much more focused and task-oriented. During the case discussions teachers were engaged in collegial problem-solving, suggesting alternatives, and considering different perspectives on the issues in the cases. The discussions around their own concerns and issues, on the other hand, were more personalized and disjointed, even though they served a function of allowing the participants to vent their frustrations.

However, Levin and Irwin (1995) also noted that the participants in these two kinds of discussions often referred to the issues raised in the case they read for discussion each week, even when they had the opportunity to discuss their own issues before getting to the case discussion. Apparently, the cases contained relevant topics for these experienced teachers, ones that they felt were worth discussing, indicating that cases are a good trigger for discussion of the kinds of issues that experienced teachers are concerned with anyway: student discipline and classroom management, parental involvement, and the roles of teachers' and parents. These topics came up repeatedly during the case discussions and during discussions based on their own concerns.

Additionally, participants' comments on a final questionnaire used in the Levin and Irwin study, corroborated by unsolicited comments from the audiotaped discussions, indicated that the cases provided a way for the teachers' to focus their discussions on important topics that they rarely have time or opportunity to discuss. Furthermore, from a teacher-educator's perspective, the case discussions provided a context to discuss issues of curriculum content, student teacher and teacher relations, and supervision in a nondidactic, more constructivist manner. Although not the original intent of this study, the case discussions offered opportunities for professional development about ways of working effectively with student teachers, a role that all of the participants were engaged in at the time of this study.

METHODS FOR STUDYING CASE DISCUSSIONS

Although it is not impossible to conduct quasi-experimental studies on case pedagogy (see e.g., Levin, 1995; Lundeberg & Fawver, 1994), research at this stage has been mainly exploratory and descriptive. In fact, it may be that the kinds of questions we have at this stage about the efficacy of case-based teaching methods best lend themselves to qualitative methods and to the ecology in which they are studied. The classroom contexts in which most case discussions occur also make controlled studies quite difficult. In addition, because understanding what and how teachers learn from cases and case-based teaching methods is varied and complex, testing hypotheses does not seem possible. However, as seen in the research summarized above, there are some empirical examples for understanding what is learned from case discussions, along with some viable methods for collecting data. A description of some typical and some potential sources of data is presented next, followed by discussion of the strengths and weaknesses of various data analysis procedures used in studying the results of the discussion of cases.

Data Sources. Two primary sources of data are used most often in studying what teachers learn from case discussions: verbatim transcriptions of actual case discussions, and written responses to prompts or questions about the case, usually before or after case discussions. Taken together, these are good sources for analyzing teachers' thinking before, during, and following a case discussion. They provide information about teachers' prior beliefs and knowledge about the content of the case, serving as a window into teachers' thinking. They also can provide information about knowledge gains and shifts in thinking. However, there are limitations in using writing to study the effects of case discussions, not the least of which are the variability in participants' skill in written self-expression and the concerns about using verbal self-reports as single data sources. Nevertheless, by comparing participants' writing with detailed analyses of the discussion from video- or audiotaped transcriptions, researchers can track changes in thinking.

In addition, researchers can maximize their confidence in the resulting interpretations of these kinds of data by calculating agreement among more than one person who analyzes the same data using the same coding scheme. Some researchers have also compared the participants' self-analysis of their written responses to cases with the researchers' codes (Lundeberg & Fawver, 1994; Lundeberg et al., 1996) to further check their interpretation of the data gathered.

Although transcriptions of case discussions and analysis of participants' case writing are good sources of data, we would increase our understanding of what is learned during case discussions, by whom, and how, if we included additional kinds of data. For example, it would be beneficial in analyzing what is learned from case discussion to include data from (a) facilitator's notes written on the board or chart paper that capture ideas presented during the discussion; (b) facilitator's reflective notes following the discussion that might capture both the content and the tone of the discussion from his or her perspective, (c) notes from an observer of the case discussion; and (d) spontaneous, unsolicited, "off the record" comments or reactions from participants in the case discussion, whether captured on tape or written down. In addition, alternative forms of data could be collected from participants, such as concept maps created before and after the case discussion, or other graphic forms that represent participants' knowledge including Venn diagrams, tree diagrams, and flow charts. If participants' attitudes about case discussion were also deemed important, these could be solicited through questionnaires, interviews, or focus groups. All of these possible sources of information have the potential of providing insight into teachers' thinking and increase the database available for analysis.

Data Analysis Procedures.   Most methods of collecting and analyzing data from case discussions are very exacting and time-consuming. For example, a content analysis of a case discussion might yield several dozen topics, which may or may not readily lend themselves to pattern analysis or categorization into themes. A thorough discourse analysis of a case discussion can also be very labor-intensive, depending on the level of detail deemed important. However, both of these methods of qualitative data analysis, when coupled with other analyses of the participants' writing and comparing with other sources of data, are invaluable in determining what is learned from the case discussion, by whom, and how.

Often transcriptions of the actual case discussion are made from video- and audiotapes and then subjected to some form of qualitative data analysis, such as detailed discourse analysis or a content analysis. Based on the researcher's questions these data may be analyzed inductively from an *emic* perspective, or deductively from an *etic* perspective based on a set of prede-termined questions or guided by a theoretical framework. Simple, descrip-tive statistics can also be used (such as proportional frequencies) to describe these data. However, it is problematic to employ more sophisticated statisti-cal tests because of the difficulty of arranging quasi-experimental designs in research on case methods. This is often due to the small the number of par-ticipants in the case discussion and because of real-world limitations in teaching settings that preclude random assignment to conditions. Further-more, the unit of analysis is actually the discussion itself and not the number of members in the discussion group.

One example of a simple but useful data collection technique is Morine-Dershimer's: asking participants to write what they think are two or three key ideas in the lesson (referring to the case and the discussion) and anything they heard anyone else say during the lesson (discussion). This in-formation, although based on self-report, offers a simple way to learn what the participants consider to be the most salient issues in the case and to de-termine what influences the participants during the discussion. These data provide a means to determine the content and perspectives that the partici-pants in case discussions deem notable. Furthermore, they lend themselves to categorizing, coding, and then counting to determine proportional fre-quencies, which is one viable way to report such data. Furthermore, the use of proportional frequencies allows us to compare the data from case discus-sions held in different classes or in different groups within the same class. And because these data are collected in writing from each participant, the unit of analysis is no longer the discussion as a whole but the individual par-ticipants' written remarks. This is also the case for longer written reactions to cases, whether in response to a set of questions or more open-ended. This makes such written responses a valuable source of data.

Another example of data analysis procedure is the method Lundeberg and her colleagues (1994, 1996) have used with students in a course that in-cludes several case discussions. They ask the students to analyze in writing the same case at the beginning and end of the course and then to compare their own analyses for changes. This is a clever technique for gathering addi-tional data on what participants' learn from cases; it also offers them the chance to practice metacognitive thinking about the content of a case and what they learned from the discussion. This method is also effective for the researcher if the goal is to determine how students' knowledge gained from the course is applied to the case, to see if there are shifts in students' devel-opment toward "thinking like a teacher," or to determine improvement in metacognitive thinking, problem-solving skills, or ability to take multiple perspectives—all potential outcomes of participating in case-based teaching. However, like all self-reported data, it is problematic and should not be the only source used for data analysis.

In addition, by going back and tracing what participants write to find the source of their ideas in the transcriptions of the discussions, as both Levin (1995) and Morine-Dershimer (1996b) have done, the researcher can corroborate the source of participants' thinking, assess if there are any changes in thinking, or if prior beliefs brought to the discussion are held on to or altered in some way. Of course, independent analyses using any or all these methods of data analysis would certainly improve the "validity" and "reliability" of any findings as well.

SUGGESTIONS FOR FUTURE RESEARCH ON CASE DISCUSSIONS

> It is easy to have a stimulating and exciting class discussion. The question is whether such discussion leads to learning or whether it amounts to little more that loose talk. To use cases productively, you must have a clear idea of what the case can teach and what you want the class discussion to accomplish. (Kleinfeld, 1988, p. 15)

So how do we move the level of research on cases, case-based teaching, and case discussions from exploration and description to the level of explanation and prediction? How can we conduct research in a way that will provide clear evidence to educators that case-based teaching is a viable pedagogical tool, effective for helping teachers learn the kinds of things we want them to learn? Can we do this carefully enough so that we can answer conclusively the question posed in the subtitle of this book: Who learns what from cases and how? How can we systematically conduct research to examine the multitude of claims made for case-based instruction in general and for case discussions in particular?

When undertaking any research, and certainly when conducting research on cases and case methods, it is imperative that we are clear about what the purposes are for using a particular case and what the intended outcomes are as well. Not all the studies described in this chapter were explicit about their purposes for using cases. Without careful attention to these considerations up front, it is nearly impossible to conduct a good study and answer any of the many questions we need to be asking.

Anyone choosing to use cases and conduct case discussions should be clear about their reasons for doing so. Is it the instructor's purpose, or the researcher's goal, to teach specific content and concepts, or to teach certain processes or skills? Is the goal of using cases to help teachers connect theory and practice, to develop teachers' problem-solving skills or critical thinking abilities, to increase cognition or metacognition, or to help teachers consider multiple perspectives when confronted with problems, issues, or dilemmas in teaching? These decisions must be made before conducting the case discussion and certainly before undertaking research on case-based pedagogy. However, we should also remain open to unintended outcomes. As Saunders (1992) states: "Clearly, any case's success in encouraging specific behaviors in prospective teachers is dependent on the degree to which the case's goals are congruent with the instructor's goals and behaviors" (p. 23). Furthermore, as Saunders (1992) recommends:

> As we research case-based instruction when discussions are the pedagogical technique used, we must attend to the fact that discussions are a form of discourse having both cognitive and social elements and that the different communication and interactional styles demonstrated by the participants may facilitate or hinder discussions. We need to examine ... how teachers mediate case-based instruction attending simultaneously to cognitive, affective, and social dimensions, and identify the multiple outcomes that are realized when cases are used. (Saunders, 1992, p. 24)

Future studies on case methods, and particularly on the role of the discussion, need to start with clear definitions of what is meant by problem-solving, critical thinking, or perspective-taking, for example. These concepts, and others such as cognition, metacognition, and reflection, need to be clearly defined. What would problem-solving look like and sound like, for example, in a written response to a case? What are effective ways to measure problem-solving or critical thinking that have been used in other studies? What are some related tasks that could be used to measure application and transfer in order to demonstrate increased problem-solving or perspective-taking in teachers? And how would we go about tying this to the case discussion? Are we assessing only cognitive outcomes for case discussions, or are affective and social goals also important? Should we separate the processes or skills learned from content or must we look at the interaction of these? These and many other questions need to be carefully considered in the next round of research on case-based teaching methods.

One way to begin is to carefully match the kinds of data gathered, especially the kinds of writing asked for before and after discussion and the kinds of questions posed during the discussions to the purposes for conducting research. Obviously, the kinds of questions asked generate different kinds of outcomes. For example, if you ask participants to write about and discuss the problems in a case versus the issues or the dilemmas in the case, you get different responses written at different levels of abstraction (Levin, 1997).

That is, discussing or writing about problems tends to produce concrete solutions, whereas addressing issues tends to lead toward more issues and
fewer solutions, or to ones that are not under the control of the teacher. If
you ask about facts in a case and clearly delineate facts from inferences, you
also get different kinds of responses than when you don't make these distinctions. Furthermore, if you are interested in measuring perspective-taking
and never elicit responses about how different players might view the case,
then you may not be able to measure perspective-taking.

The research reviewed in this chapter provides evidence that case discussions can help preservice teachers become more critically reflective thinkers, although this is influenced and moderated by their level of development
and their individual experiences. Besides trying to tease out which aspects of
biography, culture, and context are most influential on teachers' learning
from cases, we still need to understand more about when cases might be the
most effective—early in teacher education or later when they have more experience and knowledge? Related to this are questions about what kinds of
cases might be most effective at different points in a teacher education program and where they should be included—in specific methods courses? in
foundations courses? in courses with related field experiences? The studies
reported in this chapter used mainly text-based cases or videocases but
when are other kinds of cases (such as exemplary cases, or multimedia cases,
or self-written cases) most effective in helping preservice teachers continue
to develop as critically reflective thinkers able to take multiple perspectives?
These questions and others remain to be answered in future research.

There are many possible studies of case methods that could focus on what
is learned from case discussions. For example, it might be valuable to see
what homogeneous groups of teachers with respect to experience and expertise (such as all preservice teachers) learn from case discussions, and how
this is the same or different from case discussions with heterogeneous groups
of teachers with different amounts of experience and different expertise. In
preservice teacher education, where most of the student teachers are inexperienced, it will also be very important to continue to study the role of the
facilitator in the discussion, because the instructor will likely be the most experienced teacher in the group. We also need many more studies conducted
with inservice teachers. A comparison of facilitated and unfacilitated case
discussions would also be of interest, as would a comparison of case discussions with other kinds of discussions. Studying different case formats, such
as cases that use commentaries or video or multimedia cases, is also important to pursue, although we want to remember that quality cases can come
in many forms. Perhaps the more important question to pursue is what constitutes a "good" case for teacher education? It would also be valuable to see
if teachers also benefit from discussion of non-narrative material, such as

journal articles, reports, or the like. The question would then be: What are the unique benefits of *case* discussion versus other kinds of discussions that teachers might participate in? There are also questions to be answered about when and where to use case methods optimally in teacher education, and what teachers might learn from writing their own cases. All of these are empirical questions that need to be addressed by those interested in pursuing case-based teaching.

CONCLUSIONS

The data presented in this chapter presents evidence from several studies to support the claim that the *discussion* of a case is a valuable pedagogical tool in case-based teaching for the learning and development of teachers because it has the potential for triggering cognitive conflict, hence for fostering changes in teachers' thinking. Nevertheless, I believe that case methods should not be considered a panacea, but should be used as just one tool among many for teacher education. The selection of the right case at the right time for a specific purpose rests with the teacher-educator, as does the proper facilitation of the case. Case-based teaching is not easy, and there is always the danger of miseducation with cases, although probably not any more so than any other approach.

Based on the studies presented in this chapter and on other research conducted to date on case-based teaching found in this volume, I would recommend teacher-educators include case discussions and opportunities for written case analysis in their pedagogical tool kit. I believe we have good empirical evidence and enough testimonials and anecdotal evidence based on years of experience with cases to support the continued use of cases in educational settings. What we need are careful studies that continue to test the multitude of claims made about the case method.

Commentary on
"The Role of Discussion in Case Pedagogy"

Judith H. Shulman
WestEd

This chapter provides a significant review of the literature on the impact of case discussions with preservice and veteran teachers. I appreciate the efforts of the author, Barbara Levin, for tackling this challenging topic. As one who has supported a range of educators (e.g., teachers, teacher-educators, administrators, and staff developers) to both develop and use cases, I welcomed the opportunity to reflect on what we have learned to date. My comments focus on these questions: How can we use these research findings in our own practice? How can we ensure that participants learn something from the discussions? What are important avenues for future research?

After reading through this chapter, my first reaction was, "We have come a long way in a short time!" It has been just 8 years since approximately 20 people—several of whom are authors or cited in references in this volume—gathered at the Claremont Hotel in Oakland for a working conference titled "Case Methods in Teacher Education," sponsored by Far West Laboratory (now WestEd) and the American Association for Higher Education. Although case methods had been part of established preparation programs for years in professions like law, business, social work, and medicine, education had been slow to come on board. At the time, we knew of no studies on case-based teaching, so we asked experts from these professions why they use case methods. Typically, the response was, "because it works!" Clearly, no one had taken the time or effort to study these questions systematically. "These are educational questions, not ours," they responded. Because the group had decided to promote the use of case methods in the teacher education community, we also emphasized the importance of doing research on its use. And slowly, as the case literature and presentations at professional conferences grew, so did the research literature. This chapter—in fact, this entire volume—is an excellent example of its growth.

I am struck by the array of findings that researchers have generated about what can be learned from case discussions, many of which ring true with my own practice and research. We can now point to a variety of studies that suggest why case discussions work. Yet, I'm also a bit troubled by the apparent disregard by many scholars in relating their findings to the variations among facilitation strategies and purposes of the discussion leader. What is learned can and should be connected to the discussion itself. We can see this clearly in Morine-Dershimer's study (1996a), where she examined what students learned from three instructors who taught the same case. These faculty members taught different sections of the same course and routinely planned their teaching together. Not only were they surprised at the differences in student learning, as Levin described in this chapter, they also found it interesting how Morine-Dershimer was able to trace these differences to the discussion style (e.g., opening question, probes, use of tension, etc.) and intent of each instructor. They had simply assumed that students would learn the same things. A case is like any other curriculum material. There is a difference between the "curriculum potential" of the material and the curriculum-as-taught (Ben-Peretz, 1990).

This link between what was learned and the instructor's facilitation was markedly absent in a recent AERA symposium I attended, during which each researcher presented on what students learned from a case discussion. Like those in Morine-Dershimer's study, these scholars—from four different universities—taught the same case in a course that each of them was teaching, and preplanned their data collection procedures. Given that the cases were used in different courses with different reading lists, it was not surprising that students learned different things. But it was not until the discussion after the papers were finished that we realized the extent to which each discussion leader used a different style of discussion and had different ground rules and purposes for their discussions. What a missed opportunity to link what was learned to the facilitation strategies! Such an analysis would not only help us as a research community, it would also be useful to practitioners who want to improve their pedagogy as discussion leaders. Levin alluded to the need for researchers to be explicit about their facilitation strategies.

I think this recommendation is terribly important, although I might add to it. Researchers must also attend to the substance of the particular case when making generalizations about what case methods can and cannot accomplish. Recently, I reviewed a paper that suggested limitations of "the case method." Although I do not want to imply that case methods are a panacea for all of the problems in teacher education, the specific cases used for analysis in this study were quite narrow and, in my estimation, less likely to stimulate deep learning. We have to be as critical of the cases used in our research as we are of our facilitation strategies.

Much of the research examined in this chapter deals with pre- and postdiscussion analyses of what was learned from a single case discussion. This kind of research is helpful, but it is only a starting point. Some research reviewed in this chapter suggests that fundamental changes in teaching and beliefs can occur from case methods, but only after a case-based seminar or, at the very least, several case discussions. Moreover, sometimes we cannot know how cases may influence learning until several months later (see the case of George in Wilson, 1992).

In conclusion, I refer to Levin's quote from Judy Kleinfeld about the importance of distinguishing between a stimulating and exciting case discussion and one in which learning occurs. I will never forget participating in one of those discussions that Judy conducted at the Claremont conference. There was lots of animated dialogue, our assumptions were challenged, and tension was heightened during disagreements; it was certainly a stimulating discussion. But during a debriefing session, Judy asked what we had learned during the discussion. Although she too had enjoyed it, she was uncertain whether she had learned any new ideas. Now that was a sobering thought. I have spent the better part of the last decade studying and promoting case development and use. Although I strongly believe that case methods can be critical to the most promising reforms in teacher education and professional development, I have also seen evidence of questionable learning occur during a case discussion. Cases can easily lead to misconceptions when poorly selected, badly facilitated, or embedded in an inappropriate context.

We must never forget that—if you will forgive my pun—a case of beer and a case of pretzels are not equivalent in their consequences. If we wish to understand the efficacy of teaching cases in teacher education, we must always ask: cases of what? taught in what manner? within what kind of program? to teachers in what stage of teacher development? Levin's review is a positive contribution to raising the quality of that discussion.

PART III

RETHINKING CASES

8

What Is a Case?
What Is Not a Case?

Kathy Carter
University of Arizona

The question of what constitutes a case is, on the surface at least, straightforward and simple. We certainly need to know what is and is not a case if we are to have intelligent conversations about using cases to educate teachers. A clear definition is equally important if we are to study case methods and become cumulatively smarter about their utility. The idea of cases as educative tools is old and venerable, having been introduced into the preparation of lawyers and physicians around the turn of the century. Interest in cases for teacher preparation has, until quite recently, been sporadic. But certainly we can gain a head start by borrowing lessons from professions that have had nearly 100 years of experience with case methods.

Turning to other professions for clarity and reassurance has been tried before (e.g., Carter & Unklesbay, 1989; Sykes & Bird, 1992), but the results have been less than satisfactory. Few of us really feel that the question has been answered, so we persist in calling for more research in the hope that someone will capture the definition in precise terms. Some of this preoccupation with terms may well be a vestige of earlier habits developed when we were obligated to have "operational definitions." I am not persuaded, however, that the response is habitual, as most of us have learned that a multiplicity of meanings signals richness rather than confusion. At issue here, I think, is a haunting sense that things are different in teacher education;

165

that, despite many parallels across professions, preparing teachers is not completely like preparing lawyers, physicians, or corporate managers. These visceral tinges have been given expression, I argue, in the turn toward event and narration in our professional discourse in teacher preparation.

Thus, the task for this chapter is set. I revisit the conventional approach to definition by looking outward to other professions more experienced in case traditions. This excursion has two purposes: First, to assess what we have attained in our understanding of case and case method; and second, to look for junctures, to explicate differences between the case tradition in general and the intellectual currents in teacher preparation. This discussion leads naturally to an examination of story and narrative as central motifs in teacher education and as ideas quite harmonious with our emerging sense of case and case method. I make no claims to unraveling with precision the puzzle of what a case is. What I hope to do is outline a case idea that more fully integrates our awakening understandings of what it means to prepare teachers. Such an idea should move us a bit closer, at least, to a sense of what it means to introduce cases into the processes of learning to teach.

CASES AS TEACHER EDUCATION METHOD

If we look outward from teacher education to other professions that are more experienced with case practices, most notably law, medicine, and business, we can discern two broad notions of what a case is: namely, an exemplar and a problem situation (see Doyle, 1990; L. Shulman, 1986b). As is seen here, each of these meanings highlights a different aspect of professional preparation and, thus, a different facet of the case idea.

Case as Exemplar

One prominent use of cases is to illustrate a general category or to exemplify a practice. Such cases are common in medicine to illustrate the symptoms of a disease (as in "This is a case of meningitis") or to demonstrate a surgical procedure or treatment protocol. They are also commonly used in teacher preparation to depict vividly such matters as the complexity of teaching environments, the way in which a method is actually carried out in a classroom (such as teaching for understanding), or the complicated ways a general proposition about learning or development might manifest itself in concrete situations.

At a minimum, exemplar cases are inserted into a text or presentation to increase clarity or make the information more interesting. In this form, a case is usually a brief episode that clearly epitomizes a concept or issue. At a more sophisticated level, exemplars are used to concertize or operationalize "theory" or intricate practices. Diagnostic categories related often to concepts of learning or development are given concrete expression in a carefully chosen case. Similarly, issues of diversity or inequality in schooling can be dramatically represented through cases. Finally, teaching skills or instructional approaches (e.g., cooperative learning or inquiry teaching) are made concrete by portraying a teacher using the method in an actual classroom, perhaps over several days or weeks. As Laframboise and Griffith (1997) observe, "The use of cases is seen as a way to contextualize the knowledge students typically receive in a linear and fragmented way in separate courses during their teacher preparation" (p. 370).

Case as Problem Situation

A frequent alternative to exemplification is the use of cases for analysis, inquiry, and problem-solving. Here the purpose is to prepare candidates for the exacting processes of interpretation and decision-making in teaching. Laframboise and Griffith (1997) define cases in this way, as "problem-centered stories of teaching practice that are used to examine and clarify the complexities and connections in teaching practice" (p. 370). Problem cases, then, are written to exemplify "not only how a lesson was conducted but also what the problematics of the performance were" (Doyle, 1990, p. 10). Rather than simply illustrating, a case as problem situation becomes a canvas on which various types of information are combined and arranged to resolve an issue or dilemma.

Laframboise and Griffith (1997) also emphasize that "discussion during case method sessions is an essential part of the meaning making process" (p. 370). The focus, in other words is not simply on the cases themselves but also on group deliberation about cases to stimulate analysis, decision-making, and reflection. This stress on problem-solving through the analysis of precedents reflects the origins of case method in law (see Carter & Unklesbay, 1989).

Implications

This brief examination of how cases are generally seen in professional preparation underscores two important facets of conventional case methods:

1. The answer to the question of what a case is depends on intended uses and purposes. When the goal of using a case is exemplification, the emphasis is on comprehension rather than deliberation. Cases are then constructed to achieve clarity and specificity and to simplify the modeling of a concept or

practice. Problematic elements may be minimized or removed to increase lucidity. In contrast to exemplars, problem cases are often more complex and less well-formed representations of teaching. Several pages of text and perhaps even audio- or videotapes are required to present the case and supply the necessary context to understand the events portrayed. In working with such cases, students take an active role in analyzing situations and bringing their knowledge to bear on specific problems of teaching practice. Multiple interpretations of a case are encouraged. In creating exemplars, in other words, the thrust is toward convergence. In creating problem situations, the emphasis is on divergence.

2. In both conventional uses, cases are subordinate to propositional knowledge. To call an episode a case is to classify it as a piece of curriculum, that is, to impose a framework in which it becomes an instance of something that we wish to convey to students in a teacher education program. A case, then, carries a specific educative purpose as a representation of what it means to think and act as a teacher. This subordination is especially true in constructing exemplars: The case is asserted to be an instance of a concept or issue and is molded to fit this framing. Problem cases are perhaps more open ended and divergent, but the emphasis is still on "the integration of information from multiple experiences, that is, course lectures and discussions, readings, and in-class observations" (Laframboise & Griffith, 1997, p. 370). Cases in other words, are viewed primarily as pedagogy. Content with respect to teacher education resides elsewhere. Unfortunately, the difficult issues of what might constitute a curriculum for teacher education are either presupposed or ignored in most discussions of case method.

This analysis suggests that, as conventionally understood, work on cases is largely a branch of program pedagogy and an undertaking ancillary to the larger enterprise of knowledge generation and curriculum development in teacher preparation. Herein lies, I believe, the crux of the issue of what a case is. There is a growing sense, emerging from the recent work on story and narrative, that cases are more centrally located and substantively important in learning to teach. It is to this aspect case and case methods that I now turn.

CASE AS STORY

Over the past 10 or more years the very foundations of teaching and teacher education have shifted dramatically from science, with its emphasis on variables, laws, and proofs, to literature, with its emphasis on events and narration. Indeed, the idea of "story," which surfaced within the teacher education community only a few years ago (see, e.g., Carter, 1993), has rapidly captured the imaginations of investigators and teacher-educators. Today the term is widely popular; one can hardly pick up a contemporary book or journal that doesn't contain some reference to this flourishing literature.

With this outburst of enthusiasm for story has come a swift expansion of vocabulary and a rapid diversification of the meanings of terms. For purposes here, I focus on two basic concepts—story and narrative—as representing two closely related movements within the teacher education community that have particular relevance to expanding the case idea.

In the conventional approach to case method, stories are turned into cases—that is, they are assimilated as representations of various aspects of a "knowledge base" of teaching. Stories are made, in other words, to fit pre-existing categories, to serve preordained purposes, and not allowed to have their own intrinsic space and meaning. Such a practice marginalizes "storiness" in the service of formalistic discourse. My intent here is to free story from these constraints so that we might understand better the possible functions and importance of story for teachers and teacher educators.

The Nature of Story

At a very basic level, "Stories consist ... of events, characters, and settings arranged in a temporal sequence implying both causality and significance" (Carter, 1993, p. 6). Thus, a story carries information about how things work and what meaning events have. In addition, stories are told to someone, an imagined reader, by someone, an implicit or explicit observer/narrator who recounts the events and often presumes to know what the characters are thinking. Thus, a story also contains information about presumed intention and motivation as well as a sense of audience, of who is looking in on events. Finally, a story by its very nature resists singular interpretation. Thus, a story captures nuance, indeterminacy, and interconnectedness in ways that defy formalistic expression and expands the possibilities for interpretation and understanding. In Iser's (1996) words, story "launches multifarious patterns" (p. 19).

There are, of course, several clear reasons why the general notion of story has proved to be so immediately attractive to teacher-educators. At one level, an emphasis on story is a natural outgrowth of the critique of the technical rationality that characterized research and policy in teaching and teacher education for several decades. In contrast to the reductionistic accounts of process–product research, story seem to be a much more authentic way of grasping the richness and ambiguity of our experiences as teachers, the complexity of our understandings of what teaching is, the expanse of our feelings about being teachers, and our instincts about how others can be prepared to engage in this profession.

At the same time, with an expanding awareness that much of the actual work of teaching is carried out by women, there is increasing attention to gender issues in the control of teaching practice and the way knowledge about teaching is rendered. In particular, "voice" has become a central theme in teaching and teacher education (see Carter, 1993; Elbaz, 1991; Richert, 1992). "Grand theory"—that is, broad generic formulations of rules or principles—is being rejected in favor of individual stories of teachers' lived experiences as women, mothers, and professionals (see Gore, 1993; Grumet, 1988). Thus, stories are beginning to emerge as cultural capital to stand against the canonical texts of measurement, statistics, and psychology (see Iser, 1996).

This examination of authenticity and voice as features of story can be extended by reference to Iser's (1996) recent analysis of why literature matters. Iser underscores the extent to which literature, compared to the dominant technological discourse of the age, is inherently a "perturbing noise" (p. 16). In contrast to the smoothness and order of formalized or propositional discourse, story is "basically a noisy transmission channel" (Iser, 1996, p. 17). This noise results in part because story itself is constituted by "pattern breaking patterns" (Iser, 1996, p. 17) or disjointed levels of information. Interpretations of statistical tables are written to achieve essence and precision. Stories are written to embellish, enhance, and enrich. Thus, the parts of a story text compete for attention and interpretation. Moreover, the act of reading a story contextualizes it into a larger system of information the reader uses to make sense of the disjointed levels of the text, thus introducing more noise.

The value of this is profound: "the noise of literature carves out a space for unpredictability and invention that allows an unfettered imagination to impinge on cultural circulation" (Iser, 1996, p. 18). Thus, story is not simply an alternative way of expressing or illustrating propositional knowledge, but rather an idiom that tells something very different. In addition, story can be a staging ground for human self-enactment, "a panorama of what is possible, because it is not hedged in either by the limitations or the considerations that determine the institutionalized organization with in which human life otherwise takes its course" (Iser, 1996, p. 19). Story can transport us, in other words, not only to experiences we have not had but to insights that cannot be expressed in conventional discourse.

This analysis suggests an autonomous rather than subservient role in teacher preparation for cases as story. Cases, in this light, matter to teacher education not simply as instantiations of an element in a network of propositional knowledge, or as evidence for the practicality of various methods and conceptions, or as embodiments of political and social issues, or even as canvases for integrating knowledge and fostering reflection. Rather, they give rise to meanings unattainable in any other way.

Storied Knowledge

Having argued for an autonomous status for story as an expression of knowledge, I now want to push further for the centrality of story in the lives of teachers and, thus, in teacher education. One of the dominant contemporary themes across a number of specialty areas is that human knowledge is storied—that is, much of what we know and understand is embedded in stories. I have already argued that story is a way of grasping the richness and indeterminacy of our experiences as teachers and the complexity of our understandings of what teaching is and how others can be prepared to engage in this profession. Here I want to extend this point to emphasize that story is itself a way of knowing and thinking that is particularly suited to explicating teachers' practical understandings—that is, the knowledge that arises from action (see Bruner, 1985; Gudmundsdottir, 1991; Mitchell, 1981). Along these lines, Doyle (1997) contends that teaching can only be known, by practitioner and by researchers, as story:

> a classroom is an realm in which events take place, and it is through participation (i.e., action) in these events that students come to understand what the enacted curriculum embodies as content. If teaching is event and action with respect to a curriculum, then story is a quite appropriate, if not the only, way of knowing teaching. (p. 95)

This analysis suggests that knowing teaching is knowing its stories. If story is the knowledge base for teaching, then case, as story, is the nucleus rather than simply a medium of the teacher education curriculum.

CASE AS NARRATIVE

Within teacher education, the term *narrative* has taken on a somewhat distinct meaning within the general emphasis on story, a meaning that extends even further our understanding of the possibilities of case.

Although there are exceptions, narrative has come to refer primarily to an emphasis on lived experience or personal life stories (see Carter & Doyle, 1996). This approach, with its concern for biography and autobiography, places special emphasis on the view that we live storied lives: that "My acting-in-the-world ... is the continuous plotting of a narrative, interpreting the past and projecting the future according to my image of myself"

(Funkenstein, 1993, p. 22). It also reflects more fully than the traditional case approach a feminist perspective. As Bateson (1989) notes: "When one has matured surrounded by implicit disparagement, the undiscovered self is an unexpected resource. Self knowledge is empowering" (p. 5).

"Overall, work that is grounded in a biographical perspective involves intense and extended conversations with teachers (see Woods, 1985) and is based on the premise that the act of teaching, teachers' experiences and the choices they make, and the process of learning to teach are deeply personal matters inexorably linked to one's identity and, thus, one's life story" (Carter & Doyle, 1996, p. 120). Biographical investigators argue that a great deal is learned from the actual practice of teaching in classrooms and that these situated and personalized understandings form the core of teachers' work. From this perspective, attention to teachers' personal lives is considered essential in knowledge generation and policy formulation at all levels of schooling.

Several distinct approaches are being taken to personal narrative. Connelly and Clandinin (1990) focus, for instance, on narrative inquiry, which is grounded in the premise that "education is the construction and reconstruction of personal and social stories" (p. 2). Connelly and Clandinin work closely over long periods of time with a small number of teachers through observation, journal writing, conversation, documents, and the mutual construction of narrative, to achieve an understanding of how the teachers give meaning to practice and come to terms with the interplay of self and situation. Central to the process is the teacher's story, which is a "narrative-in-action"; that is, an "expression of biography and history ... in a particular situation" (Connelly & Clandinin, 1985, p. 184).

Connelly and Clandinin give special attention to "image" as a form of knowing that is nonpropositional, holistic, imbued with emotionality and morality, largely tacit, and continuously under revision. Clandinin (1989)argues that image

> draws both from the present and future in a personally meaningful nexus of experience focused on the immediate situation that called it forth. It reaches into the past, gathering up experiential threads meaningfully connected to the present, and it reaches intentionally into the future and creates new meaningfully connected threads as situations are experienced and new situations are anticipated from the perspective of the image. Image is the glue that melds together a person's diverse experiences, both personal and professional. (pp. 139–140)

This knowing embodied in images stands in sharp contrast to the formal structures of academic discourse.

Others have developed approaches similar to that of Connelly and Clandinin. Butt, Raymond, and their colleagues have constructed an approach called "collaborative autobiography" in which teachers write personal statements that cover: "a depiction of the context of current working reality, a description of current pedagogy and curriculum-in-use, reflections on past personal and professional lives that might facilitate understanding present professional thoughts and actions, and finally, a projection into preferred futures through a critical appraisal of the previous three phases" (Butt & Raymond, 1989, p. 407). These statements are done in a group setting, so that individuals hear other autobiographies that can prod memory. Knowles and Holt-Reynolds (1991) have focused on "personal history" in their studies of the early development of novice teachers. At the center of their analyses is the internal dialogue in which teacher education candidates interpret coursework and field experiences and construct their own understandings of how they will behave as teachers. This dialogue occurs within the belief systems that have accumulated from candidates' personal histories in families, peer groups, schools, and classrooms.

The work on personal narrative in teaching and teacher education is vigorous and important. With respect to our concern here for cases and case methods, this line of inquiry underscores the importance of collaboration in the construction of cases and an active role for the teacher in coming to understand what a case might mean. And these are cases from within stories of personal experiences rather than exemplars or problem scenarios constructed from the outside by observers or case writers.

The work on personal narrative also suggests a frame for interpreting all stories of teaching. Rather than seeing teaching "out there" as something happening to an anonymous someone, we can imagine a case as a personal account and construct an image of who the person in the case is. Such a frame connects the reader to a person who teaches in important ways.

From a narrative perspective, to know teaching is to know self-as-teacher. This tradition underscores the power of personal experience in teachers' understanding of their work but can easily neglect the important sources of knowledge and practice that are external to the individual. Personal narratives must be contextualized. Teachers should be grounded in their own life stories but not prisoners of their own experiences. For many, this contextualizing means that teachers should focus on the interplay of self with the broader world of educational ideas and stories (Grumet, 1988). Curiously, there is only limited attention in the area of narrative on learning from the personal stories of others (see Schubert & Ayers, 1992). A more richly developed connection between narrative and curriculum would seem, however, to be an important avenue to explore.

CONCLUSION

What, then, is a case? Traditionally, a case is an embodiment of propositional knowledge about teaching or a canvas for applying that knowledge to practical situations. From this perspective, a case is any description of an episode or incident that can be connected to the knowledge base for teaching, that can be interpreted, in other words, as a segment of the teacher preparation curriculum. Such descriptions can be succinct to illustrate a point or comprehensive to allow for the integration of several lines of information in analyzing and resolving an issue or problem.

In this view, a story becomes a case when it can be interpreted as an instance of the technical knowledge base of teaching. Such an outlook makes story subservient to propositional knowledge and a tool for pedagogy. As pedagogy, story is a container for academic knowledge but is not, in itself, a source of legitimate knowledge and curriculum.

The argument set forth in this chapter is that story has independent functions of its own as a special mode of expression and as a store of knowledge unique to teaching practice. Practice, like story and narrative, is multifarious and disjointed rather than smooth and precise, is perturbing rather than confirming. This synchronicity between story and practice implies that teaching can only be known as story and that the curriculum for teacher preparation is, at the core, indeterminant.

I am not suggesting that propositional forms of knowing teaching are to be rejected outright or that using cases in the traditional sense as example or canvas is illegitimate. Rather I am arguing for a recentering of our conceptions of knowledge for teaching to embrace the indeterminacy and complexity of teaching practice, that is, the storied nature of knowledge and knowing in teaching as it actually takes place in the world. To teach is not so much to apply science as it is to activate story and narrative in response to organic events. In such a view, story is the repository of teaching knowledge and thus, moves to the nucleus of the teacher preparation curriculum.

If this recentering takes place, our understanding of what a case is must fundamentally change. The construction of cases can no longer be simply a matter of determining what a story or narrative is a case of. Rather, case must be seen as a point on a array of interconnecting and largely disjointed and indeterminant understandings of what it means to teach. In this light, a case is judged for its storiness rather than its exemplification.

A reformulation of our notion of what a case is and how it connects to knowledge and knowing in teaching has profound implications for the field of case methods. Traditionally, research on the effects of case methods could rely on an independent and often manageable domain of information to frame assessments. Did case method improve understandings or practice on indicators derived from the knowledge base? Case as story will be much more difficult to pin down, not because effects aren't real but because they elude our powers of observation and measurement. Perhaps one approach to this issue is to reframe our conceptions of outcome, of what excellence might mean in teaching. This reframing would shift attention from enacting "the best way" to variability as a standard of good practice. A good teacher is not one who can master the teaching model but rather can master diverse situations, that is, come to terms with a wide range of events and contingencies. Excellence would then be a reflection of the stories a teacher knows.

Commentary on
"What Is a Case? What Is
Not a Case?

Sigrun Gudmundsdottir
Norwegian University of Technology and Science

In this chapter Carter takes one more step along the path that she has been paving her recent publications—that is, when it comes to doing research on teaching and teacher education, story is the most natural, or privileged, approach. Carter wants emancipate story from the constraints of pre-existing categories imposed on them by conventions in educational scholarship so that we might better understand the ways it can function to enhance our understanding of teaching and teacher education. She is not alone in calling for the primacy of story in the human sciences, because narratives are emerging as a primary unit of analysis in the sociohistorical psychology inspired by Vygotski and his Western interpreters in social psychology, education, and cultural anthropology (Bruner, 1996; Kessen, 1993). I want to focus my comments on why I think Carter is right when she says that story is privileged when it comes to understand practice and teachers' practical understanding.

As one of cultures' primary meaning-making tools, narratives are emerging as an important unit of analysis. We meet narratives in the social interactions that shape our perceptions of the social reality we meet. As social beings, we routinely adopt narratives when trying to make sense of complex social situations. Classrooms are complex social situations where people (teachers, students, and researchers) are constantly constructing meaning. One short visit to a staff meeting in a school provides ample evidence for the storied nature of life in classrooms. Staffrooms and classrooms, are places where stories meet. Students and teachers alike bring their stories to school, and these stories shape the collective meaning making process. That meaning emerges *first* as a narrative, but is later transformed into something else; numbers, tables, descriptions, and matrixes. The core of Carter's argument in her chapter is that the meaning should remain in its original form throughout, as narrative or story, and should continue be true to the context that gave rise to it. If it does not, it is likely to neglect some of the very essences that captures the richness of practice, and it will, as a consequence, loose its power to teach.

Human experience is storied and the meaning making process of the researcher is also storied. This is what Connelly and Clandinin (1990) mean when they claim that narrative is both the phenomenon and the process. The "object" of inquiry is the storied nature of human experience, and the inquiry process itself is storied. Collectively these processes make story and narrative form privileged to capture the richness of teachers understanding of practice. The consequence of Carter's argument in this chapter is that the educational research community should take that extra step in the "narrativization" of research on teaching and teacher education and consider case studies of practice and practical understanding as stories and narratives.

The question of what transforms a mere case study into a narrative or story is a logical consequence of Carter's narrative project. As with any genre in literature, language is they key. Teaching has its own language of practice. This language corresponds to typical situations where the meaning of words are connected to a concrete reality. This means that teachers and researchers who speak the language of practice do not have a complete freedom in combining thoughts and reality. They draw upon historical and institutional contexts in when thinking, speaking, and writing about practice. This constraint makes the language of practice in teaching more than just words. It is a cultural reservoir of beliefs, ideas, ways of doing and seeing, all embedded in a distinct social activity called teaching—all ventriloquating through an individual's practice, as well as the spoken and written word.

The language of practice of teaching is a "privileged" mode of talking about practice. I prefer the word *privileged* rather than any other term, because I want it to capture the feeling that arises when participants in a practical (teaching) context feel that this is the only possible mode of expressing their thoughts and ideas (although other modes are theoretically possible). Having achieved such a high degree of intersubjectivity, the conversation partners automatically and unconsciously fill in the appropriate missing word with the right meaning and infuse it with the appropriate emotional expressions. If the cultural reservoir of practice is ventriloquated through the language of practice, then the language of practice in turn speaks through narrative inquiry because it is the privileged mode (as cultures primary meaning making "tool") of capturing and expressing teachers practical understanding.

9

Culturally Relevant Teaching With Cases: A Personal Reflection and Implications for Pedagogy

Sonia Nieto
University of Massachusetts

I don't believe I'm doing this. But I don't really like to build myself too high …
because the higher you are, the harder you're gonna fall. I don't want to fall.
—Paul Chavez (Nieto, 1996, p. 258)

Paul Chavez was 16 years old when he uttered these words, words filled with the terrible fear that the largely positive experience he was finally having in school would somehow come to an end. Paul had already had a difficult life of gang activity, violence, drugs, and disappointment. What was difficult for him to believe was that he was actually staying in school and being a successful student. This had not generally been the case. In fact, Paul had been successful in school on only one other occasion, when he was in fifth grade and Ms. Nelson was his teacher. Although he had gotten in trouble since third grade, Ms. Nelson saw something in Paul that others did not. As he said: "she put me in a play and that like tripped me out. Like, why do

179

you want *me* in a play? Me, I'm just a mess-up. Still, you know, she put me in a play" (Nieto, 1996, p. 252). He had gone on to explain what fifth grade had been like, how he had been excited by schooling and about the "pretty nice things" that Ms. Nelson did.

When Mac Morante, a colleague and friend of mine who is a school psychologist in California, located and interviewed Paul in 1994, he found a young man who had many strikes against him: Paul was a gang member; he lived in poverty in a large female-headed family; his father was in a halfway house after having spent time in prison; much of his nuclear and extended family, including an older brother, had been involved with the gang; and Paul had been suspended and expelled from numerous schools. Given this scenario, many teachers might despair that Paul could be successful in school. Yet throughout his interviews, Paul made it clear that he had two goals in life: to be respected and to make something of himself. Early on, Ms. Nelson had probably sensed these wishes, but it is doubtful that many other teachers had believed Paul really wanted to make something of himself. They saw in Paul what he allowed them to see: a "mess-up," a young man with abundant problems who seemed to favor gangs over academics.

Paul's deeply held wishes were also understood and appreciated by the teachers in the alternative school that he was currently attending, but his previous behavior had made it difficult for other teachers to see beneath his tough veneer. It was through his interviews that Paul admitted that he was afraid of failing once again, and he confided that he wanted to become a teacher or a counselor, a revelation that would probably have astounded his former teachers. But the interviews gave Paul a way of exposing his vulnerabilities without losing face. I subsequently used Paul's words in developing a case study (Nieto, 1996). Paul's case study has taught many teachers and other educators important lessons about him and other youngsters like him.

In this chapter, I consider how culturally relevant cases can help teachers transform their attitudes and beliefs about the students they teach, by stripping off the veneer that many young people have learned to adopt in school settings. Specifically, I discuss the need for culturally specific cases, my own process in developing culturally specific cases, and a number of implications for pedagogy. It is my hope that teachers and teacher educators can move beyond prevalent stereotypical notions of culture to understand the complexity and context of the individual lives of students in order to reflect on their own responsibilities as teachers.

THE INESCAPABLE DEMOGRAPHIC IMPERATIVE

The growing diversity of the U.S. population is by now well known and amply documented. The United States has, of course, always been a multicultural society, from the many indigenous nations that were already here when the Europeans arrived, to the millions of Africans who were forcefully brought here and enslaved, to the many millions more who immigrated from Europe, Asia, and Latin America in the past two centuries. But the new immigration of the past several decades has made our diversity even more pronounced. Immigration to the United States was higher during the 1980s than at any other time in our history except during the great migration of the first two decades of this century (O'Hare, 1992). Moreover, the nature of immigration to the United States has also changed dramatically: whereas previous immigrants came almost exclusively from Europe, most now come from Latin America and Asia. Between 1980 and 1992, the percentage of citizens of European descent increased only modestly (5.5%), whereas the percentage of Latinos increased by more than 65% and that of Asians by 123.5% (U.S. Bureau of the Census, 1993a). In addition, about 14% of the nation's population speaks a language other than English, compared with 11% in 1980 (U.S. Bureau of the Census, 1993a; Waggoner, 1994). These population shifts are most evident in our public schools: as of 1992, 50 of the largest 99 school districts in the United States had more than a 50% enrollment of *minority* students (National Center for Education Statistics [NCES], 1994), a curious use of that term in these circumstances. It is expected that the percentage of students of color in the nation's schools will grow from some 30% in 1990 to 38% in 2010 (Hodgkinson, 1991).

The growing racial and cultural diversity of the student population is not matched in the teaching staff, which remains overwhelmingly White, and this has serious implications for the nation's schools. It has been documented, for example, that there are currently about 2.3 million public school teachers; of these, fewer than 10 percent are members of African American, Latino, Asian, and American Indian communities (U.S. Bureau of the Census, 1993b). In general, most teachers and prospective teachers are White, middle-class females who speak English exclusively. The majority of them have had neither extensive personal experiences nor professional training in cross-cultural issues and most would prefer to work in a suburban setting teaching White, middle-class youths (Aaronsohn, Carter, & Howell, 1995).

A problem related to the lack of diversity among teachers in elementary and secondary schools is the lack of diversity among faculty at the college and university level. According to the U.S. Department of Education, in 1993 there were 915,474 faculty members in all institutions of higher education. Of these, less than 5% were African American, fewer than 2.5% were Hispanic, under 4% were Asian, and just about one quarter of 1% were Native American (NCES, 1993). The immense majority (almost 90%) was of European American heritage. For professors in schools and colleges of education, this is a serious issue, because their job is precisely to prepare students to become effective teachers of students who are increasingly diverse in culture, language, and experience. For professors in other disciplines, the issue is equally serious, because they provide the general education for those who will become the nation's teachers. That general education is still largely Eurocentric in content and focus. The truism that teachers cannot teach what they do not know is unmistakable in this context.

Given these statistics, how do educators prepare for their role to teach students of such immense diversity, students who are different from the cultural "mainstream" and from one another in race, ethnicity, culture, social class, native language, and residence in the United States, among other differences? This dilemma has been recognized as a major challenge to teachers, schools, and teacher preparation programs, and it has received widespread attention among professional organizations, and among schools and colleges of education (Dilworth, 1992; Zeichner, 1996). A number of proposals concerning what needs to be done have been made; these range from aggressively recruiting teachers from underrepresented groups, to developing the cultural knowledge teachers need in preservice and inservice teacher preparation programs (Dilworth, 1992; Irvine, 1997). Reforms such as these are sorely needed, of course, but they are long-range strategies for problems that cry out for solutions now.

THE NEED FOR CULTURALLY RELEVANT CASES

One way in which educators can be prepared to effectively teach the students who are in their classrooms right now is to use culturally relevant cases. By using these kinds of cases, teachers can learn more about how culture, language, social class, and other differences are manifested in the lives of their students, and how these differences might influence students' experiences in school. Culturally relevant cases do this not by providing decontextualized depictions of "ideal" types, but rather by presenting concrete *examples* of real students. Consequently, in this chapter, I understand culturally relevant cases to be *profiles of individual students from particular cultural backgrounds*. In this sense, they fit within the framework of the case study approach as defined by Merriam (1988): "an intensive, holistic description and analysis of a bounded phenomenon such as a program, an institution, a person, a process, or a social unit" (p. xiv).

Using cases has a number of advantages for teachers. The main purpose of using case studies is to gain a deeper understanding of specific issues and problems related to education practice. That is, case studies can help educators look at particular contexts so that solutions for more general situations can be hypothesized and developed. But because culturally relevant cases are based on real students from real families living in particular situations, culturally relevant cases concern flesh-and-blood individuals, not fictitious or group-based depictions. In the final analysis, the young people in culturally relevant cases are unique individuals who can no more be "representative" of their cultural group than any other individual can. As such, cases can provide educators with pertinent information about cultural groups without at the same time presenting a static "model" of youths from a specific group. In this way, individual cases have the potential to shatter stereotypes that teachers may have of students from specific cultural groups, an outcome that is especially welcome when used with teachers who have had little or no experience with students of the same backgrounds as those in the case studies.

In what follows, I describe the process I followed in developing culturally relevant cases to conceptualize how they can be used in teacher preparation.

USING CASES TO TRANSFORM TEACHER PREPARATION

A number of years ago, when it was becoming increasingly clear to me that most teachers were unprepared to teach students who were different from themselves, I set out to write a book on multicultural education. Several excellent books about multicultural education already existed, and they provided teachers and other educators with important insights on making school more meaningful and effective for students of diverse backgrounds. Most books focused on the history and culture of specific groups, or they suggested appropriate lessons and units for classrooms. These are important and necessary components of multicultural education and they have proven to be valuable for teachers concerned with successfully teaching students of diverse backgrounds. But I wanted to focus on a different angle: I wanted to investigate what *students* of various backgrounds brought to their education and how their differences could be used in the service of their learning. In order to do this, I decided to develop a series of case studies of students from diverse backgrounds.

At the same time that I decided that developing culturally relevant case studies was an interesting endeavor, as well as the contribution that I felt I could best make to multicultural education, I was nervous about the implications of developing them. That is, I wondered if case studies would simply perpetuate the negative assumptions that teachers already might have of students of diverse backgrounds. I worried that case studies would harden teachers' preconceived attitudes about the families of their students. And I pondered about whether they would lead to further stereotypes about students. My fears were not without some substance: when I received feedback from the anonymous reviewers of the prospectus I had submitted to my publisher, each mentioned grave reservations about the use of case studies of young people from diverse backgrounds. Had I been less convinced about the need for culturally relevant cases, or about their tremendous potential as teaching tools, I would have given up the project then and there. But I did not. I continued to develop the idea and the process for developing culturally relevant cases of individual students from diverse backgrounds, and the book *Affirming Diversity: The Sociopolitical Context of Multicultural Education* (Nieto, 1992, 1996) was the result.

Using and writing culturally relevant case studies is not a neutral activity, but one that has a great many implications for how central questions about diversity and education are addressed. In the next section, I discuss several of the key decisions I made as I began to develop the idea for the case studies.

Making Decisions About Culturally Relevant Case Studies

I began the development of the case studies by inviting a number of friends, colleagues, and doctoral candidates in my program to join me in finding and interviewing students of diverse backgrounds in order to develop case studies that I might use in the book I was planning to write. As others found out about the project, they asked if they could be included, and we ended up with a wonderfully diverse and committed group of educators who shared my vision of using case studies to help change how teacher education is done.[1] We met numerous times during that year to discuss how the book could use case studies as a central organizing theme. We also discussed the criteria for selecting students; we reviewed what case studies were and how to prepare them; we developed the questions we would ask; and we thought about what other information concerning the students' families, backgrounds, and experiences we needed to get.

---

[1]The people who met to discuss and plan the interviews and format of the case studies with me were Paula Elliott, Haydée Font, Maya Gillingham, Diane Sweet, and Carol Shea. Later, Mac Lee Morante of California and Carlie Tartakov of Iowa also took part in the project by interviewing young people in their communities. For the second edition, I decided to include not only students who had done relatively well in school, but also others who had had difficult and unsuccessful experiences in school. Two students were selected, one from Boston, Massachusetts and the other from East Los Angeles, and they were interviewed by Beatriz McConnie Zapater and Mac Lee Morante, respectively. I remain grateful to these friends and colleagues for the valuable insights they have provided to me from the beginning of the project.

Who Should Be Interviewed?   From the outset, I had decided that I wanted to focus on secondary school students because I thought the recollections they had of their experiences and their suggestions for improving schools would be particularly valuable for teachers. Another early decision had to do with the kind of diversity to be included in the case studies. Although I was eager to include as many examples of diversity as possible, I was also realistic that readers would probably not get much out of a litany of case studies. For this reason, I settled on 10 case studies, roughly equal in terms of females and males (the number was expanded to 12 in the second edition), and I decided to focus my efforts on cultural, racial, and linguistic diversity. Needless to say, the cases also ended up being diverse in social class, lifestyle, family structure, urban–suburban–rural mix, sexual orientation, and other differences, although these differences were not always evident. For instance, one of the interviewers was quite certain that one of the young men she interviewed was gay, but because he did not volunteer this information, she did not probe. Although I considered many kinds of differences in my book, I chose to emphasize race, ethnicity, and language. No one book can possibly give all issues of diversity a fair treatment and it was my hope that the focus of other educators on gender, social class, exceptionality, and sexual orientation, among other differences, would provide teachers with the same careful treatment that I hoped to give to race, ethnicity, and language.

I had decided from the beginning that students of so-called "minority" groups, that is, students who are members of African American, Latino, Asian American, and Native American backgrounds, would be central to my book. These are the students who are the usual focus of multicultural education books and, given the legacy of educational inequality and their history of poor achievement in our public schools, I wanted to make sure to include them. But I also made the decision early on that I wanted to include White students of various ethnic backgrounds who are normally invisible in discussions of multicultural education. That is why we included Vanessa, a young woman of European American and Protestant heritage, and Avi, a Jewish American youngster. My colleague and friend, David Bloome, gave me invaluable help when I began the project. He suggested that I include an Arab American student because this was a growing population in our country but usually an invisible group in discussions of multicultural education. The case study of James was the result.

Some choices were serendipitous: Carol Shea, a counselor in a Boston high school, had met and worked with Manuel, a Cape Verdean student, and she was interested in interviewing him. Cape Verdeans are a large and vibrant community in parts of the northeast and in California, but people in most other parts of the United States have never met them. Manuel's case turned out to be a poignant example of the trials and triumphs of newly arrived immigrant youths and many teachers have commented to me that they learned a lot from his case. Similarly, although I had not initially intended to include a biracial or biethnic student, Linda, the student who had been identified as Black by Paula Elliott (her interviewer), insisted instead on identifying herself as "Black American and White American." It was due to that insistence that we were fortunate to end up with a wonderfully rich case study of a young woman who refused to be pigeonholed and who struggled against the identities that were foisted on her by others. Given the dramatically growing numbers of students who identify as bicultural or biethnic in our society, it turned out to be a happy coincidence that we found Linda. As a result of all the choices we made, the Black–White dichotomy that often characterizes multicultural education was challenged.

Who Should Interview Whom?   Another issue that concerned us was the ethnicity and gender of interviewers. We began by insisting that students from a particular ethnic group needed to be interviewed by somebody of the same gender and ethnicity. I, for instance, selected Marisol, another Puerto Rican female. This decision made sense on a lot of levels, but it turned out that it was not always possible and, in some cases, interviewers had other ideas. For instance, Haydée Font, another Puerto Rican woman, was working as a teaching assistant in a tutoring project at the university and she had access to the many high school students who were being tutored. She was particularly interested in interviewing a Vietnamese student, and because of this, she found Vinh. Carlie Tartakov, a long-time friend of mine who was living in Iowa, suggested that rather than select an African American female like herself, she had found a Native American student she was interested in interviewing. That is how Fern's case study was developed. Diane Sweet first interviewed Avi, who although male, was Jewish like her. Having taught English on the West Bank, she was also interested in interviewing an Arab American student, and she found James.

We learned some useful lessons from these decisions. For example, Diane found striking similarities between Avi and James, and she thought that these young men would surely have become good friends if they had ever met. Although she came from a middle-class family in Puerto Rico, Haydée discovered that she could relate on a personal level to Vinh's experiences as an immigrant. Carlie's decision to interview Fern was enriching for both of them. As a multicultural educator, Carlie had always been eager to learn about the experiences of young people from many backgrounds. She was able to compare her own experience as a young African-American woman growing up 30 years earlier in California to Fern's life in a small midwestern city. These interethnic dialogues provided a distinct kind of learning from the intraethnic dialogues, and using both resulted in case studies that were multifaceted and fascinating.

How Should We Look for the Students?   The students we selected were not a random sample, nor were they meant to be. Because I wanted to develop culturally relevant cases of real-life young people, I was not interested in finding "model" students, so we usually went with the first ones we interviewed. My major criteria were *diversity* in terms of ethnicity, race, or language, and a fairly even mix of young women and men. Given that we wanted students to speak candidly about their school experiences, I thought it would make sense to look for them in out-of-school settings, especially in community centers or through other informal channels. This did not always happen; sometimes teachers or counselors suggested students who had interesting stories to tell and we followed up on their suggestions. In most cases, we interviewed students in their own homes, sometimes in restaurants or other community settings. In all cases, we used pseudonyms, although there were a number of students who were anxious for me to use their real names. I decided against it because I felt a responsibility to protect their identity, especially if in the future they might regret that they had used their real names.

We also asked friends and colleagues to recommend students from diverse backgrounds. But sometimes we found students in unpredictable ways. For example, Diane Sweet went to a local Arab bakery. When she told the proprietor about the project she was working on, the woman immediately went to the telephone and called a friend of hers who had a son in high school, and that is how Diane located James.

What Else to Include in the Cases?   Although individual stories of young people are frequently engaging, I wanted to provide teachers with more than just interesting stories. I wanted teachers to know the context of students' lives. Why did Marisol's family migrate to the United States? Why was speaking Vietnamese at home important to Vinh? Why did Paul join a gang and why was it so hard for him to leave it? In order to answer questions such as these, teachers needed to know about the history of the people of Marisol, Vinh, and Paul. That is, without knowing something of the history of Puerto Rico and its colonial relationship with the United States; or the impact that the Vietnam War had on the lives of the Vietnamese people; or the development of gangs in East Los Angeles, it was impossible to understand the stories of these young people. As a consequence, I decided that I too needed to read, study, and learn about not only the particular context of the lives of Marisol, Vinh, and Paul, but also about the sociopolitical and sociocultural contexts of their lives.

Developing the case studies took much longer than I had expected, and it was precisely because of my decision to include the broader context of the young people's lives that it became a lengthy process. For each case study, I needed to learn something about the history of the cultural or ethnic group of the student, their national origin, the city or town or region where each lived, and the group's educational experiences in the United States. The emphasis in each case was different, but in all of them information about the context added depth to the stories. This was probably the best decision I made about constructing the case studies; had I not added elements of the sociocultural and sociopolitical context to them, the case studies would have been less textured and more simplistic. Case studies without this kind of context become one-dimensional representations of very complicated individuals, and this does little to inform teachers about the reality of the lives of their students.

These, then, were the key decisions I made concerning the case studies. For the first edition we ended up with 10 young people who were tremendously diverse in race, ethnicity, native language, social class, geographical location, and worldview, among many other differences. At the time they were interviewed, all of them were students, and they ranged in age from 13 to 19. Following are their names and identities as they defined themselves (except in the case of Vanessa, which I discuss later): Linda Howard (Black American/White American), Vanessa Mattison (European American), Rich Miller (African American), Avi Abramson (Jewish), Fern Sherman (Native American), Marisol Martinez (Puerto Rican), James Karan (Lebanese), Hoang Vinh (Vietnamese), Manuel Gomes (Cape Verdean), and Yolanda Piedra (Mexican). For the second edition (1996), I added two more case studies: Paul Chavez (Chicano/Mexican American) and Ron Morris (African American).

LEARNING FROM CULTURALLY RELEVANT CASES: IMPLICATIONS FOR PEDAGOGY

There are many lessons to be learned from culturally relevant case studies. In what follows, I focus on what I learned, and I give examples that may prove helpful to other teachers as they think about developing and using their own case studies.

Culture is Complex, Situational, Dynamic, and Socially Constructed

An important consequence of doing case studies is that one comes face to face with real-life culture, and it is an encounter that complicates simplistic notions of the concept. In my own experience, I found that I had to reconsider what it meant to be African American, Jewish, Mexican American, or anything else. Although culture is manifested in everybody in a particular group, it shows up in different ways in each person. Being a member of a cultural group is thus different for each individual, and it differs as well based on age, gender, social class, the historical moment, and many other factors. Being a young African American living in Boston in the 1990s is quite different, for example, from being a young African American from Mississippi or Montana, or an African American living 50 or even 10 years ago. As a result of the shift in my thinking, I have come to define culture as dynamic; multifaceted; embedded in context; influenced by social, economic, and political factors; created and socially constructed; learned; and dialectical (Nieto, 1999).

I had never been happy with what I call the list approach to multicultural education (lists of characteristics that supposedly describe the people of any given culture) because such lists often cause more problems than they solve. For example, knowing that Vietnamese youngsters prefer to work on their own is a gross oversimplification of what may indeed be a cultural value, but it does little to explain the enormous individual differences that can be found in the entire Vietnamese population. In the case of Vinh, we found that he loved to work in groups and to engage in dialogue, neither of which would have been expected if teachers had heeded traditional lists of characteristics of Vietnamese students. Vinh liked group work, as he stated, "[b]ecause when we learn another language, we learn to discuss, we learn to understand the word's *meaning*, not about how to *write* the word" (Nieto, 1996, p. 176). Whether it was because working in groups gave Vinh his only opportunity during class time to speak Vietnamese with the few other Vietnamese students in his school, or because it was simply his learning preference is not important. What matters is that Vinh complicated the notion of learning styles for me by demonstrating that not all students from the same cultural group learn in exactly the same way.

Culture is regularly presented in teacher preparation courses as a fixed and flat concept. Given the growing number of universities in which multicultural education courses are being required in teacher preparation programs, it is crucial that both professors and prospective teachers learn to look at multicultural education in a more reflexive and critical way. Paradoxically, even when multicultural education is criticized, the criticism seldom extends to culturally responsive pedagogy (Hoffman, 1996). The implication seems to be that culturally responsive pedagogy is always above reproach, as if all students of a particular group would benefit from the same pedagogical practices.

Culturally specific information, in fact, can sometimes serve to provide fuel for having low expectations of students, or for unfair treatment of youngsters from particular backgrounds. For instance, a truism concerning Mexican American and other Latino students is that they are most comfortable working cooperatively. But a study by Flora Ida Ortiz (1988) found that when teachers used the *cooperative* attribute from the learning style literature, Hispanic children tended to receive a lower quality education than other children. In the classrooms that she studied, Ortiz found that teachers used the research to justify a number of clearly discriminatory pedagogical decisions: teachers rarely gave Hispanic students solo performances in plays or leadership activities in other situations, and they made Hispanic children share books when there were not enough for everybody. As a consequence, teachers' preconceived negative assumptions concerning children's abilities were reinforced by their faulty interpretation of research that, in other situations, might prove to be very helpful.

Culturally relevant case studies of individual students help to challenge stereotypes and conventional wisdom. They can even lead to questioning the validity of educational theories that, although useful in explaining general situations, are sometimes accepted uncritically by teachers and professors. No case study of a single individual can adequately or legitimately portray the complexity of an entire group of people. This is an especially important reminder because educational theories, no matter how helpful or insightful, are generalizations that do not explain every case. In fact, as seen earlier, sometimes theories can reinforce negative assumptions and lead to ineffective teaching strategies. Using another example, despite the very useful theories developed by Fordham and Ogbu (1986) concerning Black students and school learning, not all Black students interpret academic success as "acting White." The perceptions and reactions of Black students to school success are also influenced by their social class, gender, family experiences with schooling, and so on. Cases can help to challenge theories that, after a while, take on a life of their own. Teachers need numerous examples of real students who behave in incredibly idiosyncratic ways, not as representatives of their entire cultural group.

Cases are Situated in Sociocultural and Sociopolitical Contexts

It is interesting to read stories of young people of diverse backgrounds and their experiences in school. But effective case studies are more than this;

they also describe in vivid detail the sociopolitical context in which students live. For instance, the case of Manuel cannot be understood without knowing something of the history of the Cape Verde Islands, the legacy of colonialism, and the reasons for the massive emigration of the Cape Verdean people to the United States. So despite the fact that on some level, Manuel's case tells the story of an individual young man struggling to make sense of his world, on another level it is the history of immigrants within the specific sociocultural and sociopolitical context of large-scale diasporas of formerly colonized people. In addition, Manuel's story is placed within the urban context of a city, in this case Boston, that had seen millions of immigrants come and go and that had developed particular policies and programs within the public schools to deal with them. The fact that the Boston Public Schools was the only school district in the country to offer a bilingual program in Crioulo, his native language, was instrumental in Manuel's academic success. Details such as these need to be included in culturally relevant case studies so that the influence of other contexts can be taken into account in explaining students' school experiences.

The importance of situating case studies within a broader context is exemplified in the example of Vanessa, the only young person of European American heritage interviewed. As I mentioned previously, Vanessa was the only student who had a hard time defining her identity. In every other case, students were quick to answer the question by saying, "I'm Chicano," or "I'm Jewish." But Vanessa faltered: when she was asked how she described herself, she answered, "I generally don't. ... Wait, can you explain that? Like, what do you want to know?" When pressed, she said,

> Well, I would [describe myself as White], but it doesn't matter to me, so that's why I said it's a tough question. 'Cause I usually just describe myself as like what I believe in or something like that. Rather than like what culture I am, whether I'm Black or White. 'Cause that doesn't matter. (Nieto, 1996, p. 77)

Confronting racial and other differences was difficult for Vanessa because, unlike the other young people we interviewed, she had not often needed to think about these questions. In her reaction, she was reflecting the value of being "color-blind," which all teachers are taught to believe is fair. However, in many ways, being color-blind means refusing to see cultural differences because cultural differences are perceived as deficits or disadvantages. Yet the fact that Vanessa understood that some people were rewarded for their identity while others were punished for it made her discomfort even greater. Because Vanessa was a young woman committed to honesty, fair play, and social justice, she found it abhorrent to benefit from her race or social class privileges. In her case study, we see a young woman grappling with the contradictions between the lofty ideals in which she was taught to believe, and the discrimination she was beginning to see more clearly. She understood, for instance, that being White meant having more opportunities than those who were not White, and she resented this. But confronting White privilege was difficult especially when these issues were never addressed in school.

Vanessa's case is important because it demonstrates the dilemma faced by many young people of trying to reconcile ideals with reality. Furthermore, although issues of diversity and equality are crucial for young people to think about, these topics are rarely included in the schools' curriculum. All of these questions are related to the broader context of Vanessa's family, school, community, and society in general. I have found in my own courses that using specific cases such as these open up spaces for dialogue about issues that otherwise are too dangerous to broach. Concrete cases offer opportunities for teachers, and in this case especially White teachers, to consider their own identities and why they have been formed in particular ways. When White teachers can begin to question why they are comfortable with "color-blindness" but uncomfortable discussing their White privilege, they will have taken an important first step in the long journey toward becoming effective teachers of students of diverse backgrounds.

Students Have Important Insights About Differences That Can Inform Pedagogy, Curriculum, and Other Policies and Practices

Another lesson that was reconfirmed for me through developing the case studies was the immense value of listening to what students have to say. Sometimes we forget that students spend more time in school than anyone else except their teachers. Student voices reveal the deep pain young people feel when schools are unresponsive and cold places. Students know the lay of the land, they know what works and what doesn't, they can tell who cares for them and why. But, incomprehensible as it might seem, those who spend the most time in schools and classrooms usually have the least opportunity to talk about their experiences and perspectives. Consequently, although students have important insights to offer about education, educators are losing a compelling opportunity to learn from them.

What are the implications of the case studies I developed of students for the school's curriculum, pedagogy, and tracking? One implication is that schools and teachers need to find ways to affirm students' cultures and languages so that their school experiences are affected in positive ways. Young people are not a blank slate; they come to school with a language, culture, and a variety of experiences that can assist them in their learning. In addition, teachers need to consider not only the individual weaknesses or strengths of particular students, but also how students are assigned a specific status based on their identity. In too many cases, the identities of non-mainstream students are disparaged because they are not thought to have valuable "cultural capital" (Bourdieu, 1977). As I learned from the case studies I developed, when culture and language are acknowledged by the school, students are able to reclaim the voice they need to successfully continue their education.

The case study students in my book provided impassioned examples of the effect that affirming their languages and cultures had on them, and conversely on how negating their languages and cultures negated a part of them as well. A good example was Yolanda, a young Mexican girl who was very successful in school. The attitudes and behaviors of the teachers in her school were reflected in policies that were based on an appreciation for student diversity. Given the support of her teachers and their affirmation of her language and her culture, Yolanda concluded, "Actually, it's fun around here if you really get into learning ... I like learning. I like really getting my mind working. ... " (Nieto, 1996, p. 223). Manuel, the Cape Verdean student, also commented on how crucial it was for teachers to become aware of students' cultural values and backgrounds. Because Manuel's parents were immigrants who were largely unfamiliar with U.S. schools and society, this awareness was especially significant for him. He said, "If you don't know a student there's no way to influence him. ... There's no way you're going to influence him if you don't know where he's been" (Nieto, 1996, p. 213).

Although "Americanization" (cultural assimilation) has been an almost undisputed goal of public schools since the beginning of the 20th century (Appleton, 1983; Dickeman, 1973; Katz, 1975), the question remains whether this kind of assimilation is healthy or necessary. A number of studies have pointed to the destructive result of assimilation, not only for self-esteem but also for students' academic progress and even for their mental health (New Voices, 1988; Poplin & Weeres, 1992; Rumbaut & Ima, 1987). The students in our case studies mentioned numerous ways in which their languages and cultures were left out of schools. In James' case, his culture and language were invisible in both the curriculum and in special school activities such as the International Fair and the school cookbook. Marisol, the young Puerto Rican woman I interviewed, told me about a teacher who prohibited Puerto Rican students from speaking Spanish in school. And Vinh spoke about how his teachers simply did not know very much about his culture. Little wonder that these young people had conflicted feelings about their backgrounds.

Using culturally relevant cases helps us look more critically at policies and practices that encourage students to leave their cultures and languages at the schoolhouse door. For instance, although it is still common to hear some teachers urge parents to "speak only English" with their children, practices such as this are called into question when culturally relevant cases are used. As an initial step in learning about their students, teachers can use cases to learn about other students who may be facing similar challenges. Vinh's words about the superficial knowledge that most teachers had about Vietnamese culture are telling: "They understand something, just not all Vietnamese culture. Like they just understand something *outside*. ... But they cannot understand something inside our hearts" (p. 179). Using culturally relevant cases might just provide the kind of information that teachers need to understand that "something inside our hearts."

Developing Cases Can Be a Powerful Pedagogical Strategy

Shortly after the first edition of *Affirming Diversity* was published, I was speaking at a conference about the case studies included in the book. A teacher in the audience asked me how on earth I had found such incredibly gifted and special students. I answered by suggesting that Vinh, Linda, Avi, Vanessa, and all the other students in the case studies were the students in all of our classrooms. Yes, they were special but, for the most part, they were not "stars." In fact, we did nothing special to find these particular students, and we found some completely by chance. In Vinh's case, for example, Haydée Font asked the director of the tutoring program to suggest one of the students in the program. When she called information to get the student's telephone number, the operator gave her the number of another Vietnamese family in the same town, obviously confusing the last name. Although the young girl who answered said that it was a wrong number, she asked Haydée what she wanted; when Haydée told her, the girl suggested that her brother, Vinh, would be a good person to interview!

Students such as these are in our classrooms, but how do we uncover those special qualities so evident in the case studies although perhaps not as evident in their everyday behavior in classrooms? One way is by using case studies as a pedagogical strategy at both the school and the university level. For example, preservice or inservice teachers can be assigned the task of developing case studies based on interviews with students they teach. This is often an inspirational activity because teachers discover things about young people that they might never have thought about. They learn, for instance, what young people care about, how they perceive school, and the importance of their families in their lives. Also, teachers' practice is frequently changed as a result of such case studies because they are led to think about curricular and pedagogical adaptations to help particular students learn. Developing cases can have important consequences for the students who are interviewed as well. When they are treated as if they know something, students become energized and motivated. For the 12 young people in my study, the very act of speaking about their schooling experiences seemed to act as a catalyst for more critical thinking about them. Most of them were so enthusiastic that they did not want to see their interviews end, and they frequently asked when we would be back to do the next one. On one of the tapes, I remember a student saying, "This is so much fun!" There are several implications for practice, including using oral histories, peer interviews, interactive journals, and simply providing students time to talk with one another through group work and other cooperative strategies. (In the forthcoming third edition of *Affirming Diversity* [Nieto, 2000], I provide guidelines for developing case studies.)

CONCLUSION

I began this chapter with Paul's case study. His story is his alone, of course, and it is not meant to teach educators about all young people who are unsuccessful in school, gang members, Mexican American, poor, or raised by their mothers. But despite the fact that it is not *representative*, his case study is *instructive* on all of these counts. For instance, it provides an important lesson about educational adaptations that can help young people such as Paul succeed in school, in this case, the alternative school he attended that was multicultural in focus and that encouraged student responsibility and involvement. His case study also gives a moving example of a mother who cared deeply about her son's academic success, and it might help to challenge the widely held stereotype among many people that poor, disempowered, and uneducated parents are apathetic about their children's education. Most of all, however, Paul's case study reveals the kinds of insights and ideas that most teachers do not get a chance to see in their daily interactions with students.

If they are to be effective with all of the students they teach, educators need to find ways to learn about the backgrounds and experiences of the increasingly diverse student population in our schools. Courses in anthropology, sociology, and urban and ethnic studies can all be helpful in preparing teachers more adequately than is currently the case. But courses alone are not enough because they are limited by the knowledge, experiences, and perspectives of the particular faculty who teach them. Textbooks, biographies, and fiction concerning the experiences of different cultural groups can also be helpful, but they too are limited, especially if they describe culture in static, abstract, and decontextualized ways. Because they provide both particular characteristics of individual students and of the broader context in which they live, culturally relevant cases can help teachers be-

come aware of and sympathetic to the experiences of young people of diverse backgrounds.

Paul's story has touched a great many teachers over the years, and it has
caused some of them to question their assumptions and biases. But no program or school can reach all students, and Paul was a particularly difficult
young man to reach. A year or so after he interviewed Paul, I asked Mac how
he was doing and he said that it was touch and go; although Paul was still in
the gang, he was also still in school. A year after that, I ran into the principal
of Paul's school, and she told me that Paul would be graduating that year and
he still wanted to become a teacher. I wish I could say that all young people
in Paul's situation were as successful, but this is far from true. But I do know
one thing: It was teachers and a particular school that made the difference
in Paul's life. In the end, it is teachers who believe in students such as Paul
who can help turn their lives around.

Commentary on "Culturally Relevant Teaching With Cases: A Personal Reflection and Implications for Pedagogy"

So-young Zeon
University of Wisconsin—River Falls

As educators, we are continuously searching for innovative methods of instruction that foster learning environments that represent the complexity of our society in its views, beliefs, perspectives, and makeup. To capture the diversified reality of our society, a case-based method of instruction may provide such an environment (Kagan, 1993). Traditionally used in classrooms of law and medicine, the case-based pedagogy is becoming more widely implemented in education classrooms. There has been support for the use of cases to facilitate critical thinking and promote the study of one's own personal attitudes and beliefs. This can lead to a classroom setting where teachers and students can explore a world beyond their personal experiences and perspectives (Reffel & Bartelheim, 1993). The use of cases can encourage dialogue and an opportunity to practice reflective thinking in the classroom.

The concern, however, of many educators that wish to use cases for effective teaching is finding well-written and culturally relevant cases. In addition, once we locate such cases, how we use them for instruction also poses serious concerns and further questions. This chapter by Sonia Nieto provides concrete examples of cases portraying real students and addresses the above mentioned concerns by sharing her reflections about writing and teaching with cases.

The development of cases is a collaborative group effort of the observer, writer and the observed or interviewed persons. It is extremely important to present the key players in a manner worthy of justifying authenticity. How do we reveal individuals who are embedded in a context with complexities while satisfactorily depicting the culture he or she belongs to with accuracy and meaningfulness without losing the individual? How do we avoid creating more stereotypes or misconceptions? As a person who has collected data, written cases, and used them to teach, I realize that this is difficult to accomplish. Nieto offers insightful information and reflections about the process of developing cases. The categories mentioned—Who should be interviewed? Who should interview whom? How should we look for the students? and Who else to include in the cases?—were helpful guidelines not only for writing but also for selecting cases for instruction.

As a professor who has been using *Affirming Diversity: The Sociopolitical Context of Multicultural Education* as the main text for a multicultural education course, I have had a chance to grapple, fail, and succeed with the various cases presented in Nieto's book. Did my students become fully acquainted with James Karam, a Lebanese student? Or was it a superficial encounter where no transformation will occur in their beliefs or their teaching practices. For the most part, students who take my class are from small towns in midwestern communities and many will find jobs teaching in similar settings. They may never meet another Lebanese student during their entire teaching career. I questioned whether cases could really assist in teacher preparation and whether some cases were so far removed from the setting in which these pre-teachers were entering that without making purposeful connections to content these cases may be less effective. I found also that asking the "right" questions made an enormous difference in how the case discussions progressed and found myself spending more time searching for appropriate questions. I agree with Nieto that listening to what my students had to say was a valuable experience. Not only was it a chance to hear how they felt and what they thought but it also allowed me to reexamine content that had been previously presented and what impact it had on the students.

Toward the middle of the chapter, Nieto offers a revised definition of culture that comes out of her personal experiences with writing and implementing cases. In our quest to write and use culturally relevant cases to help students learn about people of diverse cultures, I question whether we may have overlooked how we as educators conceptualize and implement the notions of culture in our classrooms (Hoffman, 1996). The important questions are "What constitutes a culture?" and "What do we mean by relevant?" If culture is indeed fluid, situational, dynamic, and socially constructed as Nieto sees it, how does one evaluate whether a case is truly "culturally relevant" or how long does it stay "relevant"? We need to ensure that discussion of cases do not lead to a local and oversimplified presentation of culture. It is imperative that we explore how other disciplines have used this term and the history of the term *culture* (Wax, 1993). There have been drastic changes in the way culture is being used and taught today especially in the field of multicultural education and more specifically as exploration continues into the relationship of culture to school curriculum and instruction. It seems as if at times, culture has been elevated to some social entity that does something to us as members of a particular culture and "it" gives us our identity (Hoffman, 1996).

I think the efforts of teachers and educators should be to continue on a more purposeful and rigorous study of such terms as culture and they should look for more effective instructional tools to enhance the quality of instruction. I applaud Nieto's efforts to help in the endeavor of teaching through examining a potentially powerful tool called *cases*.

10

Revisiting Fieldwork in Preservice Teachers' Learning: Creating Your Own Case Studies

≁ ≁ ≁

Susan Florio-Ruane
Michigan State University

When the editors of this volume invited me to contribute a chapter, I eagerly proposed republishing (and revisiting) my essay, "Creating Your Own Case Studies: A Guide For Early Field Experience." This short piece was not originally intended for use beyond my undergraduate class. It was meant to invite students to visit and view classrooms productively during their first course in teacher education, Exploring Teaching.[1] When I first began drafting the piece more than 10 years ago, both my students and I were beginners. They were learning to teach after having experienced classroom and school life from the perspective of pupils. I was learning to be a teacher-educator. We shared a concern for learning to see and make sense of teaching and learning in ways not entirely bound by our previous experiences, but open to discovering the perspectives of the teachers and youngsters into whose lives and classrooms we would step for one academic term.

---

[1]This course is documented in detail in a book by Feiman-Nemser and Featherstone (1992).

Field experience, especially very early in one's professional studies, is both exciting and intimidating. This is a time that is too early in one's preparation to assume the role of the teacher, yet early enough to begin to see and think like one. The beginner anxiously confronts a situation both familiar and newly complex. It is easy in these first days and weeks in the field to have one's entering (and usually unexamined) biases reinforced rather than challenged or expanded.

On first visiting the classroom as a preservice teacher, the beginner is apt to be unclear about his or her purpose and feel obliged to try to "act like a teacher" (usually either imitating or resisting the cooperating teachers' behavior as a model). The focus is apt to be methods, materials, and management. In these circumstances, the initial field experience can be a missed opportunity for examining our own entering biases, uncovering the dynamics of complex interactions between teacher and learners or among learners, or coming to a more critical understanding of how classrooms are contextualized by wider environments of school, community, and culture.

As I worked with such beginners in my first years as a teacher-educator, it struck me that many of the problems of "making the familiar strange" confronting the novice teacher bore a family resemblance to those confronting the ethnographer who works within schools, classrooms, and communities within her or his own society. My experience as an ethnographer who had grappled with and read about similar problems of initial field experience in research (see, e.g., Geer, 1969) led me to try to design accessible ways for beginners to "break the frame" of their entering points of view about both teaching and learning to teach. In both cases, the observer is called to interpret what he or she sees in ways sensitive to the local complexity of situations, the various perspectives of participants, and the ways that communication within the observed situation is shaped by wider systems and contexts. And, in both cases, the observer also finds her or himself participating in the situation's activities and relationships as a part of learning about them.

Calling this a "phenomenological approach" to the field experience, my colleague Christopher Clark and I wrote about the challenge of interpretive research within classrooms and how the spirit and methods of this approach might inform beginning teachers' learning as follows:

> In phenomenology, one seeks to describe rather than to explain what has been observed. What is observed is taken, not as given, but as made by human beings engaged in social transactions. Entering the field with such a perspective, the would-be teacher becomes less an apprentice and more a "field worker" in the ethnographic sense. As a participant observer in the scene, the student's goal is to discover the sense-making of teachers and children and to

study the social contexts in which that sense is made. Technique, previously figure ("teach me to do what you do"), is subordinated; and what was previously ground—the normative structures within and outside the classroom which shape and limit the tactical choices that teachers make—become figure. Teachers are seen as negotiating complex reconciliations between their own values, theories, and aspiration and the multiple social forces that limit and shape what is possible in the classroom. This critical stance potentially transforms the student teacher's way of seeing in the classroom and, it is hoped, aids in self-examination throughout her or his career. (Florio-Ruane & Clark, 1990, p. 21)

As I worked to help beginners learn to see in new ways, I was drawing heavily on the interdisciplinary conversation underway at the Michigan State University Institute for Research on Teaching (IRT). Under the leadership of L. Shulman and J. Lanier, the IRT was breaking ground in the qualitative study of classroom teaching, integrating theory and method drawn from ethnography, cognitive psychology, and sociolinguistics with the insights of teacher researchers (see, e.g., L. Shulman, 1986a). The focus of this effort was to come to understand teacher thought and action (and by implication, pupil thought and action) in its immediate social context of classroom and school. Read in this historical context, my essay was an early attempt to link educational research with my emerging practice as a teacher-educator.

I said at the outset that the essay reproduced here was not intended for use beyond my class. This accounts for its personal, informal tone and for a writing style devoid of technical terms and references. In writing it, I was emboldened to think that my students would embrace new ways of seeing and describing classrooms by their great interest in a book I shared with them in class—Spradley and McCurdy's *The Cultural Experience: Ethnography in Complex Society* (1972). Much of this book is comprised of case studies written by undergraduates in the authors' introductory course in ethnography. They deal with activities as diverse as the social organization of children's play at recess and the experience of being an airline flight attendant. My students were fond of the cases—especially, but not limited to, those dealing with school settings. Why, I thought, couldn't my students do likewise and create their own case studies of life in the classrooms to which they had been assigned? Thus began their work to develop "outsiders' guides" to the classroom that might be richly descriptive to a newcomer yet resonant with the perspectives of the teachers and students.

The modest, unpublished piece reprinted here was intended to help my students get started in their new roles as preservice teachers. Curiously, it struck a resonant chord among other teacher-educators and beginning teachers. Photocopies of it began to circulate long before it was ever published—first in my college, and later on other campuses. It was not uncommon for people to contact me to say that they were using it in their courses. Ultimately, J. Shulman invited me to publish it in a theme issue of the *Teacher Education Quarterly*, entitled "Case Methodology in the Study and Practice of Teacher Education." Since its publication, I have I received more requests for permission to reprint this piece than I have for any of the more "highfalutin" articles I have written about educational research. This both delights and surprises me. I am pleased to reproduce the article here, along with some concluding remarks and examples from my current teaching illustrating what I now think should be addressed as beginners enter the field to create their own case studies as a part of learning to teach.

CREATING YOUR OWN CASE STUDIES:
A GUIDE FOR EARLY FIELD EXPERIENCE

Most students of teaching spend some time in classrooms before they actually take charge of a lesson or a class. That time is usually intended to be one of observation and limited participation. Often, however, that time is spent in confusion. Beginning teachers find themselves wondering how and how much to participate in the everyday life of the classroom. They wonder about the definition of their role. How much authority are they expected to have? And they wonder how to make sense of the myriad of activities in the classroom now that their perspective is changing from that of a student to that of a teacher.

One of the ways beginning teachers can make the most of early field experiences is by applying some basic skills of observation and inference to the complex and interesting new scene in which they find themselves. In a sense, it is the beginner's job to be a participant observer in the classroom. What the beginner learns from this perspective resembles the knowledge presented in ethnographic case studies of classroom life.

Most authors of case studies began as interested outsiders trying to learn about the ways in which teachers and students worked together to teach and learn. They chose to learn about these questions by entering the places where the action was. However, in order to observe that action and come to understand it, they had to structure their participation. All persons structure their participation and make their daily rounds meaningful in three key ways. First, people see in constructive ways, bringing past experience into the picture, noting some things and neglecting others. Second, people simplify what they attend to in complex situations because the mind can only handle a limited amount of information at once. Third, people make sense of experience. They impose meaning on events and work with others to reach some consensus on what those meanings might be.

When you enter a new classroom to observe teaching and learning you engage in the same processes of seeing, simplifying, and sense-making as the teacher and the students. However, your job as a student teacher is also to understand how the teacher and students are making meaning of *their* world. Thus, a problem for you and the authors of case studies is "How can I observe in classrooms to try to discover both my own ways of seeing, simplifying, and sense-making and to discover how those same processes are undertaken by an experienced teacher and her students?"

The job that a student teacher faces is a difficult one. The observer of teaching must try both to understand the teacher and students as they make sense of their everyday lives *and* to monitor his or her own responses to what is observed. This second task of discovering one's own ways of seeing, simplifying, and sense-making is critical to becoming an insightful teacher. The suggestions offered in this paper are intended to help the student of teaching with both of these tasks.

The pages that follow offer some suggestions for how to become a participant-observer in the classroom. Trying out these suggestions in your own situation, you may or may not choose to write a case study, but you will go a long way toward thinking about what you see as a case study author might. You will distance yourself a bit from the action and ask yourself basic questions like "What is going on here?" "How are teacher and students making sense of their everyday lives?" "How are time, space, activity, and social relations being worked out in this classroom?" and "What does all of this have to do with the work of teaching?"

WHAT IS OBSERVATION?

Observation is not passive. Observers look, listen, ask, record, and analyze. When you enter a classroom to observe it is a good idea to be ready to do all of these things. Tools of the trade that you might need are simple ones—a notebook, a pencil, and a friendly and open manner. The following sections break observation into several activities—looking at space and its social meaning and use, considering time and how it is used in the classroom, logging and categorizing activities, and listening to what teachers and students have to say.

Learning to Look—Mapping the Classroom

Some case studies include maps of the classroom. Probably these maps helped the author to orient to the places in the room "where the action is." Mapping is a good way to begin to explore unknown territory. As you grow more familiar with the territory, your maps will change to reflect both what you have already begun to take for granted and what you now notice that you missed on your first days in a new place. It is a good idea to begin your observation by drawing a map of the classroom and to make maps often during your visits.

As we all know, space is important to people. Certain people in the classroom have rights to certain places; others may not go there. Some activities happen in special places. Different rules apply in different parts of the classroom These things are important to observers of teaching not only because some day they may have to plan the use of space in their own rooms, but because an observer's job is to figure out how teacher and students work together to achieve both the social and academic aims of education.

Figure 10.1 (pp. 208–209) contains is a series of classroom maps made in one open-space kindergarten/first-grade classroom. You can see how the use of space changes over time for both teacher and children. How to use space is one important thing the kindergarten children in this class learned when they first came to school. When they were asked to map their classroom you can see that they already had a sense of what important activities take place in what parts of the classroom.

Try your hand at making a map of the classroom you are observing. As you map your classroom, think about what you are including and what you are leaving out. Think as well about the importance that appears to be attached to places in the classroom by the teacher and students who spend their time there. Does the use of space change over the course of a school day or week? Are different parts of the room the sites for different kinds of teaching and learning? Are there different rules for different parts of the room? What is there room for in this room? What kinds of space are not provided? (You may want to ask the teacher or some of the students to make similar maps. Comparing them, you can compare how participants see, simplify, and make sense of the classroom space.)

Real-Time Observation—Making a Classroom Log

Another unobtrusive way to learn about classroom life is by logging the activities that occur during an hour, day, week, term, or even a year. Again, many case studies include such logs for a day to a week or even longer. Teachers and children may not always share the same view of "what we are doing now." For example, what the teacher considers to be "sharing time—an opportunity to use and practice oral language," may, to the children around the circle, be a time for friendly socializing or a time to relax. As an observer, you will want to find out how the different members of the class construe the units of time into which their typical days are divided. What importance, both social and academic, may be attached to these units of time? By whom? What does this imply for the teaching and learning that takes place within those chunks of time?

Logging classroom activity will probably also reveal that plans are seldom realized perfectly. Ask the teacher in whose classroom you are observing to show you his or her plan book—or check the chalkboard for a calendar of the day's planned events. Figure 10.2 (p. 210) shows a sample calendar of events from one elementary classroom: In the manner of this calendar, carefully record the official times and sequence of a day's activities in your classroom using the teacher's plan book or the calendar on the chalkboard as your source. Then record the times and sequence of activities that actually happen during the day. No doubt you will find that some activities take longer than the plans implied, some take less time. Some plans are interrupted by unexpected happenings, some are abandoned in midstream either because time is short or because they are not working out as well as the teacher had hoped. Sometimes students introduce activities that are incorporated by the teacher on the spot. Plans are revised in action as they are shared and worked out by teachers, students, and others who may enter the classroom during the day.

In summary, logging the day should help you to learn more about several important aspects of teaching and classroom life. First, it should help you to see that different people can use time differently even in the same classroom. Second, it should demonstrate the difference between plans developed in the "empty classroom" and the enactment of those plans in the course of everyday classroom life. Third, it should help you to discover how teachers and students use time. In some classrooms, time is a commodity in short supply. You will observe people concerned with "fitting in" all the things they have to do in a day. In other classrooms (or in the same classroom on a different day) there may seem to be a great deal of time to fill and you may observe flexibility in the use of time. What does time and its use tell you about what is valued in a given school or classroom? What does it tell you about the limitations placed on teachers and students by forces outside their control? What does the use of time as it is worked out by teachers and students tell you about the shared or differing ideas they hold about school and its purposes?

Observing Classroom Activities

Once you have gotten a feel for the flow of everyday classroom life by logging classroom activities, you'll no doubt want to zoom in for a closer look. Many case studies are concerned, at least in part, with the content, pacing, and substance of classroom activities.

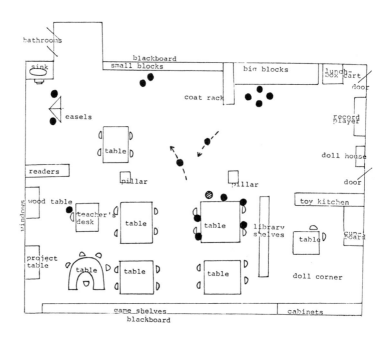

figure   floor plan of kindergarten/first grade
classroom **during worktime** (10/15/75)

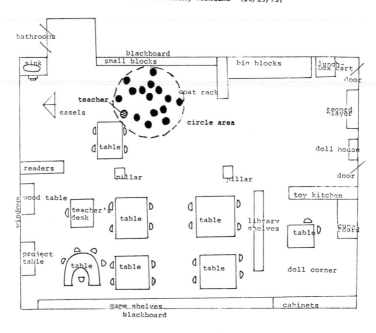

figure   floor plan of kindergarten/first grade
classroom **during the first circle** (2/27/76)

(a)

FIG. 10.1. Classroom maps: (a) Participant observer maps

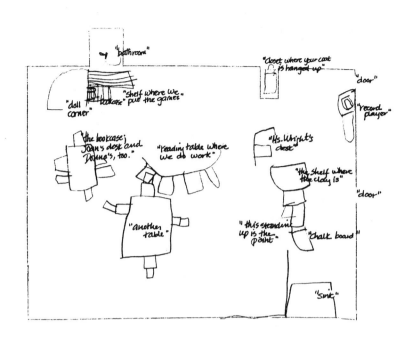

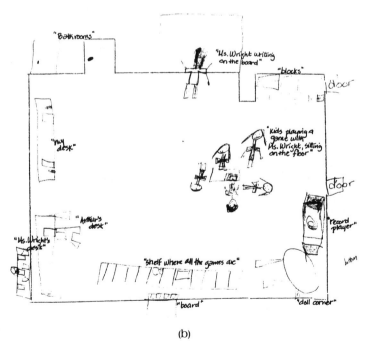

(b)

(b) Student maps.

Today is September 17, 1979

9:20–10:05	11:30–12:15	2:15–2:45
Assembly*	Language Arts	Science (2)
		Soc. St. (3)
10:05–10:30	12:15–12:50	2:45–3:00
Gym	Lunch	Clean up
10:30–11:00	12:55–1:15	3:00–3:10
Reading	Centers	Diaries
11:00–11:15	1:15–1:55	
Recess	Math	
11:15–11:30	1:55–2:10	
USR	Recess	

*The assembly included a film on bicycle and pedestrian safety and a talk on the same subject

FIG. 10.2. Sample classroom log.

Some students of teaching assume that the only activities that merit a close look are those we usually call "lessons." Often what we mean by lessons are those activities in which the teacher does most of the talking, the students (in small groups or whole class) sit facing the teacher and speak primarily to answer his or her questions, and where the content of interaction is something "academic" (e.g., reading, social studies, science, math). Certainly in U.S. schools this kind of teacher-directed activity can be readily observed, but you should also treat yourself to close study of some of the other ways in which teaching and learning occur. Be sure to observe students at work independently or in small groups outside the direct supervision of their teacher. Observe times when students move from one activity to the next. Do not overlook impromptu activities and those that seem at first blush to lack academic content. Observe children (and teachers) at lunch and at recess. Follow students to special activities such as art, gym, or assembly. Observe children and teachers at rest.

When you observe activity closely you will realize that you need to look, listen, ask questions, and record what is happening. Moreover, you need to analyze the meaning of what has transpired. Observation is never passive. Because you play such an active role in observation you need to be aware that there are three levels of observation—you will *record facts* about what is happening (e.g., by writing down word for word what someone says, by audiotaping an activity or photographing it), you will find yourself *making interpretations* of those facts (e.g., making educated guesses about what they might mean to people involved), and you will likely *make value judgments* about what is observed. The anthropologist Margaret Mead pointed out long ago that human beings are excellent "instruments" for the observation of other human beings, but their very closeness to and affinity for the situations they observe can obscure the meaning of events as much as it can illuminate that meaning. If we are to understand what behavior means to the people doing it, we must be willing temporarily to hold our interpretations in question and to suspend our value judgments so that our observations can be more complete and reflective of the people we are studying.

Think about the last time you saw fourth-grade boys and girls together. Did you observe behaviors that seemed like avoidance of the opposite sex? How did you interpret chasing, hitting, or running from one another as avoidance? Might these youngsters have meant something else by these behaviors? Is there evidence in the situation that they meant to attract rather than to avoid one another? How did you feel while observing them? Did you feel inclined to judge them as "silly" or "immature"? Did watching them bring back happy or uncomfortable memories of your own pre-adolescence? Try to find an activity in the classroom where you are working and take it apart. What factual descriptions of behaviors can you write down? What interpretations of meaning are you inclined to make about those behaviors? What other interpretations might be drawn? How does the activity make you feel? What is your judgment of its worth, goodness, value? Awareness not only of "what's happening" outside of yourself but of "what's happening" inside is the essence of good observation.

Field Notes—An Observer's Record

Researchers who write case studies use a special kind of note-taking to help them record behaviors they observed, keep track of interpretations that they were making of what those behaviors meant, and discover their own feelings and value judgments about what was seen. These notes, called "field notes," can be a very valuable record of your own classroom observations. They will teach you about classroom life as well as about differences in people's interpretations of it. At the top of Appendix A, there is a sample of field notes taken by a case study author (Example 1). In this sample, the observer has jumbled together her observations, interpretations, and value judgments. Note how difficult it is to sort out what actually happened from her own impressions, and note as well how little we learn about what the teacher or children might have thought of what was going on.

Now look at Example 2. Here is another record of the same event in which the observer has enriched her record of behavior, separated and reserved for further consideration her interpretations, speculated on the interpretations of teacher and children, and separated her own value judgments from the behavioral account. These notes, especially when taken over a number of days in the classroom, become a rich source of information and leave open the possibility of discovering the many perspectives of the people participating. The notes can tell the recorder not only about her own experience, but also about the experience of others.

On your next visit to the classroom try to take notes like the second example. One easy way to start is to set up your notebook pages to separate observations from inference and value judgments. Another way might be carefully to reread notes after you have come home from the classroom and underline or circle in a different color ink all of these inferences and judgments that are sprinkled throughout your descriptions. You might ask a friend or classmate to exchange notes with you and help you to see where your own point of view may be blinding you to others.

With a bit of practice, you'll get used to taking notes this way. Field notes can be the heart of a case study. They are also an excellent basis for discussion of teaching and learning. Experienced teachers often try to record in journals at the end of a day their recollections of what has happened in their room. Using the technique described above helps them to think in new ways about their teaching.

LISTENING AND THE ART
OF ASKING QUESTIONS

While observing in a classroom, listening is as important as looking. To learn about teachers' and students' experiences, you can listen to what they are saying in three ways. The first way of listening is the most obvious and least intrusive—*eavesdropping*. A good observer will be alert to the things people say to each other as they go about their usual business. Embedded in what they say can be important information about how they see, simplify, and make sense of their classroom life. For example, pay attention to the things a teacher says when a rule has been broken. Perhaps an exchange will go something like this:

Teacher:	Bobby, what are we supposed to be doing now?
Bobby:	(no response)
Students:	Seat work.
Teacher:	And how are we supposed to act during seat work?
Mary:	We're not supposed to talk.
Bill:	And we should not interrupt you at the reading table ... we should wait until our group is called to the table if we have questions about our work.

In this fictional exchange, teacher and students are making explicit the usually hidden understandings that organize their activity during reading instruction. As an astute observer and careful listener, you can learn a great deal about reading instruction, student relationships, and teacher–student interaction in this classroom without having to interrupt with direct questions about what is going on.

A second source of information used by case study authors to learn about classrooms is also readily available to you. This is *informal conversation*. On most of your visits to the classroom, you'll find that you have ample time to chat with students, your cooperating teacher(s), and other people in the school. You should consider this conversational time an important opportunity to learn about the school, the classroom, and the points of view of teachers and children. Unfortunately, in a new setting, we are often so concerned about the impression *we* are making that we neglect to make notes of or think about what others say to us. In addition, if our focus as classroom observers is merely on "how to do something" (be it run the movie projector or teach a concept), we may fail to note the many other kinds of information we can get from our conversations with teachers and children. Be sure to listen for information about the "why" of things, about the things people take for granted, those they choose to comment upon, and the themes that recur in their talk.

Sometimes a student of teaching is fortunate to have one or several special conversations with teachers or students. These conversations are special in that participants in the classroom have agreed to give you some of their valuable time for the third form of talk—*an interview*. Interviews are really quite specialized conversations. If you are the interviewer, you will note this right away, because even before the conversation begins you will need to decide what you want to learn about from the interview, why you want to learn it, and how best to get the answers you need. If you are fortunate to be able to interview a teacher, student, or other member of the school community while you are learning to teach, you'll want to keep some of the following things in mind:

- People are busy, so plan and use the time they give you carefully,
- Think about your interview in advance and write up a set of questions that will guide the conversation,
- Interviews can be open-ended (just a few major questions that a person can answer freely) or tightly controlled by the interviewer (where you ask a planned set of very specific questions),
- If you can answer a question by a method other than interview, do so. Save interviews for finding out about the things you can't ordinarily see or pick up by eavesdropping and casual conversation (e.g., thoughts, feelings, memories, values),
- Rehearse interviews with a friend before you actually give them so that you can get used to asking your questions and so that someone else can check the interview for clarity of its sequence and wording,
- Keep interviews short (perhaps 20 minutes is a good rule of thumb), and record what is said either in notes taken on the spot to be elaborated later, or on audiotape that you can review later (be sure you have the speaker's permission to make an audiotape),
- Remember that for all the things you can learn in an interview, it should never be your sole source of information. People cannot always tell you all they know. Sometimes this is because they are not aware of all that motivates their actions, sometimes it is because your questions are not clear to them, and sometimes it is because it would be indiscreet or impolite for them to tell you all that they know.
- Like all good things, a little interviewing can go a long way to help you fill in the gaps in what you have heard and seen and to help you check out your own inferences and interpretations.

PUTTING IT ALL TOGETHER

As stated at the outset, your goal in applying these techniques for looking, listening, recording, and thinking may or may not be to write your own case study. Although this is something that your professional education courses might require or that you might find personally valuable to do, it is more likely that you will gain the greatest benefit from case study research simply by learning to think carefully and systematically about classroom experience. Your carefully collected field notes, maps, logs, and interviews—taken together—will tell you far more about teaching than you might otherwise have learned. These ways of working will insure that you have a clear role to play in the classrooms you visit and that you can get the most out of what you see, hear, and do there.

One way to organize what you collect is in the form of an "outsider's guide" to the classroom you studied. Try to frame what you have learned in the form of rules and informational tips that an outsider would need both to comprehend what's happening in this classroom and to behave appropriately there. If you can do this, and if you can share it with the teacher and children with whom you have worked, you will have gone a long way toward discovering the ways of seeing, simplifying, and sense-making operating in the classroom. In addition, you'll have learned a lot about your own ways of making sense—of your knowledge about teaching, your values, your biases, and the things you still need to learn.

AFTERTHOUGHTS

As Appendix B illustrates, my thinking has changed somewhat over the past decade. When I teach entering teacher education students, I still use many of the ideas just presented (and, in fact, the essay) in my own teaching (see, e.g., the assignment in Appendix B). But I have added more dimensions to the work—both in the field and in the university classroom. I have, for instance, pushed back the borders of classroom case work so that my students can look within and across sites and, in so doing, begin to situate each within wider social ecologies such as school, community, family, state, and nation. In doing this, students are moved to ask the following kinds of questions about the classroom in its own right and the other systems of meaning in which they are nested:

1. What is happening, specifically, in the social action that takes place in this particular setting?
2. What do these actions mean to the actors involved in them, at the moment the actions take place?
3. How are the happenings organized in patterns of social organization and learned cultural principles for the conduct of everyday life—how, in other words, are people in the immediate setting present to each other as environments for one another's' meaningful actions?
4. How is what is happening in this setting as a whole (i.e., the classroom) related to happenings at other system levels outside and inside the setting (e.g. the building, a child's family, the school system, state, and federal mandates, etc.)?
5. How do the ways everyday life is organized in this setting compare with other ways of organizing social life in a wide range of settings and at other times? (Erickson, Florio, & Buschman, 1980; paraphrased in Erickson, 1986, p. 121 and Florio-Ruane, 1987, p. 187)

In that spirit, I now encourage more cross-talk among my students when they return from their field experiences bearing "data" from different schools, grades, classrooms, neighborhoods, and communities. I ask them to compare classroom life in these diverse contexts. I have also pushed back borders of time so that my students can compare what they see and describe with accounts of schooling in other historical periods and societies. And I am just beginning to encourage them to find ways in their visits to the field to locate learning in students' activities outside the classroom in clubs, sports, churches, and other nonformal learning sites.

Heath (1997) points out that such cross-site analysis is drawn more from ethnology than from ethnography. She recommends it to accompany ethnography, overcoming some of the limits of that method's tendency to freeze social processes in narrative form and generalize inappropriately from setting to setting on the basis of analysis of discrete particulars culled in one time and place. In this light, it is important in doing classroom observation to realize that this classroom is not the basis for generalizations about all classrooms; that this particular learning experience is not the only one in the youngsters' everyday lives; and that what we observe of youngsters in this particular context is limited by the social context and relationships within which it occurs.

In addition to pushing back the borders, I also have framed and focused classroom participant observation a bit. In my teaching these days, students still engage in fieldwork, but they are asked to view what they see, hear, and ask in the classroom through the lens of literacy. Of course, other teacher-educators might choose other lenses, but because a great deal of my own research pertains to the teaching and learning of oral and written language—and because literacy is such a foundational part of elementary school teaching, I choose this lens. As the assignment in Appendix B illustrates, this focus gives beginning teachers a curricular frame for viewing learners, teachers, and their activities—both inside the classroom and outside it.

Finally, I have come to realize that to do a good job of observing and coming to know others, one must begin and end by looking inward (Ferdman, 1991). This is particularly important if one is to discover the biases inherent in one's point of view. Even as we work to recruit a more diverse cohort, teaching and teacher education remain fields dominated by Euro-American, native English-speaking, middle-class (and at the elementary level, female) people (The New York Times, 1995). Because they are the so-called "mainstream," most teachers are isolated from the diversity of experience held by their pupils. It is difficult in such circumstances to be self-conscious about the norms and beliefs one holds about learning, teaching, and communication. Lacking such self-consciousness, it is exceedingly difficult to realize that these norms and beliefs may be neither universal nor inherently superior to other ways of behaving and making sense—for other people and in other contexts.

For "White teachers," both novice and experienced, it is essential confront as part of professional development the idea that our social, racial, linguistic, and gender identities limit our ability to serve an increasingly diverse pupil population (Paley, 1995). And for those entering the profession from diverse social, cultural, and linguistic backgrounds, examining and articulating entering beliefs and perspectives brings new voices into the ongoing professional conversation about how to educate the next generation (Galindo & Olguin, 1996). Paraphrasing one of her colleagues, Vivian Paley (1995) describes the necessary interplay of perspectives in our conversations about teaching this way: "I know its not easy. We need practice in asking people sensitive questions about themselves and, in turn, being asked about ourselves. But after awhile, we are not afraid to ask" (pp. 136–137). To help beginners practice asking sensitive questions (and listen sensitively to answers), I have chosen in recent years to focus their interviewing of experienced teachers around the theme of home and school—and the ways teachers think about family involvement.

I have also paid more attention to writing up the case studies. Crafting the brief "outsiders' guide" turns out to be a very challenging task. Just as experienced field workers in anthropology must struggle with voice, stance, theme, and genre as they write about themselves and others, so must the beginning teachers. As they work to craft texts in which readers will be able to see, hear, and sense a bit of the richness and complexity of what they have observed in the classroom, the beginning teachers discover that description, inference, and evaluation are interwoven. As teacher researchers such as Paley (1986b) and Y. Goodman (1978) have shown us, this insight—and the management of its implications—is essential not only to good research but to good teaching. It is used daily by thoughtful teachers to frame, check, and revise both their assessment of student learning and pedagogical next steps.

The essay I wrote for my students was a beginning—but only that. It should be read and used with several important provisos. First, it is important to acknowledge our expectations and how they bias what we see and how we evaluate it. Second, the opportunity to look comparatively at teaching and learning across diverse settings enables us to learn more than we could be focusing in just a single time or place. Third, we need to resist coming to early and simplistic explanations of what we see and ask more questions—of ourselves and of those whose lives and learning we want to understand. In short, we need to look deeper—into our own lives, into the lives of those in whose classrooms we work, into our society's institutions and history—in order to understand teaching and learning in the classroom.

In this way we will begin to create, not static case studies that simplify, silence, sort, and separate, but stories of teaching and learning in context which illuminate complexity, explore possibility, risk disagreement, and foster conversation about and across diverse perspectives. All of this is a part of teaching and learning to teach—a part accessible to us from our very first days in the field.

APPENDIX A: SAMPLE FIELD NOTES

Example 1: Inappropriate Field Notes
Mixing Observation, Inference, and Value Judgments

Today I watched Mrs. N. teach reading to the low group in a third-grade classroom. After she called the group to the reading table, there was a lot of commotion in the room. The other students did not seem to know what they were supposed to do while Mrs. N. was reading with the low group. They talked loudly and wandered around the room. Mrs. N. had trouble controlling them. She had to stop to reprimand them. Finally, the students who were supposed to be doing seat work settled down.

Meanwhile, at the reading table, the low group (called the "Mustangs") spent a lot of time whispering and hitting one another. It took a long time for Mrs. N. to get them quiet and ready to read. She had them open their books to the table of contents and read the name of the story for today. When she called on one student to read it, he couldn't. A lot of the other students in the group called out the story's name. Mrs. N. had to tell them not to call out. I think the reading group would have gotten off to a better start if Mrs. N. had controlled the students better. The students doing seat work didn't know what they were supposed to do and broke a lot of rules. The students in the Mustangs group fooled around a lot and did not try to read.

Example 2: More Appropriate Field Notes, Where the Observer Attempts to Separate Observation From Inference,
Value Judgment, and Questions

On March 25, 1984, I observed Mrs. N. and her students during the morning. On the calendar at the chalkboard, Mrs. N. had written: "9:15 am—reading and seat work." This activity lasted for 90 minutes. During this time, Mrs. N. called each of three named groups (the "Mustangs," the

This is my first chance to see Mrs. N. teach reading!

Is this a regular part of the school day?

"Tigers," and the "Kangaroos") to the corner of the room where there is a horseshoe-shaped table she calls "the reading table." While the small groups were there with her (for about 30 minutes each), they read from three different books. Other students were sitting at their desks with printed worksheets from the same book as the one they read in their groups.

The groups seem to be ranked by reading level. Are the Mustangs the lowest? How can I be sure? How did Mrs. N. decide to group the students?

This morning I heard a lot of talking and observed a lot of moving around the room after Mrs. N. called the first group, named the Mustangs, to the table. Mrs. N. said to the other students in a loud voice, "How are we supposed to behave during seat work?" One student (I think his name was Billy) replied, "We're supposed to sit quietly and do our work and not interrupt you at the Reading Table." "That's right!" Mrs. N. replied. After about 5 minutes, students at their seats were quiet. Most were writing on their printed sheets; a few were looking at other students or gazing around the room.

Is "seat work" a time familiar to the students? Why don't they seem to be following rules they apparently know? What do students do at this time?

Meanwhile, the five students in the Mustang group went to the reading table. They chose their own seats. They talked to each other about other things besides reading while Mrs. N. was busy with the other students. Several talked about a game they had played yesterday at recess. Others talked about a new fishing pole Bob had gotten for his birthday. Ken laughed and pushed Jenny. At this point, Mrs. N. sat down in her seat at the U-shaped table and told the students, "I want you quiet and ready to read. Bob,

It seems surprising that the transition in to reading for the Mustangs is taking such a long time. Why didn't the teacher talk with the kids a little bit at first to help them get ready to read? It appears that the rules for reading involve students taking turns to read aloud after Mrs. N. calls on them.

turn to the table of contents." With that, the students turned to the front of the book. Bob did not read the story's title when asked to. Three of the other students said the name out loud. It was "A Surprise for Pat." Mrs. N. said, "that's right, but do we call out? The students said, "No" softly. Then some of them leaned back and bent their heads so that they were looking down and away from Mrs. N.

APPENDIX B: SAMPLE COURSE ASSIGNMENT

As we begin the second part of our course, you will visit the classroom. This is an exciting and important part of your professional education, and I am pleased to be able to help you think about what you are seeing and learning in the field. I have developed this hand-out to guide you through the field assignments from our course. This hand-out will also be given to your cooperating teacher so that he or she knows what you have been asked to do in the classroom. These assignments are not too time consuming, and you should have ample time and flexibility to take your lead about how to participate in the classroom from you cooperating teacher. When we meet weekly in class, however, we will take time to talk, think, and write about the field experience, exchange experiences with classmates in other field settings, and link the field experiences to our course readings and other learning activities. Please do not hesitate to contact me if you have questions about the field assignments during the coming weeks.

Before you go into the field, read "Creating Your Own Case Studies" in the packet. On Monday, 2/5, come to class prepared to discuss it. Also bring you spiral notebook to class that day.

Classroom Visit 1: Classroom Map

As is described in the reading, make several maps of the classroom in your notebook. The first map should be done as soon as you enter the classroom. The last map should be done at the end of your first day in the field. In the interim, you may want to make several maps during the visit as people's use of space changes with their activities. If possible, you might also ask one or several youngsters to map the classroom for a glimpse of the space from their point of view. Although you are only required to map the classroom on your first visit, you may elect to make maps throughout your field experience noting how they change as your understanding of space and its meaning in this classroom grows.

In class, we will analyze the maps and compare and contrast use of space (a) as you learned about it during your visit, (b) as it changes from activity to activity, and (c) as it occurs in other classrooms. The maps you make should identify room areas, resources within the spaces, as well as paths participants take from one part of the room to another in conducting their activities. Keep careful notes of this assignment in your field notebook.

Classroom Visit 2: Classroom Log

As described in the case studies article, logging the class activities during your visit this week will shed light on time and how it is used in the class-room. It will also highlight transitions between activities and the management strategies used by teacher and pupils. Logging can have several parts. If the teacher has written a daily schedule of activities on the chalk board, you should copy that one as an example of the "official" record. (Some teachers may also have such a log written down as part of their daily plans, and you might ask to see it.) We all know, however, that official schedules have, in reality, some degree of flexibility.

This week, keep careful track of the clock and the class members' activi-ties, making your own log of activities—what happens when? In class we will look at the logs both to discover the difference between formal plans for time allocation and the actual unfolding of classroom activities and also for in-sight into the priorities of the class for the time in which you visited—On what do they spend time and how does this give insight into their curricu-lum? How does time allocation compare across different classrooms, differ-ent grade levels, and so on? As with the mapping assignment, you may wish to do more logging on subsequent visits to the classroom. Keep careful notes of this assignment in your field notebook.

Classroom Visit 3: The Literate Environment
and Textbooks

This week look closely at the classroom as a literate environment (see our textbook, *Literacy Instruction for Today*, by Au, Mason, and Scheu, 1995). Take note of the kinds of encounters with print, drawing, talk about text, and other literacy-related activities (e.g., dramatic play; storytelling) it pro-vides. Even if you are not visiting during language arts or reading time, examine the kinds of textual materials the pupils use for learning. If possible, ask to borrow a few examples for sharing at our class meeting this week. The teacher will be a resource in helping you to discover the classroom as a literate environment. Keep careful record of the textual materials you observe in your field notebook.

Classroom Visit 4: Observing Youngsters' Learning in the Classroom

To prepare for this visit, read "Kidwatching" by Yetta Goodman (1978) and "On Listening to What the Children Say" by Vivian Paley (1986b). These articles, along with the "Case Studies" article should help you observe youngsters in learning activities. This week, focus on learners. Try to see the classroom and its activities from their perspective(s). You may select to follow one youngster closely as he or she goes about the afternoon of your visit, or you may choose to focus on several youngsters, following each closely for a period of time. The youngster(s) you follow should be referred to in your notes with a pseudonym to protect their privacy.

Negotiate with your teacher how best to observe youngsters. He or she may suggest that you ask a child if you can spend some time with her or him watching as he or she works and plays. Or she or he may suggest that you unobtrusively observe youngsters. In either case, your objective is to see and hear how youngsters engage with teacher and peers in learning activities. Some of these activities may be academic in nature; others may involve recess or special areas. Some may involve whole-group interaction, others may occur in peer groups or individually. Make sketchy notes of your observations while in the classroom, and fill out the details as soon after leaving the classroom as you can. Keep a careful record of all your notes in your field notebook. In class we will compare pupil observations, especially noting differences and similarities across age/grade levels and diverse classroom activities.

Classroom Visit 5: Teacher Planning, Instruction, Assessment

Building on your growing observation and note-taking skills, this week you will turn your attention to observing the teacher. As in last week's assignment, you are trying to get a sense of classroom activity from an insider's point of view—this time, the teacher's. Again you may briefly negotiate this assignment with him or her. She or he may prefer that you remain unobtrusive and make observations as you go about routine classroom activities with her or him and the class. Or she or he may prefer to "think-aloud" about some of those activities, describing what she or he did and why as part of the observation.

As in the prior assignment, refer to your teacher with a pseudonym to protect her or his privacy. Your goal, as above, is to learn about, not to judge, the insider's perspective. Take sketchy notes while on the site, and fill them out in more detail as soon as possible after the visit. In class, we will discuss different approaches teachers take to such important responsibilities as planning, instruction, classroom management, and assessment as they are available in your observations.

Classroom Visits 6 and 7: Interviewing the Teacher about the School–Community Context and Parent Involvement

To help prepare for this assignment, read the International Reading Association's booklet on *Parents and Literacy* (Morrow, Neuman, Paratore, & Harrison, 1995). Sometime in the last 2 weeks of your field experience, make arrangements to interview your teacher for about 20 minutes. Please attempt to make this interview minimally inconvenient for your teacher. In class, we will plan and practice the interviews, refining the questions and sharpening your listening skills.

The focus of the interview will be your teacher's perspective on the challenge of making connections between home and school, the classroom and the community. This is a very important part of teaching in modern times, and it is likely that your teacher will have much to say about the challenge of fostering communication with the other adults (both family- and community-based) who play central roles in the child's development. The interviews will give you a chance to learn more about the teacher's thinking on this topic and to access information about teaching not easily available by other means (e.g., direct observation). We will draw on these interviews as we meet to discuss issues of parent and community involvement in class. As always, these interviews will use pseudonyms and be kept confidential. Record the interview questions and notes in your field notebooks.

Post Field Experience Writing Assignment

I will read and write comments on your field notes during the field experience period. After you leave the field, you will be asked to use the field notes to develop an "outsider's guide" to your classroom. This will be a written narrative (five to eight pages, typed; additional pages for maps, logs, or other examples) describing the classroom you visited to an outsider who is unfamiliar with it. The guide will synthesize both your assigned observations and the knowledge you have gained from visiting the classroom generally to offer a richly descriptive account of what life is like in the classroom—from the perspectives of teacher and pupils. It should touch on topics we have studied including use of time and space, materials, pupil activities, and teacher thought and action as well as the ways in which the classroom is connected to families and the wider community.

ACKNOWLEDGMENTS

This work was sponsored in part by the Institute for Research on Teaching, College of Education, Michigan State University. The IRT was funded primarily by the Program for Teaching and Instruction of the National Institute of Education, U.S. Department of Education (Contract No. 400-81-0014). The opinions expressed in this chapter do not necessarily reflect the position, policy, or endorsement of the U.S. Department of Education. A version of this chapter was originally published in the *Teacher Education Quarterly* special issue on "Case Methodology in the Study and Practice of Teacher Education" (Winter 1990), volume 17, number 1, pp. 29–41.

Commentary on "Revisiting Fieldwork in Preservice Teachers' Learning: Creating Your Own Case Studies"

Helen Featherstone
Michigan State University

When the youngest of my three daughters was 3 years old, I read *Mollie is Three*, Vivian Paley's narrative study of the 3-year-olds in her nursery school class. The conversations that Paley described astonished me. I was used to the fact that 3-year-olds say things differently, but I realized as I read that I usually assumed that their sometimes odd declarations simply reflected their inexperience with language. Paley's stories focused my attention on new possibilities: how often, I wondered, had I absentmindedly read commonplace meanings into enigmatic questions and comments, assuming that the 3-year-old saw the world more or less as I did? Paley made no such assumptions, she just continued the conversation, always investigating meaning. The ensuing conversations were often startling.

Reading Paley, I realized how much I had probably missed. Convinced that I understood "what's going on here," I had too rarely asked the questions that would have shown me that I had leapt to unwarranted conclusions. In the weeks that followed I listened far more carefully to what my 3-year-old *actually said.* And when her observations surprised me, I tried to follow where they led me. I learned that some of my daughter's ideas about reality were considerably more interesting than I had realized.

I was reminded of what I had learned from Paley about my own limitations as an observer when I read Florio-Ruane's chapter, "Revisiting Fieldwork in Preservice Teachers' Learning" and reflected on her insight that seeing requires effort, discipline, and some conviction that there is something to see: "It is easy in these first days and weeks in the field to have one's entering (and usually unexamined) biases reinforced rather than challenged or expanded." If college students are simply sent off with directions to "observe," they will miss much of what goes on in the elementary classrooms—just as I missed much that was interesting in my conversations with 3-year-olds. The prospective teachers' familiarity with this setting can blunt their curiosity and stifle their questions. Not realizing that there is anything to see or hear, they miss major landmarks of the social landscape, fascinating clues to the meanings and intentions of teachers and children (as Thoreau says, "Objects are concealed from our view not so much because they are out of the course of our visual ray as because there is no intention of the mind and eye towards them. ... The scarlet oak must, in a sense, be in your eye when you go forth"). With her tasks, suggestions, questions, and examples, Florio-Ruane helps her students to locate a few of these landmarks, to peek below the familiar surfaces of school life.

The skills and dispositions of the ethnographer—the ones that the prospective teachers in Florio-Ruane's classes begin to learn as they tackle her assignments with the gentle guidance of "Creating Your Own Case Studies"—are as useful to the experienced teacher as they are to the inexperienced student of teaching. Just as the teachers-to-be must find ways to recognize their own biases and look for the assumptions hidden inside of commonplace exchanges, veterans must regularly examine many of their own assumptions in order to teach all of their students well. Unless they make a conscious effort to dig beneath the surface of classroom life they are unlikely to learn how children with different backgrounds and strengths are making sense of school life, and they will be likely to misread some children's behavior. But the pace, volume, and complexity of the work of teaching can prevent even the expert teacher from stopping to observe, and hence from seeing children and their work fully. The work of the Philadelphia Teacher Learning Cooperative (TLC)[1] suggests ways in which disciplined observation and conversation can help teachers to connect with children who worry them and to reframe problems that appear intractable.

---

[1]The Philadelphia TLC is a group of public and private school teachers with about 30 active members. It is independent of university or school system affiliation and has met weekly since 1979.

Since the 1970s, teachers in the TLC have used descriptive processes created by Pat Carini and colleagues at the Prospect Center in North Bennington, Vermont, to investigate the experience of their students and the complex realities of their classrooms (see Featherstone, 1998; Kanevsky, 1993). These descriptive processes—the most commonly used is the descriptive review of the child—guide the observations a teacher makes in preparation for the review; they also frame the conversation within the TLC—the review itself. After a teacher schedules a review for one of her students, she observes the child as often as she can, making notes that will enable her to describe the child as fully as possible to the other TLC teachers. Five headings organize both her observations and her description: physical presence and gesture; disposition; connections with other children and adults; preferences and abiding interests; modes of thinking and learning. The rich rounded description that emerges helps the teacher to see any problematic behavior or learning problem in the broader context of the child's life at school. In addition to shaping the teacher's observations, the descriptive review format guides the TLC's conversation, ensuring that the teacher will present her description uninterrupted, that an experienced chairperson will then summarizes themes he or she heard in this presentation, and that other group members will ask clarifying questions before anyone offers interpretations or suggestions. Like "Creating Your Own Case Studies," the descriptive review process helps participants to step outside the action of the classroom to observe and reflect. Teachers report that the discipline of these processes enables them to see particular children in new ways, to locate strengths and interests that had been less visible before the review, and, in consequence, to teach their students better.

For prospective teachers, learning to teach is about learning what to *do*. They want to know how to manage a busy classroom, how to teach mathematics in ways that will ensure both understanding and success on standardized tests, how to plan literature units that engage both the nonreader and the book worm. Although admitting the importance of doing, we teacher-educators often try to focus more of our students' attention on learning to listen carefully to children and to raise questions. "Constructing Your Own Case Studies" provides students with valuable tools for seeing, hearing, and asking questions. The challenge for teacher-educators is to help their students to connect observing and reflecting with doing—to convince them, as the teachers in the TLC are convinced, that what they learn by stepping back and watching a child or a group, by describing what they see to others, by attending to questions that direct further wondering and looking helps them to teach more effectively. Learning more about how to forge this link is critical—it defines an agenda for research and for practice—because our students will carry these tools and dispositions forward into their professional work only if they see and feel their usefulness—if the looking and questioning they do as teacher candidates allow them to connect with children in more productive ways, to teach a successful lesson, or, in general, to develop into the kind of teacher on whom nothing is lost.

PART IV

FUTURE DIRECTIONS

11

Reflections
on Methodologies
and Future Research

Mary Anna Lundeberg
University of Wisconsin—River Falls
Barbara B. Levin
University of North Carolina at Greensboro
Helen L. Harrington
University of Michigan

Case-based instruction has been around at least since 1927, when the first casebook was published (Kagan, 1993). Experienced teacher-educators have long used classroom cases, such as vignettes and simulations, as instructional tools. "Good teachers have always used stories in their teaching," writes Noddings (1997), as she describes how biographical, historical, personal, humorous, literary and psychology-of-learning stories enliven instruction (p. 19). In teacher education, problem-based cases allow students to vicariously explore the complex world of teaching and encourage them to think about how they might resolve future dilemmas. It is only recently that cases have been used to study teachers' thinking, to facilitate growth in preservice teachers' thinking (Kagan, 1993), and to inform our practice as teacher-educators (e.g., Moje, Remillard, Southerland, & Wade, chap. 4, this volume).

In this final chapter, we look across all of the previous chapters and the work reviewed in them to examine patterns in the research. We reflect on some of the questions, methods, and procedures used to study what is learned from cases; we highlight the strengths and weaknesses in studies of the ways in which case-based pedagogy is enacted; and we suggest directions for future research based on those reflections.

WHAT CAN BE LEARNED FROM STUDYING CASES AND CASE METHODS?

Which Research Questions Are of Value?

Zeichner points out, in his commentary on chapter 4, that researchers need to move beyond merely deciding whether case discussions are a valuable pedagogical tool, and instead should try to understand what students actually learn and, in turn, how what they learn affects our pedagogical goals. Most of the research questions reflected in this book can be classified as "teacher research"; that is, educators studying what students in their own classes are learning. In addition to Moje et al., several other researchers in this book ask variations of this basic teacher research question: "What do my students actually learn from case pedagogy?" (e.g., Barnett & Tyson, chap. 3; Harrington, chap. 2; Lundeberg, chap. 1; Richardson & Kile, chap. 6). Another basic teacher research question central to chapters in the second section of our book asks, "How does the way I structure my classroom environment matter?" (e.g., Levin, chap. 5; Richardson & Kile, chap. 6). Finally, the chapters in the third section of our book pose questions about the nature of cases (Carter, chap. 8), what kind of research needs to be included in the cases we use with our students (Nieto, chap. 9), or in the kinds of cases we ask our students to write (Florio-Ruane, chap. 10).

Some educators may wonder why we have neglected to include research attempting to answer the question: "Do students learn more from the case method as compared to X?" In the early stages of many innovations, researchers typically compare the innovation with what has traditionally been done. For example, in one of her foundations courses, Kleinfeld (1991a) randomly assigned students to one of two discussion sections to answer the question: "Do students learn more from case discussions than from discussions of readings?" Kleinfeld then compared students' written analysis of a case by classifying their problem solving skills as "well-developed, moderate, or low" (p. 22), and found (not surprisingly) that preservice teachers assigned to sections of case discussion analyzed cases better than those without this experience. A major design flaw in studies such as these is instructor bias. Moreover, is it fair to compare the case-analysis skills of students with experience analyzing cases to those with no experience?

Kleinfeld (1991a) also attempted to answer a question that several researchers (e.g., Merseth, 1996; Sykes & Bird, 1992) believe is an essential question regarding the use of cases: "Does case use influence teacher or student performance in classrooms?" To answer this question, Kleinfeld tried to determine if case use influenced preservice teachers' abilities to analyze actual classroom experiences. She compared differences in students' analysis of 2 days of observations in a classroom by asking them to answer a set of structured questions. Unfortunately, because almost half of the students in one section failed to respond to these structured questions, her results were inconclusive.

Although we agree with the importance of this question, we would argue that horse race studies (e.g., is case pedagogy better than X ... in preparing future teachers for the classroom) are not fruitful areas of research, because this kind of research question is unanswerable. We believe it is impossible to make a valid comparison of the long-term classroom effects of preservice teachers who have analyzed cases with those who have not had this experience. There are simply too many confounding variables that are unaccounted for and cannot be adequately controlled. Furthermore, we think cases are one of many pedagogical tools that may be used in a teacher education program and it is likely the combination of several pedagogies, rather than a single one, that will contribute to teacher development. However, research revealing what students actually learn as compared to what we assume they learn, and research informing how we structure the learning environments to include cases seem to be productive questions, if we acknowledge and counter the problem of researcher bias as thoroughly as possible.

What Is the Value in and Problem With Researcher Bias?

Engaging in action research has earned credibility in recent years as a valuable method of examining teachers' practices, especially in Great Britain, Australia, and the United States (Elliott, 1989, 1991). Action research is systematic inquiry by teachers, usually focused on promoting changes in practice (Henson, 1996). In the past decade, action research (in particular, an outgrowth of action research called teacher research) has been advocated for both preservice and inservice teacher education as a means of improving teaching and learning through critical reflection on problems in practice (Gore & Zeichner, 1991). A major value of teacher action research is the insider knowledge used to frame questions and to analyze data (Cochran-Smith & Lytle, 1993). A disadvantage, seen particularly by traditional empirical researchers, involves the lack of objectivity when researchers study their own classrooms.

Answering questions regarding what students learn or how we might improve the practice of case pedagogy involves careful reflection on the biases we bring into our research. Although we are never able to fully acknowledge all of our inherent biases, we can attempt, at a minimum, to explicate our pedagogical goals for using cases and to question conventional assumptions about case pedagogy. Discussions and collaborative research with colleagues, especially colleagues whose views conflict with our own, or colleagues who bring a different disciplinary perspective, enable us to make the implicit more explicit. Some of the major contributions of Moje et al.'s chapter in terms of methodology include the variety of perspectives brought by a team of colleagues, the clarity with which they acknowledge their goals and biases and the honesty with which they reflect on their unanticipated results. As Moje et al., remind us, good qualitative researchers seek out disconfirming evidence. Disagreements about pedagogy may also stimulate reflection on goals and balance in interpreting results, as Lundeberg and Scheurman (1997) discovered. Their initial controversy led them to design a pair of studies to determine whether students learn more when the "story" comes first (in the form of a narrative case) and "theory" comes second (in the form of classroom instruction), or when theoretical instruction comes first and case analysis comes second. Finally, as J. Shulman alludes to in her commentary, cross-institutional studies, such as the symposium presented at AERA (Levin, 1997), may also shed light on pedagogical goals and assumptions taken for granted when these are explicitly acknowledged.

The problem of bias in teacher research may also be countered by the collection and triangulation of multiple data. Barnett and Tyson (chap. 3) triangulate many different forms of data over an extensive period of time, an important consideration if we are to look for developmental changes in teacher thinking. In examining the facilitator's role in leading case discussions, Barnett and Tyson focus on fostering autonomy among the inservice teachers involved in their case discussions. Using multiple data from interviews, videotapes, personal reflections, and interviews of teachers, they found that facilitators listened carefully to the teachers' language and experiences, slowed the discussion at times by writing on the board, and pushed participants for clarity. As in the Moje et al. chapter, a methodological strength in Barnett and Tyson's work is the use of multiple measures and the triangulation of data.

A unique feature of the methodology used by Lundeberg and her colleagues (1994, 1996, 1997) involves asking preservice teachers to examine their own written case analysis from the beginning and end of the semester using an analytic framework to guide their metacognitive reflection. This methodology allows for the voices of preservice students to be included along with that of teacher-researchers. Collecting preservice teachers' qualitative perspectives on their growth in learning by asking them to closely examine their own work has more validity than some self report measures (e.g., surveys), but also poses potential problems. To what extent do students tell us what they think we want to hear? Students are not blind to which written case analysis they wrote at the beginning and end of the semester, so there may be the implicit assumption that we would expect their analyses to improve. Finally, preservice teachers may be able to identify a number of theories, perspectives, or issues in pre- and post-case analyses, but asking them to qualitatively assess changes is much more complex. Is more necessarily better? If preservice teachers can identify twice as many issues in a case or consider additional perspectives in a later analysis as compared to an initial analysis, have they improved their flexibility in thinking? Furthermore, what change really counts? As Einstein said, "Not all that counts can be counted and not all that is counted, really counts." This is an area where Harrington's (chap. 2) qualitative assessment of the complexity of students' performance of thought contributes to our thinking about how we might assess change.

What Changes Are of Value and How Do We Measure This Change?

Many researchers seem to be assuming that case pedagogy develops preservice teachers' critical reflection, problem-solving ability, or produces changes in their beliefs, dispositions, or attitudes. However, though we may be using some of the same terms, we have yet to develop shared meanings. Factors that inhibit shared meanings include the central role that classroom contexts play in our work, the multiple disciplines that frame our research, and the varied research paradigms we draw from. However, we can strive to be clearer in defining our terms. For example, what does perspective-taking mean? How will we think we know if preservice teachers have developed it? Or what would we need to understand if the goal of using a particular case is to help preservice teachers connect theory and practice? Furthermore, how do we know that the "changes" we are assessing reflect true growth in beliefs and understandings as opposed to training students to say, think, or act in certain ways—which is a question raised by Richardson and Kile (chap. 6) and Griffin (commentary on chap. 6). Finally, as Lundeberg notes (chap. 1), because beliefs may often be implicit, changes in beliefs are complicated to assess through an outsider's (researcher's) lens. Is it enough for researchers to identify what they interpret as changes in beliefs, or do such changes in beliefs need to be acknowledged by the learner as a new conception? When preservice teachers adopt new perspectives and change their beliefs, do they *value* becoming more open-minded? Do preservice teachers become more likely to consider ethical questions and the moral consequences of decisions when analyzing a case? Do they understand that teaching is contextual, that their knowledge is limited and that pedagogical knowledge about teaching changes over time?

This imperative to clarify terms extends to a call for additional explicitness in how we analyze and present data as well. For example, how do we define viewing a case from a student perspective? What is a teacher perspective? Although definitions may be given, rarely are coding schemes shared that include examples that emerge from the data. What distinguishes a student from a teacher perspective? If we are to advance knowledge in this area, we need to better understand one another's interpretations of data. This is particularly true with research in an area such as case pedagogy, given the variety of research paradigms and disciplines of the researchers. Teacher-educators' goals and methods of using cases vary considerably and need to be made explicit in their research, regardless of methods selected.

A number of researchers measure preservice teachers' development by examining changes in their writing (e.g., Harrington, chap. 2; Lundeberg, chap. 1; Richardson & Kile, chap. 6). Harrington's contribution includes a qualitative assessment of the complexity of students' thinking. In contrast to studies that examine changes by analyzing discussion patterns and participants' language (e.g., Moje et al., chap. 4; Levin, chap. 5; Barnett & Tyson, chap. 3), examining writing allows teacher researchers to compare all participant's development, rather than just those who speak during a discussion. A primary limitation in studies measuring change through written case analyses is that this methodology favors students skilled in writing. Furthermore, most written case analysis uses the individual as the point of analysis; even though Lundeberg and Scheurman's (1997) later work used pairs of students writing case analyses, this methodology still fails to capture the contributions of complex, rich group case discussion.

How Might We Study the Ways Case-Based Pedagogy Is Enacted?

In addition to examining what students learn in our own classes, and how this influences how and what we teach, other fruitful questions worth exploring are questions regarding the pedagogy of cases. Knowing more about variations in facilitation, discussion, or using written case analyses—how cases are enacted—affect changes in preservice teachers may advance the field. Both qualitative and quantitative methods have been used to analyze data in several of the studies on case pedagogy, though very few of the studies reported in this book used traditional quasi-experimental designs with random assignment of participants to discussion groups or to a facilitator. In fact, most of the studies reported are descriptive and naturalistic, with a focus on understanding what is learned from case discussion and case writing. Often this was accomplished through inductive methods for identifying the sources of understanding of written comments collected before and after a case discussion. Sometimes these were then tallied and converted to proportional frequencies.

Other researchers also used various methods of discourse analysis, ranging from inductive methods designed to elicit themes and patterns from the data to more deductive analyses, where certain questions or categories were preselected for analysis. A variety of methods of analysis seems legitimate, although collecting and triangulating data from a variety of sources is very important if results are to show any validity or reliability. For example, researchers studying the role of the facilitator could report analysis of data collected from transcriptions of case discussions, from written work completed by case participants, and from specific tasks undertaken to capture how the role of the facilitator influences the outcomes of the case discussions.

What Are Some Strengths and Weaknesses of Research on Case Pedagogy?

Facilitating Cases. A variety of data collection procedures can be used to study the role of the case facilitator, but nearly all the studies reported to date have used videotape or audiotape to capture interactions and utterances during case discussions. These tapes are then transcribed to provide a running record of the participants' discourse, which provides a textual version that is available for close analysis. However, few people describe their procedures in detail, so information is missing from reports of this research indicating, for example, where the video camera or tape recorder are placed, if there was more than one tape recorder or video camera, and who operated it. Furthermore, researchers usually neglect to report the decision rules or procedures used for transcription, the level of detail transcribed, whether or not nonverbal data were included in the transcription, and what transcription rules or conventions were followed to indicate things such as latching, overlapping speech, pauses, or prosodic cues.

Without making manuscripts unduly long, the procedural elements used during data collection and transcription would be very useful to share in future research in this field, which is so dependent on transcribed data. Although there isn't one best method for transcription, there is also no single method of discourse analysis (Cazden, 1986). Nevertheless, making this information explicit will help other researchers polish their own data collection and data analysis procedures for studying case methods.

The problems involved in interpreting the discourse during case discussions can never be solved entirely, because we can never completely understand all the shared knowledge of the participants or know all the background knowledge, beliefs, and experiences they bring to the discussion. However, we can approximate good interpretations by employing multiple strategies for analysis and looking for convergence. Research reports that include these details through microanalysis and comprehensive discourse analysis of both the participants' and the facilitator's role in case discussions would be very valuable in future research in this field.

Writing About Case Discussions. In addition to taping and transcribing the case discussions, a variety of procedures for collecting written data from the participants have been employed in studies of case-based pedagogy. Participants are often asked to write before and after the discussion, and in some research studies they are also asked to write again at a later time. The timing of data collection procedures, while perhaps dictated by expediency and limited by the practical constraints of semester or class schedules, are important to consider as they provide evidence of either immediate reactions or perhaps more lasting reactions, initial impressions of the case or perhaps deeper impressions, suggesting whether or not any transfer of new knowledge or changed beliefs has occurred as a result of the case discussion. These details should also be reported and manipulated in future research on case methods.

The kinds of writing solicited before and after case discussions range from open-ended to more focused questions and from a small number (2 or 3 questions) to a larger number (6 to 10 questions). Some researchers have also used surveys or questionnaires as part of their data collection procedures, often to collect information on attitudes toward case discussions. As one example, Morine-Dershimer (1991, 1993, 1996b) asks the participants in her studies to limit their writing to responses on a 3x5 card, asking for just two open-ended responses: "Write on the front of the card a key idea of this lesson" and "Write on the back two things you heard anybody else say during the lesson" (Morine-Dershimer, 1993, p. 6). In contrast to the majority of researchers writing chapters, who analyzed their own case discussions, Morine-Dershimer (1996a) compared the discussion styles of three teaching assistants (one secondary education, two elementary education) who led four discussions. Two of these four discussions were with small classes (21–23 students) and two were with larger classes (33–35 students). At the end of class, students were asked to report on what they remembered from the discussion using the aforementioned instructions and index cards (Morine-Dershimer, 1996a). Based on frequency counts of the types of written comments, Morine-Dershimer (1996a) concluded that less structure (i.e., more small-group processing) produced more learning in students. The large group discussions were characterized as teacher-directed, primarily because the teaching assistants (TAs) did not vary much from the teaching notes, whereas in the classes involving small group discussions, the TAs allowed students more autonomy (Morine-Dershimer, 1996a). However, the teacher-directedness of the large group discussions may have resulted more from the inexperience of the TAs than the size of the classes. Indeed, facilitating a case well requires extensive experience (Merseth, 1991a; Silverman & Welty, 1996; Wasserman, 1994). Another concern about this research involves restricting student responses (what if students do not remember exactly two things from case discussion, but only one, or five?).

Quasi-experimental research can yield important insights into ways to structure the learning environment with cases if we are careful not to confound variables and if we examine the magnitude of differences. Research that involves collecting quantitative data and calculating mean differences should include the use of statistics to enable us to analyze whether differences are significant or due to chance. Too many researchers report vague categories—for example, claiming that preservice teachers learn more or show deeper understandings—without clarifying their meanings. Limitations of space in journals or volumes such as ours constrains researchers' clarity, too, however.

In addition, whether studying case discussions, the role of the facilitator, or case writing, future studies should include a description of pre-case discussion procedures undertaken by the facilitator, which describe the degree of planning and indicate the facilitator's purposes and goals for selecting a particular case; the context for using the case including the course content, level of students, time in the semester, and the like; the kinds of questions asked; what the opening question is going to be; anticipated topics for discussion; estimated time allotted for these topics; and how the case discussion is to be structured (e.g., in small groups, whole-class, teacher-directed all or part of the time, use of the board or not). Although this level of detail is not usually revealed in the procedures section of reports on research on cases, such detail is essential to others who want to understand case-based pedagogy. At a minimum, all future research reports on cases and case-based teaching should provide the reader with information about and analysis of the facilitator's overall purpose(s) and goals(s) for using case methods and for selecting a particular case.

Teacher-educators may also make certain assumptions about how to prepare for case discussions. Unfortunately, we know little about whether, for instance, students think more critically with or without guiding questions to answer. What should be included in the notes students bring to a case discussion? Should they answer questions from their casebook or does more critical reflection occur if they use a heuristic for every case they analyze? What are the costs and benefits of reading additional information about the case (e.g., journal articles, textbook chapters, expert commentaries). Research on questions like these regarding the use of cases in teacher education classrooms will make an important contribution to the field.

What Questions Have Not Been Studied?

Finally, one area of research omitted from the literature on case pedagogy involves understanding more about how the form and content of a case influences students' learning. For example, do students engage in more critical reflection if the case includes explicit ethical dilemmas rather than pedagogical problems? What effect do dilemma-based cases have on students' understanding as compared to exemplar cases? Should case commentaries be included or do these constrain students' discussion? How complex must a case be if it is to be analyzed more than once in a semester? How do "authentic" cases, which include actual descriptions of students (e.g., Nieto's cases), compare to cases that are fictional in construction with regard to influencing preservice teachers' attitudes and knowledge? Understanding more about which kinds of cases are better suited to which goals and purposes of instructors is a neglected and needed area of research.

In his commentary, Griffin notes that the research on cases is fragmented and fragile. After reviewing the literature, we agree and disagree. Research on case pedagogy reflects the field of education, comprised of a variety of disciplines, and hence a variety of methodologies and perspectives. We view this as a strength and encourage researchers to continue to explore who learns what from cases and how using a variety of methodologies. Regardless of the methodological challenges we face in studying whether (and how) cases help our students discover understanding about teaching and learning, intuitive knowledge is not enough. Gathering empirical evidence to systematically test our assumptions will enable us to reassess our goals and to improve our practice.

References

Aaronsohn, E., Carter, C. J., & Howell, M. (1995). Preparing monocultural teachers for a multicultural world: Attitudes toward inner-city schools. *Equity and Excellence in Education, 28*(1), 5–9.

Anderson, L. M., Blumenfeld, P., Pintrich, P. R., Clark, C. M., Marx, R. W., & Peterson, P. (1995). Educational psychology for teachers: Reforming our courses, rethinking our roles. *Educational Psychologist, 30*(3), 143–158.

Anderson, J. R., Reder, L. M., & Simon, H. A. (1996). Situated learning and education. *Educational Researcher, 25*(4), 5–11.

Apple, M. W. (1990). *Ideology and curriculum* (2nd edition). New York: Routledge.

Appleton, N. (1983). *Cultural pluralism in education: Theoretical foundations.* New York: Longman.

Ashton, P. T. (Ed.). (1991). Case methods [special issue]. *Journal of Teacher Education, 42*(4).

Au, K. H., Mason, J. M., & Scheu, J. A. (1995). *Literacy instruction for today.* New York: HarperCollins.

Bakhtin, M. (1981). *The dialogic imagination.* Austin: University of Texas Press.

Ball, D. (1997). Developing mathematics reform: What don't we know about teacher learning—but would make good working hypotheses? In S. N. Friel & G. W. Bright (Eds.), *Reflecting on our work* (pp. 77–111). Lanham, MD: University Press of America.

Barnett, C. (1991). Building a case-based curriculum to enhance the pedagogical content knowledge of mathematics teachers. *Journal of Teacher Education, 42*(4), 263–272.

Barnett, C. (1998). Mathematics teaching cases as a catalyst for informed strategic inquiry. *Teaching and Teacher Education, 14*(1), 81–93.

Barnett, C., Goldenstein, D., & Jackson, B. (1994). *Dilemmas of teaching: Math cases to promote inquiry, discussion, and reflection.* Portsmouth, NH: Heinemann.

Barnett, C., & Ramirez, A. (1996). Fostering critical analysis and reflection through mathematics case discussion. In J. A. Colbert, P. Desberg, & K. Trimbel (Eds.), *The case for education: Contemporary approaches for using case methods* (pp. 1–14). Needham Heights, MA: Allyn & Bacon.

Barnett, C., & Sather, S. (1992, April). *Using case discussions to promote changes in beliefs among mathematics teachers.* Paper presented at American Educational Research Association, San Francisco.

Barnett, C. S., & Tyson, P. A. (1993a, April). *Case methods and teacher change: Shifting authority to build autonomy.* Paper presented at the annual meeting of the American Educational Research Association, Atlanta.

Barnett, C., & Tyson, P. (1993b, April). *Mathematics teaching cases as a catalyst for informed strategic inquiry.* Paper presented at American Educational Research Association, Atlanta.

Barnett, C. S., & Tyson, P. A. (1994, April). *Facilitating mathematics case discussions while preserving shared authority.* Paper presented at the annual meeting of the American Educational Research Association, New Orleans.

Barnett, C., & Tyson, P. (in press). Mathematics teaching cases as a catalyst for informed strategic inquiry. *Teaching and Teacher Education.*

Bateson, M. C. (1989). *Composing a life.* New York: Atlantic Monthly Press.

Belenky, M. F., Clinchy, B. M., Goldberger, N. R., & Tarule, J. M. (1986). *Women's ways of knowing: The development of self, voice, and mind.* New York: Basic Books.

Ben-Peretz, M. (1990). *The teacher-curriculum encounter: Freeing teachers from the tyranny of texts* (SUNY Series in Curriculum Issues and Inquiries). Buffalo: State University of New York Press.

Berliner, D. (1992). Telling the stories of educational psychology. *Educational Psychologist, 27,* 143–161.

Black, A., & Ammon, P. (1992). A developmental-constructivist approach to teacher education. *Journal of Teacher Education, 43,* 323–335.

Bliss, T., & Mazur, J. (1996). Creating a shared culture through cases and technology: The faceless landscape of reform. In J. Colbert, K. Trimble, & P. Desberg (Eds.), *The case for education: Contemporary approaches for using case methods* (pp. 15–18). Boston: Allyn & Bacon.

Bourdieu, P. (1977). *Outline of theory and practice.* Cambridge: Cambridge University Press.

Bowers, C. (1988). *The cultural dimensions of educational computing: Understanding the non-neutrality of technology.* New York: Teachers College Press.

Bransford, J. D., Sherwood, R. D., Haselbring, T. S., Kinzer, C. K., & Williams, S. M. (1990). Anchored instruction: Why we need it and how technology can help. In D. Nix & R. Spiro (Eds.), *Advances in computer-video technology* (pp. 115–141). Hillsdale, NJ: Lawrence Erlbaum Associates.

Bransford, J. D., & Vye, N. J. (1989). A perspective on cognitive research and its implications for instruction. In L. B. Resnick & L. E. Klopfer (Eds.), *Toward the thinking curriculum: Current cognitive research* (pp. 173–205). Reston, VA: Association for Supervision and Curriculum Development.

Brookfield, S. (1991). *Developing critical thinkers: Challenging adults to explore alternative ways of thinking and acting.* San Francisco: Jossey-Bass.

Brookhart, S. M., & Freeman, D. J. (1992). Characteristics of entering teacher candidates. *Review of Educational Research, (62),* 37–60.

Brown, J. S., Collins, A., & Duguid, P. (1989). Situated cognition and the culture of learning. *Educational Researcher, 18*(1), 32–41.

Bruner, J. S. (1985). Narrative and paradigmatic modes of thought. In E. Eisner (Ed.), *Learning and teaching the ways of knowing* (Eighty-fourth yearbook of the National Society for the Study of Education, Part 2, pp. 97–115). Chicago: University of Chicago Press.

Bruner, J. S. (1986). *Actual minds, possible worlds.* Cambridge: Harvard University Press.

Bruner, J. S. (1990). *Acts of meaning.* Cambridge: Harvard University Press.

Bruner, J. S. (1996). *The culture of education.* Cambridge: Harvard University Press.

Bullough, R. V., Goldstein, S. L., & Holt, L. (1984). *Human interests in the curriculum: Teaching and learning in a technological society.* New York: Teachers College Press.

Burbules, N. (1993). *Dialogue in teaching: Theory in practice.* New York: Teachers College Press.

Butt, R. L., & Raymond, D. (1989). Studying the nature and development of teachers' knowledge using collaborative autobiography. *International Journal of Educational Research, 13,* 403–419.

Calderhead, J., & Gates, P. (Eds.). (1993). *Conceptualizing reflection in teacher development* (pp. 1–10). London: Falmer.

Carnegie Forum on Education and the Economy. (1986). *A nation prepared: Teachers for the 21st century* (Report of the Task Force on Teaching as a Profession). Hyattsville, MD: Author.

Carter, K. (1989). Using cases to frame mentor-novice conversations about teaching. *Theory Into Practice, 27*(3), 214–22.

Carter, K. (1990). Teachers' knowledge and learning to teach. In W. R. Houston (Ed.), *Handbook of research on teacher education* (pp. 291–266). New York: Macmillan.

Carter, K. (1992). Toward a cognitive conception of classroom management: A case of teacher comprehension. In J. Shulman (Ed.), *Case methods in teacher education* (pp. 111–130). New York: Teachers College Press.

Carter, K. (1993). The place of story in research on teaching and teacher education. *Educational Researcher, 22*(1), 5–12.

Carter, K. (1994). The case against thinking like a teacher. *Journal of Teacher Education, 45*(3), 236–238.

Carter, K., & Doyle, W. (1996). Personal narrative and life history in learning to teach. In J. Sikula (Ed.), *Handbook of research on teacher education* (2nd ed., pp. 120–142). New York: Macmillan.

Carter, K., & Unklesbay, R. (1989). Cases in teaching and law. *Journal of Curriculum Studies, 21,* 527–536.

Cazden, C. (1986). Classroom discourse. In M. C. Wittrock (Ed.), *Handbook of research on teaching* (3rd ed.). New York: Macmillan.

Chambliss, M. J., & Garner, R. (1996). Do adults change their minds after reading persuasive text? *Written Communication, 13*(3), 291–313.

Christensen, C. R. (1991a). Premises and practices of discussion teaching. In C. R. Christensen, D. A. Garvin, & A. Sweet (Eds.), *Education for judgment: The artistry of discussion leadership* (pp. 15–34). Boston: Harvard Business School Press.

Christensen, C. R. (1991b). The discussion teacher in action. In C. R. Christensen, D. A. Garvin, & A. Sweet (Eds.), *Education for judgment: The artistry of discussion leadership* (pp. 153–172). Boston: Harvard Business School Press.

Christensen, C. R., Garvin, D. A., & Sweet, A. (Eds.). (1991). *Education for judgment: The artistry of discussion leadership.* Boston: Harvard Business School Press.

Christensen, C. R., & Hansen, A. J. (1987). *The art of discussion leadership*. Boston: Harvard Business School Press.

Clandinin, D. J. (1989). Developing rhythm in teaching: The narrative study of a beginning teacher's personal practical knowledge of classrooms. *Curriculum Inquiry, 19,* 121–141

Cochran-Smith, M., & Lytle, S. (1993). *Inside/outside: Teacher research and knowledge.* New York: Teachers College Press.

Cognition and Technology Group at Vanderbilt. (1990). Anchored instruction and its relationship to situated cognition. *Educational Researcher, 19*(6), 2–10.

Colbert, J., Trimble, K., & Desberg, P. (1996). *The case for education: Contemporary approaches to using case methods.* Needham Heights, MA: Allyn & Bacon.

Connelly, F. M., & Clandinin, D. J. (1985). Personal practical knowledge and the modes of knowing: Relevance for teaching and learning. In E. Eisner (Ed.), *Learning and teaching the ways of knowing* (Eighty-fourth Yearbook of the National Society for the Study of Education, part 2, pp. 174–198). Chicago: University of Chicago Press.

Connelly, F. M., & Clandinin, D. J. (1990). Stories of experience and narrative inquiry. *Educational Researcher, 19*(5), 2–14.

Crow, G., Levine, L., & Nager, N. (1990). No more business as usual: Career changers who become teachers. *American Journal of Education, 98*(3), 197–223.

Dana, N. F., & Floyd, D. M. (1994). *When teacher educators collaboratively reflect on their practices: A case study on teaching cases.* (ERIC Document Reproduction Service No. ED369768).

Darling Hammond, L. (1998). *Doing what matters most: Investing in quality teaching.* Washington, DC: National Commission on Teaching and America's Future.

Demastes-Southerland, S., Good, R., & Peebles, P. (1996). Patterns of conceptual change in evolution. *Journal of Research in Science Teaching, 33,* 407–431.

Desberg, P., & Fisher, F. (1996). Using technology in case methodology. In J. Colbert, K. Trimble, & P. Desberg (Eds.) *The case for education: Contemporary approaches for using case methods* (pp. 39–55). Boston: Allyn & Bacon.

DeVries, R. (1997). Piaget's social theory. *Educational Researcher, 26*(2), 4–17.

Dewey, J. (1910/1991). *How we think.* Amherst, NY: Prometheus Books. [Originally published: Lexington, MA: D.C. Heath, 1910.]

Dewey, J. (1933). *How we think: A restatement of the relation of reflective thinking to the educative process.* Boston: D.C. Heath.

Dickeman, M. (1973). Teaching cultural pluralism. In J. A. Banks (Ed.), *Teaching ethnic studies: Concepts and strategies* (pp. 4–25). Washington, DC: National Council for the Social Studies.

Dilworth, M. E. (Eds.). (1992). *Diversity in teacher education.* San Francisco: Jossey-Bass.

Doyle, W. (1990). Case methods in the education of teachers. *Teacher Education Quarterly, 17,* 7–15.

Doyle, W. (1997). Heard any really good stories lately? A critique of the critics of narrative in educational research. *Teaching and Teacher Education, 13*(1), 93–99.

Driscoll, M., & Lord, B. (1990). Professionals in a changing profession. In T. J. Cooney & C. R. Hirsch (Eds.), *Teaching and learning in the 1990s* (pp. 237–245). Reston, VA: National Council of Teachers of Mathematics.

Elbaz, F. (1991). Research on teachers' knowledge: The evolution of a discourse. *Journal of Curriculum Studies, 23,* 1–19.

Elbow, P. (1973). *Writing without teachers.* New York: Oxford University Press.

Elbow, P. (1986). *Embracing contraries: Explorations in learning and teaching* (pp. 69–98). Oxford: University of Oxford Press.

Elliott, J. (1989). Educational theory and the professional learning of teachers: An overview. *Cambridge Journal of Education, 19*(1), 81–101.

Elliott, J. (1990). Teachers as researchers: Implications for Supervisions and for teacher education. *Teaching & Teacher Education, 6*(1), 1–26.

Elliott, J. (1991). *Action research for educational change.* Milton Keynes: Open University Press.

Enright, R. D., Lapsley, D. K., & Levy, V. M. (1983). Moral education strategies. In M. Pressley & J. R. Levin (Eds.), *Cognitive strategy research: Educational applications* (pp. 43–83). New York: Springer-Verlag.

Erickson, F. (1986). Qualitative methods in research on teaching. In M. C. Wittrock (Ed.), *Handbook of research on teaching* (3rd ed., pp. 119–161). New York: Macmillan.

Erickson, F., Florio, S., & Buschman, J. (1980). *Fieldwork in educational research.* (Occasional Paper No. 36). East Lansing: Michigan State University Institute for Research on Teaching.

Ewell, P. T. (1991). To capture the ineffable: New forms of assessment in higher education. In G. Grant (Ed.), *Review of research in education* (Vol. 17, pp. 75–126). Washington, DC: AERA.

Featherstone, H. (1998). Studying children: The Philadelphia Teachers' Learning Cooperative. In Allen (Ed.), *Assessing student learning: From grading to understanding.* New York: Teachers College Press.

Feiman-Nemser, S., & Buchmann, M. (1983). Pitfalls of experience in teacher education. In P. Tamir, A. Hofstein, & M. Ben-Peretz (Eds.), *Preservice and inservice education of science teachers.* Philadelphia: Balaban International Science Services.

Feiman-Nemser, S., & Buchmann, M. (1986). The first year of teacher preparation: Transition to pedagogical thinking? *Journal of Curriculum Studies, 18*(3), 239–256.

Feiman-Nemser, S. & Featherstone, H. (Eds.). (1992). *Exploring teaching: Reinventing an introductory course.* New York: Teachers College Press.

Female and far from diverse: Report from National Center for Educational Statistics, U.S. Department of Education. (1995, January 7). *The New York Times,* p. 22.

Fenstermacher, G. D. (1994). The knower and the known: The nature of knowledge in research on teaching. In L. Darling-Hammond (Ed.), *Review of research in education* (Vol. 20, pp. 1–24). Washington, DC: American Educational Research Association.

Ferdman, B. (1991). Becoming literate in a multiethnic society. In E. Jennings & A. Purves (Eds.). *Literate systems and individual lives: Perspectives on literacy and schooling* (pp. 95–115). Albany: SUNY Press.

Florio-Ruane, S. (1987). Sociolinguistics for educational researchers. *American Educational Research Journal, 24*(2), 185–197.

Florio-Ruane, S., & Clark, C. M. (1990). Using case studies to enrich field experiences. *Teacher Education Quarterly, 17* (17–28).

Floyd, D. M. (1992). *Coming to know: Prospective elementary teachers' thinking and the case study approach.* Unpublished doctoral dissertation, Florida State University.

Fordham, S., & Ogbu, J. U. (1986). Black students' school success: Coping with the "burden of acting White." *Urban Review, 18*(3), 176–206.

Funkenstein, A. (1993). The incomprehensible catastrophe: Memory and narrative. In R. Josselson & A. Lieblich (Eds.), *The narrative study of lives* (Vol. 1, pp. 21–29). Newbury Park, CA: Sage.

Galindo, R., & Olguin, M. (1996). Reclaiming bilingual educators' cultural resources: An autobiographical approach. *Urban Education, 31*(1), 29–56.

Garner, R., & Alexander, P. A. (1989). Metacognition: Answered and unanswered questions. *Educational Psychologist, 24*(2), 143–158.

Garvin, D. A. (1991). A delicate balance: Ethical dilemmas and the discussion process. In C. R. Christensen, D. A. Garvin, & A. Sweet, (Eds.), *Education for judgment: The artistry of discussion leadership* (pp. 287–303). Boston: Harvard Business School Press.

Gee, J. P., Michaels, S., & O'Connor, M. C. (1992). Discourse analysis. In M. D. LeCompte, W. L. Millroy, & J. Preissle (Eds.), *The handbook of qualitative research in education* (pp. 227–291). San Diego: Academic Press.

Geer, B. (1969). First days in the field: A chronicle of research in progress. In G. Mc-Call & J. L. Simmons, (Eds.), *Issues in participant observation* (pp. 144–162). Reading, MA: Addison Wesley.

Gess-Newsome, J., & Southerland, S. A. (in press). Teaching science for all. In S. E. Wade (Ed.), *Preparing teachers for inclusive education: Case pedagogies and curricula for teacher educators*. Mahwah, NJ: Lawrence Erlbaum Associates.

Goodlad, J. (1990). *Teachers for our nation's schools*. San Francisco: Jossey-Bass.

Goldman, E., & Barron, L. (1990). Using Hypermedia to improve the preparation of elementary teachers. *Journal of Teacher Education, 41*(3), 21–31.

Good, T. L., & Brophy, J. E. (1994). *Educational psychology* (5th ed.). New York: Longman.

Goodman, Y. (1978). Kidwatching: Observing children in the classroom. In A. Jaggar, & M. T. Smith-Burke (Eds.), *Observing the language learner* (pp. 9–18). Urbana, IL: National Council of Teachers of English and Newark, DE: International Reading Association.

Gordon, A., Heller, J. I., & Lee, G. (1994). *Mathematics case methods: External longitudinal evaluation*. Unpublished manuscript.

Gordon, A., Heller, J. I., & Lee, G. (1995). Literacy teachers learning a new literacy: A study of the use of electronic mail in a reading instruction class. *Reading Research and Instruction, 34*, 222–238.

Gore, J. M. (1993). *The struggle for pedagogies: Critical and feminist discourses as regimes of truth*. New York: Routledge.

Gore, J. M. (1993). *The struggle for pedagogies: Critical and feminist discourses as regimes of truth*. New York: Routledge.

Gore, J. M., & Zeichner, K. M. (1991). Action research and reflective teaching in preservice teacher education: A case study from the United States. *Teaching and Teacher Education, 7*, 119–136.

Green. D., Grant, G., & Shulman, J. (Eds.). (1990). Case methodology in the study and practice of teacher education [special issue]. *Teacher Education Quarterly, 17*(1).

Greenwood, G. E. (1996) Using the case method to translate theory into practice. In J. A. Colbert, P. Desberg, & K. Trimbel (Eds.), *The case for education: Contemporary approaches for using case methods* (pp. 57–78). Needham Heights, MA: Allyn & Bacon.

Greenwood, G. E., & Parkay, F. W. (1989). *Case studies for teacher decision making*. New York: Random House.

Grossman, P. (1992). Why models matter: An alternate view on professional growth in teaching. *Review of Educational Research, 62*, 171–179.

Grumet, M. R. (1988). *Bitter milk: Women and teaching*. Amherst: University of Massachusetts Press.

Gudmundsdottir, S. (1991). Story-maker a story-teller: Narrative structures in curriculum. *Journal of Curriculum Studies, 23,* 207–218.

Haertel, E. H. (1991). New forms of teacher assessment. In G. Grant (Ed.), *Review of Research in Education* (Vol. 17, pp. 3–30). Washington, DC: AERA.

Haroutunian-Gordon, S. (1991). *Turning the soul: Teaching through conversation in the high school.* Chicago: University of Chicago Press.

Harrington, H. (1994a). Teaching and knowing. *Journal of Teacher Education, 45*(3), 190–198.

Harrington, H. (1994b). Perspective on cases. *Qualitative Studies in Education, 7*(2), 117–133.

Harrington, H. (1995). Fostering reasoned decisions: Case-based pedagogy and the professional development of teachers. *Teaching and Teacher Education, 11*(3), 203–241.

Harrington, H. (1996, April). *Learning from cases.* Paper presented at the annual meeting of the American Educational Research Association, New York.

Harrington, H., & Garrison, J. (1992). Cases as shared inquiry: A dialogical model of teachers preparation. *American Educational Research Journal 29*(4), 715–735.

Harrington, H. L., & Hodson, L. (1993, April). *Cases and teacher development.* Paper presented at the annual meeting of the American Educational Research Association, Atlanta, GA.

Harrington, H. L., & Quinn-Leering, K. (in press). Considering teaching's consequences. *Teaching and Teacher Education, 13*(1).

Harrington, H. L., Quinn-Leering, K., & Hodson, L. (1996). Written case analyses and critical reflection. *Teaching and Teacher Education, 12,* 25–37.

Heath, S. B. (March 7, 1997). *Ethnography, ethnology, and case studies: Framing and valuing distinctions.* Keynote address presented at the Eighteenth Annual Ethnography and Education Research Forum, University of Pennsylvania, Philadelphia.

Heller, J. (1995, April). *Entering a hall of mirrors: On building tools to assess the impact of case-based methods of teacher development.* Paper presented at the annual meeting of the American Education Research Association, San Francisco.

Henson, K. T. (1996). Teachers as researchers. In J. Sikula, T. Buttery, & E. Guyton (Eds.), *Handbook of research on teacher education* (2nd ed., pp. 53–64). New York: Macmillan.

Herbert, J,. & McNergney, R. (1995). *Guide to foundations in action videocases: Teaching and learning in multicultural settings* (pp. 3–6). Boston: Allyn & Bacon.

Hodgkinson, H. (1991). Reform versus reality. *Phi Delta Kappan, 73*(1), 9–16.

Hoffman, D. M. (1996). Culture and self in multicultural education: Reflections on discourse, text, and practice. *American Educational Research Journal, 33*(3), 545–569.

Holmes Group. (1986). *Tomorrow's teachers: A report of the Holmes Group.* East Lansing, MI: Author.

Holmes Group. (1990). *Tomorrow's schools: Principles for the design of professional development schools.* East Lansing: Michigan States University College of Education.

Holmes Group. (1995). *Tomorrow's school of education: A report of the Holmes Group.* East Lansing, MI: Author.

Holt-Reynolds, D. (1992). Personal history-based beliefs as relevant prior knowledge in course work. *American Educational Research Journal, 29,* 325–349.

Hunt, P. (1951). The case method of instruction. *Harvard Educational Review, 21*(3), 175–192.

Hutchinson, N. (1996, April). *Student-authored courses and critical reflection in a course on inclusive education*. Paper presented at the annual meeting of the American Educational Research Association, New York.

Ingvarson, L. C., & Merrin, M. (1997) Building professional community and supporting teachers as learners: the potential of case methods. In L. Logan & J. Sacks (Eds.), *Meeting the challenge of primary schooling for the 1990s*. London: Routledge.

Irvine, J. J. (Ed.). (1997). *Critical knowledge for diverse teachers and learners*. Washington, DC: American Association of Colleges for Teacher Education.

Iser, W. (1996). Why literature matters. In R. Ahrens & L. Volkmann (Eds.), *Why literature matters: Theories and functions in literature* (pp. 13–22). Heidelberg: Universitatsverlag C. Winter.

Jablon, J. R., Ashley, L. A., Marsden, D. B., Meisels, S. J., & Dichtemiller, M. L. (1994). *Omnibus guidelines*. Ann Arbor, MI: Rebus Planning.

Jacobson, M. J., & Spiro, R. J. (1995). Hypertext learning environments, cognitive flexibility, and the transfer of complex knowledge: An empirical study. *Journal of Educational Computing Research, 12*, 301–333).

James, F. (1991). *An analysis of case-based instruction in teacher preparation*. Unpublished doctoral dissertation, University of Virginia, Charlottesville.

Kagan, D. M. (1992). Professional growth among preservice and beginning teachers. *Review of Educational Research, 62*, 129–169.

Kagan, D. M. (1993). Contexts for the use of classroom cases. *American Educational Research Journal, 30*(4), 703–723.

Kanevsky, R. (1993). Descriptive review of a child: A way of knowing about teaching and learning. In M. Smith & S. Lytle (Eds.), *Inside/outside: Teacher research and knowledge*. New York: Teachers College Press.

Katz, M. B. (1975). *Class, bureaucracy, and the schools: The illusion of educational change in America*. New York: Praeger.

Katz, L., Raths, J., Mohanty, C., Kurachi, A., & Irving, J. (1981). Follow-up studies: Are they worth the trouble? *Journal of Teacher Education, 32*, 18–24.

Kennedy, M. M. (1988). Inexact sciences. Professional development and the education of expertise. In E. Z. Rothkopf (Ed.), *Review of research in education* (Vol. 14, pp. 133–167). Washington, DC: American Educational Research Association.

Kent, T., Herbert, J., & McNergney, R. (1995). Telecommunications in teacher education: Reflections on the first Virtual Team Competition. *Journal of Information Technology for Teacher Education, 4*(2), 137–148.

Kessen, W. (1993). Rumble or revolution: A commentary. In R. Wozniak & K. Fischer (Eds.), *Development in context: Acting and thinking in specific environments* (pp. 269–279). New Jersey: Lawrence Erlbaum Associates.

King, P., Wood, P., & Mines, R. (1990). Critical thinking among college students. *Review of Higher Education, 13*, 167–186.

Kinzer, D. K., & Risko, V. J. (1995). Improving teacher education through dissemination of videodisc-based case procedures and influencing the teaching of future college professionals. In S. P. McGraw & S. L. Newkird (Eds.), *Fund for the improvement of secondary education: Program book and project descriptions* (pp. 181–182). Washington, DC: Fund for the Improvement of Postsecondary Education.

Kleinfeld, J. (1988a). *Learning to think like a teacher: The study of cases*. Fairbanks: University of Alaska, Fairbanks, Center for Cross-Cultural Studies. (ERIC document 308–039).

Kleinfeld, J. (Ed.). (1988b). *Teaching cases in cross cultural education*. Fairbanks, AK: College of Education.

Kleinfeld, J. (1990). The special virtues of case method in preparing teachers or minority schools. *Teacher Education Quarterly, 17*, 43–52.

Kleinfeld, J. (1991a, April). *Changes in problem solving abilities of students taught through case methods*. Paper presented at the American Educational Research Association, Chicago.

Kleinfeld, J. (1991b, April). *Preparing teachers for multicultural classrooms: A case study in rural Alaska*. Paper presented at the annual meeting of the American Educational Research Association, Chicago.

Kleinfeld, J. (1992a, April). *Can cases carry pedagogical content knowledge? Yes, but we've got signs of a "Matthew Effect."* Paper presented at the annual meeting of the American Educational Research Association, San Francisco.

Kleinfeld, J. (1992b). Learning to think like a teacher: The study of cases. In J. Shulman (Ed.), *Case method in teacher education*. New York: Teachers College Press.

Knowles, J. G., & Holt-Reynolds, D. (1991). Shaping pedagogies through personal histories in preservice teacher education. *Teachers College Record, 93*, 87–113.

Kowalski, T. J., Weaver, R. A., & Henson, K. T. (1990). *Case studies on teaching*. New York: Longman.

Kuhn, D. (1992). Thinking as argument. *Harvard Educational Review, 62*, 155–178.

Laframboise, K. L., & Griffith, P. L. (1997). Using literature cases to examine diversity issues with preservice teachers. *Teaching and Teacher Education, 13*, 369–382.

Lampert, M., & Ball, D. (1998). *Investigating teaching: New pedagogies and new technologies for teacher education*. New York: Teachers College Press.

Lanier, J. (1986). Research on teacher education. In M. Wittrock (Ed.), *Handbook of research on teaching* (3rd ed., pp. 527–569). New York: Macmillan.

Lave, J. (1988). *Cognition in practice*. New York: Cambridge University Press.

Lave, J. (1996). Teaching, as learning, in practice. *Mind, Culture, and Activity, 3*, 149–165.

Lemke, J. L. (1990). *Talking science: Language, learning, and values*. Norwood, NJ: Ablex.

Levin, B. B. (1993). *Using the case methods in teacher education: The role of discussion and experience in teachers' thinking about cases*. Unpublished doctoral dissertation, University of California, Berkeley.

Levin, B. B. (1995). Using the case method in teacher education: The role of discussion and experience in teachers' thinking about cases. *Teaching and Teacher Education, 10*(2), 1–14.

Levin, B. B. (1996, April) *Learning from discussion: A comparison of computer-based versus face-to-face case discussions*. Paper presented at the annual meeting of the American Educational Research Association, New York.

Levin, B. B. (1997, April). *The influence of context in case-based teaching: Personal dilemmas, moral issues, or real changes in teachers' thinking?* Symposium paper presented at the annual meeting of the American Educational Research Association, Chicago.

Levin, B. B., & Irwin, D. M. (1995, April). *Discussion-based teaching as faculty development: What teachers learn from case discussions versus discussions based on teacher-generated issues*. Paper presented at the annual meeting of the American Educational Research Association, San Francisco.

Levin, B. B., & Powell, R. R. (1997, April). *The influence of context in case-based teaching: A collaborative inquiry into preservice teachers' cultured thinking*. Symposium paper presented at the annual meeting of the American Educational Research Association, Chicago.

Lincoln, E., & Guba, E. (1985). *Naturalistic inquiry*. Newbury, CA: Sage.

Lipman, M. (1991). *Thinking in education*. New York: Cambridge University Press.

Lipman, M. (1996). *Natasha: Vygotskian dialogues*. New York: Teachers College Press.

Liston, D., & Zeichner, K. (1991). *Teacher education and the social conditions of schooling*. New York: Routledge.

Little, J. (1990). The persistence of privacy: autonomy and initiatives in teachers' professional relations. *Teachers College Record, 91*(4), 509–536.

Little, J. (1993). Teachers' professional development in a climate of educational reform. *Educational Evaluation and Policy Analysis, 15*(2), 129–152.

Lortie, D. (1975). *Schoolteacher: A sociological study*. Chicago: University of Chicago Press.

Lundeberg, M. A. (1985). *Studying understanding in legal case analysis*. Unpublished doctoral dissertation, University of Minnesota, Minneapolis.

Lundeberg, M. A. (1987). Metacognitive aspects of reading comprehension: Studying understanding in legal case analysis. *Reading Research Quarterly, 22*, 407–432.

Lundeberg, M. A. (1993a). Case discussions in educational psychology. In V. Wolf (Ed.) *Improving the climate of the college classroom* (pp. 159–164). Madison, WI: University of Wisconsin System Office of Equal Opportunity Programs and Policy Studies.

Lundeberg, M. A. (1993b). *Gender differences in case analysis*. Paper presented at the annual meeting of the American Educational Research Association, Atlanta, GA.

Lundeberg, M. A. (1995, April). *Contexts for socially mediated learning*. (Part of a TEP/SIG symposium: Teaching educational psychology for constructivist learning; Geoffrey Scheurman, Organizer; Greg Marchant, Nancy Knapp & Tom Rocklin, Participants; Richard Mayer, Discussant.) Paper presented at American Educational Research Association, San Francisco.

Lundeberg, M. A. (1997). *Please sit and listen: Structure in case discussions*. Paper presented at the annual meeting of the American Educational Research Association, Chicago.

Lundeberg, M. A., & Fawver, J. E. (1993, April). *Cognitive growth in case analysis*. Paper presented at American Educational Research Association, Atlanta, GA.

Lundeberg, M. A., & Fawver, J. E. (1994). Thinking like a teacher: Encouraging cognitive growth in case analysis. *Journal of Teacher Education, 45*, 289–297.

Lundeberg, M. A., Matthews, D., & Scheurman, G. (1996, April). *Looking twice means seeing more: How knowledge affects case analysis*. Paper presented at the Annual Meeting of the American Educational Research Association, New York.

Lundeberg, M. A., & Scheurman, G. (1997). Looking twice means seeing more: Developing pedagogical knowledge through case analysis. *Teaching and Teacher Education, 13*(8), 783–797.

Marlow, M., Stevens, E., & Taylor, L. (1997, April). *Cultured thinking and case-based teacher education: Understanding postbaccalaureate preservice teachers' thinking about the effects of standardized testing in Colorado*. Paper presented at the annual meeting of the American Educational Research Association, Chicago.

Masoner, M. (1988). *An audit of the case study method*. New York: Praeger.

McAninch, A. R. (1993). *Teacher thinking and the case method: Theory and future directions*. New York: Teachers College Press.

McNair, M. P. (Ed.). (1954). *The case method at the Harvard Business School*. New York: McGraw-Hill.

McNergney, R., & Herbert, J. (1995). *Foundations of education: The challenge of professional practice*. New York: Allyn & Bacon.

Merriam, S. B. (1988). *Case study research in education*. San Francisco: Jossey-Bass.

Merseth, K. K. (1981). *The case method in training educators*. Cambridge, MA: Harvard Graduate School of Education Doctoral Qualifying Paper.

Merseth, K. K. (1990a). *Beginning teachers and computer networks: A new form of induction support*. East Lansing, MI: National Center for Research on Teacher Education.

Merseth, K. K. (1990b). Case studies and teacher education. *Teacher Educational Quarterly, 17*(1), 53–62.

Merseth, K. K. (1991a). *The case for cases in teacher education*. Washington, DC: American Association of Colleges for Teacher Education.

Merseth, K. K. (1991b). The early history of case-based instruction: Insight for teacher education today. *Journal of Teacher Education, 42*(4), 243–249.

Merseth, K. K. (1992). Case for decision making in teacher education. In J. H. Shulman (Ed.), *Case methods in teacher education* (pp. 50–62). New York: Teachers' College Press.

Merseth, K. (1996). Cases and the case method in teacher education. In J. Sikula (Ed.), *Handbook of Research on Teacher Education* (pp. 722–746). New York: Simon & Schuster/Macmillan.

Merseth, K. K., & Lacey, C. A. (1993). Weaving stronger fabric: The pedagogical promise of hypermedia and case methods in teacher education.*Teaching and Teacher Education, 9*(3), 283–299.

Metz, K. E. (1991). Development of explanation: Incremental and fundamental change in children's physics knowledge. *Journal of Research in Science Teaching, 28*, 785–797.

Mezirow, J. (1991). *The transformative dimensions of adult learning*. San Francisco: Jossey-Bass.

Miller, B., & Kantrov, I. (1998). *A guide to facilitating cases in education*. Portsmouth, NH: Heinemann.

Mitchell, W. J. T. (Ed.). (1981). *On narrative*. Chicago: University of Chicago Press.

Moje, E. B. (in press). Cases of inclusion in a content literacy methods course. In S. E. Wade (Ed.), *Preparing teachers for inclusive education: Case pedagogies and curricula for teacher educators*. Mahwah, NJ: Lawrence Erlbaum Associates.

Moje, E. B., & Wade, S. E. (1996, April). *What case discussions reveal about teacher thinking*. Paper presented at American Educational Research Association, New York.

Moje, E. B., & Wade, S. E. (1997). What case discussions reveal about teacher thinking. *Teaching and Teacher Education, 13*(7), 691–712.

Morine-Dershimer, G. (1991). Learning to think like a teacher. *Journal of Teaching and Teacher Education, 7*, 159–68.

Morine-Dershimer, G. (1993, April). *What's in a case—and what comes out?* Paper presented at the annual meeting of the American Educational Research Association, Atlanta, GA.

Morine-Dershimer, G. (1996a). *What's in a case—and what comes out?* In J. Colbert, K. Trimble, & P. Desberg (Eds.). *The case for education: Contemporary approaches to using case methods* (pp. 100–123). Needham Heights, MA: Allyn & Bacon.

Morine-Dershimer, G. (1996b, April). *Tracking salient comments in case discussions*. Paper presented at the annual meeting of the American Educational Research Association, New York.

Morrow, L., Tracey, D., Baker, K., Brooks, G., Cronin, J., Nelson, E., & Woo, D. (1998). *The nature of effective grade-1 literacy instruction*. Albany, NY: School of Education.

Morrow, L. M., Neuman, S. B., Paratore, J. R., & Harrison, C. (Eds.) (1995). *Parents and literacy*. Newark, DE: International Reading Association.

National Center for Education Statistics. (1993). *Integrated postsecondary education data system*. Washington, DC: United States Department of Education.

National Center for Education Statistics. (1994). *Characteristics of the 100 largest public elementary and secondary school districts in the United States: 1991–1992*. Washington, DC: United States Department of Education.

National Commission on Excellence in Education. (1983). *A Nation at risk: The imperative for educational reform: A report to the nation and the secretary of education. U.S. Department of Education*. Washington, DC: U.S. Government Printing Office.

New Voices. (1988). *New voices: Immigrant students in U.S. public schools*. Boston: National Coalition of Advocates for Students.

Nieto, S. (1996). *Affirming diversity: The sociopolitical context of multicultural education* (2nd ed.). New York: Longman.

Nieto, S. (in press). *The light in their eyes: Student learning, teacher transformation, and multicultural education*. New York: Teachers College Press.

Noddings, N. (1997). The use of stories in teaching. In W. Campbell & K. Smith (Eds.), *New paradigms for college teaching* (pp. 19–35). Edina, MN: Interaction Book Company.

Noordhoff, K., & Kleinfeld, J. (1991, April). *Preparing teachers for multicultural classrooms: A case study in rural Alaska*. Paper presented at the annual meeting of the American Educational Research Association, Chicago.

O'Hare, W. P. (1992). *America's minorities: The demographics of diversity*, 47 (2), Washington, DC: Population Reference Bureau.

Ortiz, F. I. (1988). Hispanic-American children's experiences in classrooms: A comparison between Hispanic and non-Hispanic children. In L. Weis (Ed.), *Class, race and gender in American education* (pp. 63–86). Albany: SUNY Press.

Pajares, M. F. (1992). Teachers' beliefs and educational research: Cleaning up a messy construct. *Journal of Educational Research, 62*(3), 307–332.

Paley, V.(1986a). *Mollie is three: Growing up in school*. Chicago: University of Chicago Press.

Paley, V. (1986b, May). On listening to what the children say. *Harvard Educational Review, 56*(2), 122–131.

Paley, V. (1995). *Kwanzaa and me: A teacher's story*. Cambridge: Harvard University Press.

Patton, M. Q. (1990). *Qualitative evaluation and research methods*. Newbury Park, CA: Sage.

Peterson, P. L., Carpenter, T., & Fennema, E. (1989). Teachers' knowledge of students' knowledge in mathematics problem solving: Correlational and case analysis. *Journal of Educational Psychology, 81*, 558–569.

Poplin, M., & Weeres, J. (1992). *Voices from the inside: A report on schooling from inside the classroom*. Claremont, CA: Institute for Education in Transformation, Claremont Graduate School.

Posner, C. J., Strike, K. A., Hewson, P. W., & Gertzog, W. A. (1982). Accommodation of a scientific conception: Toward a theory of conceptual change. *Science Education, 66*, 211–227.

Powell, R. R., Jarchow, E., Swafford, J., & Smith, W. (1997, April). *"Where do you draw the line?": Local thinking, situativity, and case-based teacher preparation*. Paper presented at American Educational Research Association, Chicago.

Pressley, M., & Afflerbach, P. (1995). *Verbal protocols of reading: The nature of constructively responsive reading*. Hillsdale, NJ: Lawrence Erlbaum Associates.

Pressley, M., El-Dinary, P. B., Gaskins, I., Schuder, T., Bergman, J. L., Almasi, J., & Brown, R. (1992). Beyond direct explanation: Transactional instruction of reading comprehension strategies. *Elementary School Journal, 92,* 511–554.

Pressley, M., with McCormick, C. (1995). *Advanced educational psychology*. New York: HarperCollins.

Pressley, M., Wharton-McDonald, R., Allington, R., Block, C. C., Morrow, L., Tracey, D., Baker, K., Brooks, G., Cronin, J., Nelson, E., & Woo, D. (1998). *The nature of effective grade-1 literacy instruction*. Albany, NY: School of Education.

Pressley, M., Wharton-McDonald, R., Mistretta, J., & Echevarria, M. (1998b). The nature of literacy instruction in ten grade-4/5 classrooms in upstate New York. *Scientific Studies of Reading, 2,* 159–194.

Reffel, J. A., & Bartelheim, F. J. (1993, April). *The influence of case-based instruction on reflection decision making*. Paper presented at the American Educational Research Association Annual Meeting, Atlanta.

Remillard, J. T. (1996, April). *Problems and solutions in a case-based mathematics methods course*. Symposium paper presented at the Annual Meeting of the American Educational Research Association, New York.

Remillard, J. T. (in press). Mathematics for all: Using teaching cases to prepare preservice elementary teachers for inclusive classrooms and pedagogies. In S. E. Wade (Ed.), *Preparing teachers for inclusive education: Case pedagogies and curricula for teacher educators*. Mahwah, NJ: Lawrence Erlbaum Associates.

Resnick, L. B., Levine, J. M., & Teasley, S. D. (Eds.) (1991). *Perspectives on socially shared cognition*. Washington, DC: American Psychological Association.

Richardson, V. (1990). Significant and worthwhile change in teaching practice. *Educational Researcher, 19,* 10–18.

Richardson, V. (1991, April). *The use of cases in considering methods for motivating students*. Paper presented at the annual meeting of the American Educational Research Association, Chicago.

Richardson, V. (Ed.). (1994). *Teacher change and the staff development process: A case in reading instruction*. New York: Teachers College Press.

Richardson, V. (1996). The role of attitudes and beliefs in learning to teach. In J. Sikula (Ed.), *Handbook of research on teacher education* (pp. 102–119). New York: Simon & Schuster/Macmillan.

Richardson, V., & Anders, P. (1994). A theory of change. In V. Richardson (Ed.), *Teacher change and the staff development process: A case in reading instruction* (pp. 199–216). New York: Teachers College Press.

Richardson, V., & Kile, S. (1992, April). *The use of videocases in teacher education*. Paper presented at the annual meeting of the American Educational Research Association, San Francisco.

Richert, A. E. (1991a). Case methods and teacher education: Using cases to teach teacher reflection. In B. R. Tabachnik & K. Zeichner (Eds.), *Issues and practices in inquiry-oriented teacher education* (pp. 130–150). London: Falmer.

Richert, A. E. (1991b). Using teacher cases for reflection and enhanced understanding. In A. Lieberman & L. Miller (Eds.), *Staff development for education in the 90's* (pp. 113–132). New York: Teachers College Press.

Richert, A. E. (1992). Voice and power in teaching and learning to teach. In Linda Valli (Ed.), *Reflective teacher education: Cases and critiques* (pp. 187–197). Albany: SUNY Press.

Risko, V. J., McAllister, D., Peter, J., & Bigeho, F. (1994). Using technology in support of preservice teachers' generative learning. In E. G. Sturtevant & W. M. Linek (Eds.), *Pathways for Literacy: Learners Teach and Teachers Learn*, the Sixteenth Yearbook of the College Reading Association (pp. 155–167). Pittsburgh, KS: College Reading Association.

Risko, V. J., Yount, D., & McAllister, D. (1992). Preparing preservice teachers for remedial instruction: Teaching problem solving and use of content and pedagogical knowledge. In N. Padak, T. V. Rasinski, & J. Logan (Eds.), *Literacy Research and Practice: Foundations for the Year 2000*, the Fourteenth Yearbook of the College Reading Association (pp. 37–50). Pittsburgh, KS: College Reading Association.

Rud, A. (1993). Breaking the egg crate. *Educational Theory, 43*(1), 71–83.

Rumbaut, R. G., & Ima, K. (1987). *The adaptation of Southeast Asian refugee youth: A comparative study.* Final Report. San Diego: Office of Refugee Resettlement.

Sacken, M. (1992, February). *Using cases in the education of educators.* Paper presented at the annual meeting of the American Association of Colleges for Teacher Education. San Antonio, TX.

Sargent, C. G., & Belisle, E. L. (1955). *Educational administration: Cases and concepts.* Boston: Houghton-Mifflin.

Sato, M. (1991, April). *Case method in Japanese teacher education: Traditions and our experiments.* Paper presented at the annual meeting of the American Educational Research Association, San Francisco.

Sato, M. (1992). Japan. In H. B. Leavitt (Ed.), *Issues and problems in teacher education* (pp. 155–168). New York: Greenwood.

Saunders, S, (1992, April). *The nature of preservice teachers' comments in discussing a videotaped teaching case.* Paper presented at the annual meeting of the American Educational Research Association, San Francisco.

Schlagal, B., Trathen, W., & Blanton, W. (1996). Structuring telecommunications to create instructional conversations about student teaching. *Journal of Teacher Education, 47*, 175–183.

Schön, D. A. (1979). Generative metaphors: A perspective on problem-setting in social policy. In A. Ortony (Ed.), *Metaphor and thought* (pp. 254–283). London: Cambridge University Press.

Schön, D. A. (1983). *The reflective practitioner.* New York: Basic Books.

Schön, D. A. (1987). *Educating the reflective practitioner.* San Francisco: Jossey-Bass.

Schrage, M. (1990). *Shared minds: The new technologies of collaboration.* New York: Random House.

Schubert, W., & Ayers., W. (Eds.). (1992). *Teacher lore: Leaning from our own experience.* New York: Longman.

Shulman, J. (1991). Revealing the mysteries of teacher-written cases. *Journal of Teacher Education, 42*(4), 250–262.

Shulman, J. H. (Ed.). (1992a). *Case methods in teacher education.* New York: Teachers College Press.

Shulman, J. H. (1992b). Introduction. In J. Shulman (Ed.), *Case methods in teacher education* (pp. xiii–xvii). New York: Teachers College Press.

Shulman, J. H. (1992c). Revealing the mysteries of teacher-written cases: Opening the black box. *Journal of Teacher Education, 42*(4), 250–262.

Shulman, J. H. (1996). Tender feelings, hidden thoughts: Confronting bias, innocence and racism through case discussions. In J. A. Colbert, P. Desberg, & K. Trimbel (Eds.), *The case for education: Contemporary approaches for using case methods* (pp. 137–158). Needham Heights, MA: Allyn & Bacon.

Shulman, J. H., & Colbert, J. A. (1989). Cases as catalysts for cases: Inducing reflection in teacher education. *Action in Teacher Education, 11*(1), 44–52.

Shulman, J. H., & Colbert, J. A. (Eds.). (1987). *The mentor teacher casebook.* Eugene, OR: ERIC Clearinghouse on Educational Management, Educational Research, and Development; San Francisco: WestEd.

Shulman, J. H., & Colbert, J. A. (Eds.). (1988). *The intern teacher casebook.* Eugene, OR: ERIC Clearinghouse on Educational Management, Educational Research, and Development; San Francisco: WestEd.

Shulman, J. H., Colbert, J. A., Kemoper, D., & Dmytriw, L. (1990). Case writing as a site for collaboration. *Teacher Education Quarterly, 17*(1), 63–78.

Shulman, L. S. (1986a). Paradigms and research programs in the study of teaching: A contemporary perspective. In M. C. Wittrock (Ed.), *Handbook of research on teaching,* (3rd ed., pp. 3–36). New York: MacMillan.

Shulman, L. S. (1986b). Those who understand: Knowledge growth in teaching. *Educational Researcher, 15*(2), 4–14.

Shulman, L. S. (1992). Toward a pedagogy of cases. In J. H. Shulman (Ed.), *Case methods in teacher education* (pp. 1–30). New York: Teachers College Press.

Shulman, L. S. (1996). Just in case: Reflections on learning from experience. In J. A. Colbert, P. Desberg, & K. Trimbel (Eds.), *The case for education: Contemporary approaches for using case methods* (pp. 197–217). Needham Heights, MA: Allyn & Bacon.

Siegel, H. (1988). *Educating reason: Rationality, critical thinking, and education.* New York: Routledge.

Sikula, J. (Ed.). (1996). *Handbook of research on teacher education.* New York: Simon & Schuster/McMillan.

Silverman, R., & Welty, W. M. (1996). Teaching without a net: Using cases in teacher education. In J. A. Colbert, P. Desberg, & K. Trimbel (Eds.), *The case for education: Contemporary approaches for using case methods* (pp. 159–172). Needham Heights, MA: Allyn & Bacon.

Silverman, R., & Welty, W. M. (1997, April). *The influence of local context in case based teaching: An inquiry into preservice teachers' cultured thinking.* Paper presented at American Educational Research Association, Chicago.

Silverman, R., Welty, W. M., & Lyon, S. (1992). *Case studies for teacher problem solving.* New York: McGraw-Hill.

Soloman, J. (1987). Social influences on the construction of pupil's understanding of science. *Studies in Science Education, 14,* 63–82.

Souviney, R., Saferstein, B., & Chambers, E. (1995). InterNet: Network communication and teacher development. *Journal of Computing in Teacher Education, 11,* 5–15.

Spiro, R. J., Coulson, R. L., Feltovich, P. J., & Anderson, D. K. (1988). Cognitive flexibility theory: Advanced knowledge acquisition in ill-structured domains. In *Tenth An-*

nual Conference of the Cognitive Science Society (pp. 375–383). Hillsdale, NJ: Lawrence Erlbaum Associates.

Spiro, R. J., & Jehng, J. (1990). Cognitive flexibility and hypertext: Theory and technology for the nonlinear and multidimensional Traversal of complex subject matter. In D. Nix & R. Spiro (Eds.), Advances in computer-video technology (pp. 163–205). Hillsdale, NJ: Lawrence Erlbaum Associates.

Spiro, R. J., Vispoel, W. P., Schmitz, J. G., Samarapungavan, A., & Boerger, A. E. (1987). Knowledge acquisition for application: Cognitive flexibility and transfer in complex domains. In B. C. Britton (Ed.), Executive control processes (pp. 177–199). Hillsdale, NJ: Lawrence Erlbaum Associates.

Spradley, J. P., & McCurdy, D. W. (1972). The cultural experience: Ethnography in complex society. Chicago: SRA Associates.

Stoiber, K. (1991). The effect of technical and reflective preservice instruction on pedagogical reasoning and problem solving. Journal of Teacher Education, 42, 131–139.

Sykes, G. (1989). Learning to teach with cases. Colloquy, 2(12), 7–13.

Sykes, G., & Bird, T. (1992). Teacher education and the case idea. In G. Grant (Ed.), Review of research in education (Vol. 18, pp. 457–521). Washington, DC: American Educational Research Association.

Tannen, D. (1990). You just don't understand: Men and women in conversation. New York: Morrow.

Thomas, L., Clift, R. T., & Sugimoto, T. (1996). Telecommunications, student teaching, and methods instruction: An exploratory investigation. Journal of Teacher Education, 46, 165–174.

Tochon, F. (1999). Video study groups. Madison, WI: Atwood.

Toulmin, S., Rieke, R., & Janik, A. (1984). An introduction to reasoning (2nd ed.). New York: Macmillan.

United States Bureau of the Census. (1993a). Foreign-born population in the United States. Washington, DC: U.S. Government Printing Office.

United States Bureau of the Census. (1993b). Monthly News. Washington, DC: U.S. Government Printing Office.

University Council for Educational Administration. (1987). Leaders for America's Schools: The Report of the National Commission on Excellence in Educational Administration. Tempe, Arizona: UCEA.

Van Zoest, L. R. (1995, April). The impact of small-group discussion on preservice teachers' observations and reflections. Paper presented at the annual meeting of the American Educational Research Association, San Francisco.

Wade, S. E. (Ed.). (in press). Preparing teachers for inclusive education: Case pedagogies and curricula for teacher educators. Mahwah, NJ: Lawrence Erlbaum Associates.

Wade. S. E., & Moje, E. B. (1997, March). Verbal interaction patterns in case discussions associated with critical/reflective and technical/rational thinking. Paper presented at the Annual Meeting of the American Educational Research Association, Chicago.

Wade, S. E., Niederhauser, D., Cannon, M., Long, T. (1997). Electronic discussions in an issues course: Expanding the boundaries of the classroom. Unpublished manuscript.

Waggoner, D. (1994). Language-minority school-age population now totals 9.9 million. NABE News, 18(1).

Wasserman, S. (1993). Getting down to cases: Learning to teach with case studies. New York: Teachers College Press.

Wasserman, S. (1994a). *Introduction to case method teaching: A guide to the galaxy.* New York: Teachers College Press.

Wasserman, S. (1994b). Using cases to study teaching. *Phi Delta Kappan, 75*(8), 602–611.

Wax, M. (1993). How culture misdirects multiculturalism. *Anthropology and Education Quarterly, 24*(2), 99–115.

Webb, N. M. (1989). Peer interaction and learning in small groups. *International Journal of Educational Research, 13,* 21–39.

Welty, W. M. (1989, July/August). Discussion method teaching. *Change,* 41–49.

Wilcox S., Lanier, P., Schram, P., & Lappan, G. (1992). *Influencing beginning teachers' practice in mathematics education: Confronting constraints of knowledge, beliefs, and context.* East Lansing, MI: National Center for Research on Teacher Education.

Wilson, S. M. (1992). A case concerning content: Using case studies to teach about subject matter. In J. H. Shulman (Ed.), *Case methods in teacher education.* New York: Teachers College Press.

Wilson, S. M., Shulman, L. S., & Richert, A. E. (1987). "150 different ways" of knowing: Representations of knowledge in teaching. In J. Calderhead (Ed.), *Exploring teachers' thinking.* London: Cassell Educational.

Wolf, D., Bixby, J., Glenn, J., & Gardner, H. (1991). To use their minds well: Investigating new forms of student assessment. In G. Grant (Ed.), *Review of research in education* (vol. 17, pp. 31–74). Washington, DC: AERA.

Woods, P. (1985). Conversations with teachers: Some aspects of life-history method. *British Educational Research Journal, 11,* 3–26.

Woolfolk, A. E. (1993). *Educational psychology* (5th ed.). Boston: Allyn & Bacon.

Zeichner, K. (1996). Educating teachers for cultural diversity. In K. Zeichner, S. Melnick, & M. L. Gomez (Eds.), *Current reform in preservice teacher education* (pp. 133–175). New York: Teachers College Press.

Zeichner, K., & Liston, D. P. (1987). Teaching student teachers to reflect. *Harvard Educational Review, 57,* 23–47.

Zeichner, K. M., & Liston, D. P. (1996). *Reflective teaching: An introduction.* Mahwah, NJ: Lawrence Erlbaum Associates.

Zeichner, K., & Tabachnik, R. (1991). Reflections on reflective teaching. In R. Tabachnik & K. Zeichner (Eds.), *Issues and practices in inquiry-oriented teacher education* (pp. 1–21). London: Falmer.

Author Index

Subject Index

Contributors

Carne Barnett is the director of the Mathematics Case Methods Project at WestEd in Oakland, California. She has prior experience as a teacher in urban settings and as a teacher educator at the University of California, Berkeley, where her pioneering work with cases for teaching mathematics began in 1987. Her research focuses on the characterization and growth of mathematics teachers' pedagogical content knowledge, as well as on methods for using cases as a professional development tool. She has published journal articles and book chapters in *the Journal of Teacher Education, Teaching and Teacher Education*, the *Journal of Mathematics Teacher Education, The Case for Education*, and *Mathematics Teachers in Transition*. Carne is the principle investigator of a National Science Foundation grant, whose purpose is to establish case discussions that are attended and facilitated by classroom teachers. She also directs a project to develop caselike materials for students and support materials for teachers to foster worthwhile discussions of mathematics.

Kathy Carter is a professor of education at the University of Arizona. Her research focuses broadly on understanding teachers' professional works and improving the teacher-education processes. In particular, she has attempted to learn more about the way teachers comprehend classroom processes and develop the knowledge structures that enable them to carry out their work with grace and effectiveness. To this end, she has focused on issues of story and personal narrative, teachers' well-remembered events, expertise in teaching, and cases as vehicles for teachers' understanding and development. She was an associate editor of *Teaching and Teacher Education* and has served on the editorial boards of the *Journal of Teacher Education, Teaching and Change*, and *Elementary School Journal*. She also served as vice president for Division K (*Teaching and Teacher Education*) of the American Educational Research Association. She has published numerous chapters and articles in such books and journals as *The Handbook of Research on Teacher Education, The Teacher Educator's Handbook, The Educational Researcher*, the Journal of Curriculum Studies, Teaching and Teacher Education, and the *Journal of Teacher Education*.

Helen Featherstone is an associate professor of teacher education at Michigan State University and editor of *Changing Minds*, a bulletin on school reform. She is presently researching the difficulties that experienced and prospective teachers face as they try to learn to teach mathematics in new ways and on what is involved, both for teachers and university-based teacher educators, in creating conversations within teacher groups that support and sustain the kinds of mathematics teaching that reformers are currently advocating. She was the founding editor of *The Harvard Education Letter*; her books include A *Difference in the Family: Life with a Disabled Child* and *Exploring Teaching: Reinventing an Introductory Course* (edited with Sharon Feiman-Nemser).

Susan Florio-Ruane is a professor of teacher education at Michigan State University (MSU). She served as a senior researcher in the MSU Institute for Research on Teaching from 1977 to 1987, leading a study of "Schooling and the Acquisition of Written Literacy" and co-coordinating the Written Literacy Forum, a collaborative research project bringing together the insights of campus-based ethnographers and educational psychologists with those of elementary and secondary school teachers of writing. She was the principal investigator in a study of "Autobiographies of Education and Cultural Identity: Preparing Teachers to Support Literacy Learning in Diverse Classrooms," funded by the Spencer Foundation. She also co-directed the study of "Reading Culture in Autobiography: The Education of Literacy Teachers," funded by the National Council of Teachers of English. She is currently co-directing a study within the U.S. Department of Education-funded Center for the Improvement of Early Reading Achievement on "Re-engaging Low Achieving Readers: Collaborative Research on the Role of Technology in Teachers' Development of Literacy Curriculum."

Dr. Florio-Ruane coordinated the Learning Community Teacher Education Program and lead the reform of its preservice literacy curriculum. Her paper on what beginning teachers need to know about "The Social Organization of Classes and Schools" won the 1990 Division K Research in Teacher Education Award of the American Educational Research Association (AERA). From 1996 to 1998 she served as coordinator of the MSU Masters in Literacy Instruction Program. She was president of the Council on Anthropology and Education from 1994 to 1996 and president-elect and program chair from 1992 to 1994. She was an external evaluator of the National Center for Research on Writing at University of California, Berkeley and Carnegie Mellon University. She currently serves as associate editor of the *Anthropology and Education Quarterly* and supervises intern teachers in the Detroit metro area. She teaches research methods at the doctoral level, as well as master's and undergraduate-level courses in literacy education and serves on the advisory board of the Teachers College Press Practitioner Inquiry Series.

Dr. Florio-Ruane has been published in numerous books and journals including, the *American Educational Research Journal*, the *Anthropology and Education Quarterly*, the *Elementary School Journal*, the *Journal of Curriculum Studies*, *Research in the Teaching of English*, *Language Arts*, the *International Journal of Teaching and Teacher Education*, and *English Education*. She wrote the inaugural entry on the anthropological study of classrooms and schools for the International Encyclopedia of Education and was a contributing author of *Literature Works*, a literature-based language arts–reading series for children in kindergarten through Grade 5. She is currently completing a book entitled, *In Good Company: Autobiography, Conversation and Teacher Learning About Culture and Literacy*. She authored the chapter on ethnographic research to be published in *The Handbook of Reading Research* . Her research interests include teacher-researcher collaboration in studies of culture, literacy, and autobiography; innovative models of sustainable professional development; and the role of technology in supporting teachers' and students' learning about literature and literacy.

Gary A. Griffin is a professor of teacher education and director of the National Center for Restructuring Education, Schools, and Teaching at Teachers College, Columbia University. His scholarship, teaching, and service have focused on teacher education and professional development, school change, and curriculum improvement. His current research activity centers on nontraditional contexts for learning to teach, with particular attention to restructuring schools and professional development schools as settings for experienced teacher learning. He is conducting a set of linked studies aimed at understanding the relationships among school organization features, teacher professional development, and student achievement. He has published articles in a wide variety of scholarly and professional journals and is editor of the 1999 Yearbook of the National Society for the Study of Education, *The Education of Teachers*.

Sigrun Gudmundsdottir is a professor of education at the Norwegian University of Science and Technology, in Trondheim, Norway. She also has been a school teacher in Scotland and Iceland. Her current research interests include cultural–historical approaches to the study of teaching and learning in classrooms and narrative research. She is presently associate editor of *Teaching and Teacher Education*. Her forthcoming publications are (in English): "Narrative Research on School Practice" in *The Handbook for Research on Teaching*, and with A. Reinertsen and N. Nort¯mme, "The Five Klafki Questions as a Conceptual Framework for Research on Teaching" in *The German Didaktik Tradition: Teaching as Reflective Practice*. She has also co-authored, with V. Nilssen V. Wangsmo-Cappelen, "Mentoring the Teaching of Mathematics," in *The European Journal of Teacher Education*.

Helen Harrington is an associate professor of education at the University of Michigan, Ann Arbor. Her research focuses on teacher development. She is specifically interested in how professional education programs can be designed to provide educational opportunities that support and challenge students to move toward more complex ways of thinking and making meaning. Her research is directed toward investigating if and how the pedagogical processes and techniques, incorporated in preservice programs, serve as bridges toward more complex ways of thinking. She is currently investigating how computer conferencing activities can be incorporated in preservice programs to facilitate the professional development of prospective teachers as well as investigating if case-based pedagogy is an effective way to prepare prospective teachers to deal with teaching's complexity and ambiguity. She has published numerous articles in such journals as the *American Educational Research Journal*, the *International Journal of Teaching and Teacher Education*, and the *Journal of Teacher Education*.

Robert Steven Kile (Steve) was a secondary history teacher in Flagstaff, Arizona, before becoming a doctoral student in teacher education at the University of Arizona. His dissertation focused on the differences in beliefs and approaches to teacher education of elementary and secondary, traditional and nontraditional preservice students in the first course taken in their teacher education program. He became an assistant professor at the University of Nevada, Las Vegas, where he was actively involved in the reform of their teacher education program through the development of professional schools. Steve passed away in November 1998, leaving his wife, Elizabeth Walsh, and three young sons. We will all miss Steve.

Barbara B. Levin is an assistant professor in curriculum and instruction at the University of North Carolina at Greensboro, where she works closely with her Professional Development School partners to initiate a Paideia-focused PDS for a cohort of undergraduate teacher education majors. Her research interests include cases and case-based pedagogy, longitudinal studies of the development of teacher's pedagogical knowledge, and teaching and learning with computer-based technologies. She has published in the *International Journal of Teaching and Teacher Education, Teacher Education Quarterly, Journal of Research on Computing in Education,* and in the *Journal of Childhood and Computing.*

Mary Anna Lundeberg is a professor in teacher education at the University of Wisconsin–River Falls. Her research focuses on case-based pedagogy, gender differences in confidence, and teaching and learning science with computer-based technologies. She has published articles in the *Journal of Educational Psychology, International Journal of Teaching and Teacher Education, Review of Research in Education, Journal of Research in Science Education, Journal of Teacher Education, Reading Research Quarterly* and *Journal of Childhood and Computing.* In 1995, she was awarded the Outstanding Teacher Educator of the Year award in Wisconsin. Mary is currently the principal investigator in a collaborative PK-20 partnership among the University of Wisconsin–River Falls and four school districts to restructure schools through a sustained professional development process that is technology-mediated, problem-based, and interdisciplinary. She is co-principal investigator on a National Science Foundation grant, incorporating case-based investigations into introductory biology.

Katherine K. Merseth is the director of research for the Harvard Children's Initiative and was the founding executive director of the Harvard Project on Schooling and Children at Harvard University. She is also a member of the faculty at the Harvard Graduate School of Education. She began teaching at Harvard in 1983 and has served in various faculty and leadership roles including director of teacher education and director of the Roderick MacDougall Center for Case Development and Teaching. From 1988 to1991, she was a member of the education faculty at the University of California, Riverside and director of the Comprehensive Teacher Education Institute. In addition, Dr. Merseth has served as dean for program development and as a member of the dean's senior administrative team at the Harvard Graduate School of Education. Prior to her work in higher education, Dr. Merseth was employed as a teacher and administrator in K–12 public schools in Massachusetts and in Jamaica, West Indies.

Dr. Merseth's research and publications center on the extrinsic and intrinsic influences on educational practice. She is the author of *The Case for Cases, Cases in Educational Administration,* and an important literature review entitled "Cases and Case methods of Instruction" in *The Handbook of Research on Teacher Education.* She is also the author or co-author of numerous articles, chapters, and monographs on teacher education, mathematics instruction, administrative leadership, computer networks, and case-based instruction. In 1994, she received the American Association of Colleges of Teacher Education Award for outstanding writing in teacher education. Her teaching at the university focuses on school reform and the design of structures to enhance children's learning.

Elizabeth B. Moje is an assistant professor in the educational studies program at the University of Michigan. Her research focuses on secondary teachers' and students' literacy interactions and practices in various social and cultural contexts.

Sonia Nieto is a professor of education at the University of Massachusetts, Amherst. Her research focuses on multicultural education, the education of Latinos, and Puerto Rican children's literature. Her books include *Affirming diversity: The Sociopolitical Context of Multicultural Education* and *Educating Puerto Rican Students in U.S. Schools*. She also has published numerous book chapters and articles in such journals as *The Harvard Educational Review, The Educational Forum, Multicultural Education*, and *Theory into Practice*. Dr. Nieto has served on local, regional, and national advisory boards that focus on educational equity and social justice, and she has received many awards for her educational advocacy and activism including the 1989 Human and Civil Rights Award from the Massachusetts Teachers Association, the 1995 Drylongso Award for Anti-Racism Activism from Community Change in Boston, and the 1997 Multicultural Education of the Year Award from the National Association for Multicultural Education. In addition, she was awarded an Annenberg fellowship for Urban School Reform in 1998.

Nel Noddings is Lee Jacks professor of child education, Stanford University, Emerita; professor of philosophy and education, Teachers College Columbia University. Author or co-editor of 10 books and more than 125 articles and chapters. Her most recent books include *Philosophy of Education*, and *Caregiving*, co-edited with Suzanne Gordon and Patricia Benner and forthcoming is *Caring and Justice*, co-edited with Michael Katz and Kenneth Strike.

Michael Pressley is the professor in Catholic education as well as the professor of psychology at the University of Notre Dame. His main interest is in the nature of effective classroom instruction, including work on classroom-based comprehension instruction, excellent Grade-1 teaching, and new community of learners approaches. He is the current editor of the *Jour-*

nal of Educational Psychology, reflecting in part his commitment to psychological research that advances understanding of education.

Janine T. Remillard is an assistant professor of education at the University of Pennsylvania in Philadelphia. Her research interests include mathematics teacher education, urban education, and policy-practice relationships. Over the past several years, she has studied the relationships between educational policy and classroom practice in elementary mathematics. She has particular interest in examining how teachers interpret and act on policy and the assumptions about the practice of teaching underlying policy initiatives and implementation efforts. She is also interested in examining learning and change in prospective and practicing teachers. She has published in *Elementary School Journal* and *Curriculum Inquiry* and in several edited volumes on teacher education and mathematics education. She is currently involved in two research projects in the Philadelphia area that examine teaching and learning to teach mathematics in urban classrooms and beginning teachers' learning to teach in urban settings.

Virginia Richardson is professor of teacher education and chair of educational studies at the University of Michigan. Her interests relate to teacher change, teacher beliefs, teacher education and staff development. She has published a number of books and articles in these areas, including editing a recently published book by Falmer Press called *Constructivist Teacher Education: Building a World of New Understandings*.

Anthony G. Rud, Jr. is associate dean and associate professor in the School of Education at Purdue University. His scholarship centers on the intersection of the cultural foundations of education and life in schools, with particular emphasis on the preparation and professional development of teachers, principals, and superintendents. Rud has co-edited two books and published a number of articles and reviews. His current work includes research with Alan M. Beck of Purdue's School of Veterinary Medicine on the moral and cognitive dimensions of human–animal interaction in schools.

Judith H. Shulman is the director of the Institute for Case Development at WestEd. Her research interests focus on the development and use of cases and their impact on teacher learning and on the education and professional development of teachers. Shulman's publications include *Case Methods in Teacher Education*, several co-edited casebooks with facilitator's guides, and numerous chapters and articles in such professional journals *as Educational Researcher, Journal of Teacher Education, Teaching and Teacher Education*, and

Teacher Education Quarterly. Currently, she is a principal investigator in the National Partnership on Excellence and Accountability in Teaching (NPEAT), incorporating case methods into standards-based teacher education programs.

Rita Silverman is professor of education and co-director of the Center for Case Studies in Education at Pace University. Since 1988, she has been awarded four grants from the fund for the Improvement of Postsecondary Education (FIPSE), the first of which was to develop cases in teacher education, which led to *Case Studies for Teacher Problem Solving*. The next two FIPSE grants extended the work in cases to faculty development initiatives. The fourth FIPSE grant, awarded in 1998, is to develop a PDS model to prepare preservice students for teaching in urban settings. Professor Silverman has disseminated her work in cases studies in journals and by presenting research on case teaching at national and regional education and faculty development conferences and by demonstrating case method teaching at pre-conference workshops at national and international conferences and at more than 75 colleges and universities throughout the United States and Canada. She has also written in the areas of assessment and inclusion.

Sherry A. Southerland is an assistant professor of science education at the University of Utah. Her research interests include the influence of culture and language on the process of conceptual change in science content areas, the influence of group interactions on students' conceptual change, and philosophical issues associated with the teaching and learning of science. She has published in *Journal of Research in Science Teaching, Science Education, BioScience*, and *Science & Education*. Currently, Sherry is co-principal investigator on a National Science Foundation grant, investigating the role of authentic problem-solving and structured group interactions in the facilitation of conceptual development.

Pamela Tyson is a co-director of the Mathematics Case Methods Project at WestEd. Since the spring of 1992, she has worked closely with teachers in developing their expertise in facilitating mathematics case discussions. In addition, she teaches courses on elementary mathematics methods and mathematics case discussions to preservice and in-service teachers at San Francisco State University. Prior to joining the mathematics case methods project, she directed a research team, at Far West Laboratory, to develop prototype assessments of secondary mathematics teachers' sensitivity in addressing student diversity. She has also conducted research on teachers' pedagogical content knowledge in teaching fractions. Tyson was a classroom teacher in secondary mathematics and computer programming in the

Rochester, New York area and an elementary computer software teacher in Richmond, California.

Suzanne Wade is a professor of educational studies at the University of Utah. She received her Ed.D. in 1984 from the Harvard Graduate School of Education. Her areas of specialization include teaching reading and learning strategies in the subject areas, assessment and instruction of reading difficulties, inclusive education, and the use of cases in teacher education. Dr. Wade has published in journals such as the *Journal of Educational Psychology, Reading Research Quarterly, Review of Educational Research, JRB: A Journal of Literacy, Teaching and Teacher Education,* and the *Journal of Educational and Psychological Consultation.* She presently has two edited volumes in preparation: *Inclusive Education: A Casebook and Readings for Prospective and Practicing Teachers* and *Preparing Teachers for Inclusive Education: Case Pedagogies and Curricula for Teacher Educators.* She has been supported in her work by a National Academy of Education Spencer Fellowship, awarded in 1990 and a Career Development Award from the Joseph P. Kennedy, Jr. Foundation, awarded in 1994 to design and teach a case-based course on inclusive education.

Ken Zeichner is a Hoefs-Bascom professor of teacher education, and chair of elementary education at the University of Wisconsin–Madison. He has published widely on issues related to teacher education and action research in North America, Europe, Africa, Australia, and Asia. His recent publications include *Reflective Teaching* and *Culture and Teaching* ,with Dan Liston, "Practitioner Research," with Susan Noffke in *The Handbook of Research on Teaching,* and *Critical Practitioner Inquiry and the Transformation of Teacher Education in Namibia.* He was vice president of the American Educational Research Association from 1996 through 1998 (Division K– *Teaching and Teacher Education*) and is a member of the Board of Directors of the American Association of Colleges for Teacher Education (1997–2000). His current research focuses on teacher research as a professional development activity.

So-young Zeon is an assistant professor in the Teacher Education Department at the University of Wisconsin–River Falls. Her research interests include writing cases and teaching with cases in teacher education in undergraduate classrooms, technology and instruction, ethnic identity development of college-age students, and the acculturation process of ethnic minorities in the United States, with specific emphasis on Asian Americans.